The
Technocratic
Illusion

A STUDY OF MANAGERIAL POWER IN ITALY

The Technocratic Illusion

FLAVIA DEROSSI

With a Foreword by Harold J. Leavitt
Translated by Susan LoBello

M. E. Sharpe, Inc.
Armonk, New York

This book is a translation of *L 'illusione tecnocratica: Il potere dei dirigenti
nell'industria italiana*, published in Milan by Etas Libri in 1978. Copyright
© 1978 by Etas Libri S.p.A. This edition has been revised and edited by the
author.

Library of Congress Cataloging in Publication Data

Derossi, Flavia.
    The technocratic illusion.

    Edition, originally published in 1978 under title: L'illusione tecnocratica,
edited and revised by the author.
    Includes bibliographical references.
1. Industrial management—Italy. 2. Industrial organization—Italy.
I. Title.
HD70.I8D4713   658'.00945   81-14341
ISBN 0-87332-185-5   AACR2

Printed in the United States of America

To Marshall

Contents

Foreword   HAROLD J. LEAVITT   *ix*

Preface   *xi*

1. Introduction   *3*

2. The Power of the Managers   *12*

3. The Decision Process   *26*

4. Limits and Conditions on Managerial Power   *38*

5. The Crisis of Managerial Authority   *97*

6. The Managers' Dilemma   *116*

7. The Powerless Elite   *146*

Appendix: RESEARCH METHODOLOGY   *183*

Notes   *192*

About the Author   *235*

Foreword

This is a refreshingly competent book. Unlike many recent books about managers around the world, this one radiates the thoroughness and solid work that Flavia Derossi and her colleagues put into it. It depicts in depth the Italian management system, its place in the Italian society, and also its place in the wider organizational world.

While *The Technocratic Illusion* focuses mainly on Italian managers, it is also a book about power, about decision making in organizations, and about organization-environment relations. The Italian management system is treated, in effect, as an illustrative case, as one of many possible patterns of organized human effort.

For the social scientist, no justification of this work is needed. The sheer quantity of Derossi's data is impressive. So is the quality. She examines the decision-making and policy-making powers of several levels of the Italian management hierarchy against the background of current organizational theory. She spotlights the rather unique role of the Italian manager as a member of a "powerless elite," a kind of nonprofessional professional. Derossi points to the loneliness, the anomie of the Italian middle manager, shows how and why it occurs and the consequences it generates. By doing so, she not only alerts us to such phenomena but also warns us to think ahead toward the secondary and tertiary consequences, good and bad, that might follow from our own apparently sensible current practices.

Methodologically, she specifies her group's interviewing procedures for her 663 subjects in 50 randomly selected major manufacturing firms. And she presents detailed tabular results, often in useful comparative form. But she sensibly leaves the methodological details for an Appendix, devoting the readable body of the text to concepts and findings.

For any manager, this is a very useful book indeed. It is not just for the Italian manager, nor even for the non-Italian manager working with or in an Italian firm. It extends beyond the Italian scene, using the Italian experience as a kind of backdrop against which to consider other alternatives.

Those of us close to American management are finally coming to realize that we, too, must keep learning and relearning the managing process. In the last few years we have been shaken by other nations' managerial successes, especially those of Japan. And we have been studying the Japanese model to see what we can import. Clearly, for success-oriented Americans, successful Japanese have pzzazz, while the Italians have certainly not ranked high on our list of the world's great managers. Nor will they rank much higher after this book. But Derossi's clear portrait of the Italian system's strengths and weaknesses may enrich our understanding of the managing process as much as our study of the Japanese example. Our implicit, unexamined, taken-for-granted managerial behaviors can be made more explicit, more examinable, more questioned as we come to understand the strengths and weaknesses of alternative models. This fine book about Italians can teach us a great deal about Americans.

HAROLD J. LEAVITT
Kilpatrick Professor of
Organizational Behavior
Graduate School of Business
Stanford University

Preface

This study examines the power of industrial managers in Italy, as measured by their role in decision making and their authority over subordinates. The conclusions run counter to current claims about "managerial supremacy," i.e., the notion that professional managers have totally displaced owners as the leaders of business.

Our inquiry began in the early 1970s when we conducted several hundred interviews with managers at various hierarchical levels. That interview data has been integrated with the results of an investigation of more recent developments in Italy, using new interviews and a variety of recent research reports and articles. These contemporary studies reveal the continued development of trends identified in the earlier investigation.

As every business manager knows, any complex creation is a collective work, resulting from the combined efforts of many. Our research is no exception. The 663 interviews with managers in the 50 largest Italian firms, located in various parts of the country, and the quantitative analysis of the data were only possible thanks to the dedicated teamwork of a number of talented collaborators. Those who participated throughout the investigation are Magda Talamo, Jorge Garcia Bouza, Maria Teresa Gayta, Franco Mussetta, Francesca Pennacchietti, Enrico Taliani, Viviana Vindrola. Among those who participated on a consultant basis are Anna Anfossi, Johan Galtung, and Herbert Hyman.

The present investigation was the last to be conducted by the

Center for Industrial and Social Research in Turin. Thus it concludes fourteen years of studies by this institution devoted to research on the social problems associated with industrialization.

FLAVIA DEROSSI

The
Technocratic
Illusion

Introduction

This book offers a portrait of an important figure on the Italian economic scene—the industrial manager. His role is in many respects similar to that of an American manager, but his most interesting features stem from the conditions that cause him to be different from his American counterpart. These conditions—the Italian sociopolitical environment, the characteristics of industrialization in Italy, and the social status and professional background of the manager himself—shape the role and style of Italian managers. For the benefit of the reader who is unfamiliar with the Italian context, we shall briefly examine each of these conditions.

1.1. The social and political scene

Italy was a slow starter in expanding its rate of economic development: its lack of raw materials and a poor internal market kept Italy an agricultural country decades after the economic "take-off" of most European nations. At the beginning of the century, Italian industrial production constituted only 5 or 6 percent of the Western European total. Even at the end of World War II, half of Italy's working population was still engaged in agriculture.

Today, in spite of its status as one of the world's leading industrialized countries (ranking seventh for industrial GNP), Italy presents a persistent combination of modernism and of features that are typical of the underdeveloped nations. The population's level of education is still unsatisfactory. Although recent measures have virtually eliminated illiteracy, only fifteen years ago nearly 10 percent of the people could not read; today only 25 percent have completed the eight years of compulsory education. Government services—from public works and postal and telephone services to the educational system—are archaic and ineffective; tax collection is notoriously inefficient. The government bureaucracy, which is generally unskilled and unmotivated, enjoys not only protection from any sort of disciplinary action but also lifelong job security and a promotion system based on seniority.

The juxtaposition of modernity and underdevelopment is perhaps most starkly apparent in the case of regional disparities. A skewed regional distribution of GNP and economic growth splits the country into the developed North (with 46 percent of Italy's population it provides 70 percent of total industrial employment) and the economically backward Central-Southern region. A constant flow of emigration from the latter areas to the North of Italy and to the countries of the European Common Market has only partially alleviated the tension produced by this economic division. Wide discrepancies in income distribution show up as well among individuals in Italy and the current economic crisis has only widened the gap between social classes.[1]

The social stress of these internal conditions has been exacerbated in recent years by the slowdown of economic growth in all Western European countries and by the pressure of the oil crisis (Italy, which has some nuclear and hydropower, is totally dependent on oil imports). The country failed to tackle social inequalities during the advantageous boom years of the late 1960s; now economic crisis has made problems worse and solutions more difficult. Unemployment has soared as the economic slowdown in other European countries has sealed the traditional pressure valve of emigration. The percentage of job holders in the working-age population (39 percent in contrast to 59 percent in the United States) is one of the lowest in Europe.[2] There is a mushrooming "underground" labor market that partially compensates for a low official employment. But this adds yet another feature of dualism to the Italian scene: while big private corporations are struggling to keep afloat and state-owned industry is on the verge of bankruptcy, the myriad of tiny private enterprises growing up all over the country escape statistics, taxation, and labor legislation.

Union and government control is enforced vigorously on the visible part of the economy, represented primarily by the large corporations. Indeed, confronted by economic uncertainty, the country has clung even more firmly to provisions protecting job security, imposing a firm barrier to dismissals. To maintain jobs, the unions have refused to allow overtime even on a temporary basis. These conditions have further frozen the labor market, since companies are reluctant to employ new people they cannot dismiss when conditions warrant. The most observable consequence of these developments is that they keep young people and women out of jobs. In fact, the female labor-participation rate, about 25 percent (compared to about 50 percent in the United States), is as low as it was a century ago.

Industry, as the most dynamic sector of the economy, is deemed to be the only institution capable of responding to the many unfulfilled expectations of the Italian public. But the big corporation, as the most visible of the productive structures, elicits not only demands and hopes, but also animosity. In Italy as in few other European countries, the *public* character of the industrial firm is widely stressed; yet industry does *not* enjoy social legitimation. Social problems are considered to be a result of the exploitation of workers by the ruling class; hence, social tensions quite readily translate themselves into political and class struggles. Anticapitalist ideology is widespread.

Thus, in the eyes of the Italian public, industry is both the tool for achieving economic well-being and the culprit behind all social evils. Capitalist entrepreneurs and major corporate shareholders (easily identified thanks to the concentration of ownership) are viewed as personifications of an exploitative ruling class.

In the "Hot Autumn" of 1969, waves of strikes and worker unrest gave dramatic expression to the widespread social dissatisfaction. Wages were not the main source of anger; a more important factor was a deeply felt frustration over the delay of badly needed reforms in the areas of health, education, transportation, low-cost housing, and regional development.[3] These social tensions have persisted. Italian society today is marked by chronic industrial conflicts, increasing support for leftist parties,[4] and the terrorist behavior of fringe groups at the extreme left and right of the political continuum.

How does such a social and political situation affect managers? On the one hand, the Italian manager is usually less free to act than his U.S. counterpart, and therefore less responsible for what goes on in the firm; however, since he is likely to be a scion of the higher classes, he is considered one of the villains of the situation.

ment," and also for some of the very largest firms, in which the concentration of share ownership grants control to the members of a family or a closely knit group.[8] Dynasties of Schumpeterian-type entrepreneurs are still very much alive in the Italian economic scene, where they play an active and open role.

The control of state-owned enterprise is a more complicated matter. The massive presence of the state-owned firms places Italy midway between the capitalist and the socialist economies. State companies differ from private firms in their history, goals, and type of top management. State ownership of companies started in the depression of the 1930s, when it was used as a device to rescue jobs in private firms threatened by bankruptcy. (A parallel rescue effort was made in the same period in the United States, but there, ownership was usually left in private hands.) The same need to protect employment presented itself again after World War II. Later, state firms came to be used as a tool for developing the Southern, depressed areas of the country.[9] Thus for many of the state-owned enterprises the orientation of the firm has been shifted —from industry's traditional focus on productivity and profit to social achievements such as saving communities from the disruption of job losses, guaranteeing job security, and the creation of new jobs. It should also be noted that the state firms are important political power centers, and they are used as such by the political parties.

These two drives, the social and the political, explain why the choice of top management to run state companies is dictated not only by technical and professional criteria but also by political considerations. One of the anomalies of Italian industry is that although the president of a state-owned firm may happen to be a good administrator, he will not necessarily be judged by his administrative skills. And, if he employs a group of managers who still think in terms of efficiency, they may well be required to curb their efforts, in order to accommodate the social goals of the firm.

While in state industry top management is selected in a complex political interplay and in private industry family connections count the most, the selection of middle management follows technical and administrative criteria in all types of industry (although obviously a measure of nepotism is present in all of them). But in small firms—let us remember that 94 percent of Italian firms employ fewer than 100 workers—the professional manager operates under the strict control of the owner-manager. Throughout Italian industry "patrimonial management" clearly coexists with "professional management."[10]

1.3. The social and professional background

It is a distinguishing feature of the Italian manager that his job in Italy enjoys legal recognition. He is even represented by his own special union.

In 1937 the Italian Civil Code introduced an article describing the profession of the *dirigente* (manager) and separating him from the other categories of subordinate workers.[11] In the same year a royal decree further reinforced his separation. It differentiated the managerial group from the company owner by creating the Federation of Italian Managers, in all respects a union, whose task was to negotiate a separate national contract with the employers.

Both the legal recognition granted to the managerial role and the legitimization of the managerial group arose in large measure from the wider and ambitious design of the Fascist regime. The concept of the Corporate State fostered a view of society that consisted of diverse economic groups (and not of single individuals), each to be represented in the central governing body.

But why in prewar Italy was it decided that *managers* should be set apart in a specific legally defined group? In 1937 industrial managers totaled about 6,000 people. Most were scattered in small family businesses and their role and influence was quite limited. The government could have simply included them in a legal box along with other industrial employees; but it did not, probably because of the class distinctions existing in the society at the time. Special recognition had to be given to an employee group comprised mainly of people from the higher socioeconomic strata— a group that could not identify with the lower working class nor even with the petty bourgeoisie, and yet could not be placed on a par with the affluent class of the company owners. The government recognized that the rigid stratification that existed within the firm was in a broad sense a mirror of the social classes of the nation.

This social and professional partition exists in all countries in varying degrees. The Italian case is made notable by the tightness of the links between social class origin, job, and social status (that is, a pervasive lack of social mobility) and by the rigidity of career patterns in Italian industrial firms (that is, a general lack of professional mobility). Of course, no social system is so rigid as not to allow some individuals to filter to higher positions. A few workers are given a chance for modest upward mobility by promotion to the position of foreman or low-level supervisor. And occasionally a white-collar worker can become a service-head or, in the rarest of cases, a *dirigente*.

The separation of the managers from other employees and the higher status and salary they enjoy are usually explained by reference to the professional responsibilities of their jobs. Managers' status within the firm does not depend on their social class origin *per se*, but on the higher level of education they are required to possess. But higher education and university attendance have been almost exclusively a privilege of the higher economic classes. Even today the Italian manager is still largely the product of the middle and upper classes. (See Table 1.3.) His career mobility is jointly influenced by his education and social origin. (See Table 1.4.)

Founded with a constituency of 6,000, the industrial managers' association today represents nearly ten times that number. In 1954 managers were less than 0.3 percent of the Italian industrial labor force; today they are 1 percent. The number of managers has

Table 1.3

Social Class Origin of Managers (Father's Occupation)
(in %, *n* = 663)

Working class (workers, artisans, farmers)	13
Middle class (white-collar workers, primary school teachers, commercial, etc.)	47
Upper middle class (liberal professions, university professors, judges, high civil servants)	18
Industrial upper class (entrepreneurs and managers)	17
Nonindustrial upper class (entrepreneurs and managers in nonmanufacturing firms, bankers, landed proprietors)	5
	100

Source: Unless otherwise indicated, all tables were compiled by the author on the basis of data collected in the present study.

Table 1.4

Managers Achieving Rapid Career Mobility:
by Social Class Origin and Education
(in %, *n* = 655)

| Education | Social class | | | |
	Lower class	Middle class	Upper class	Difference
High school or less	4	12	36	−32
University degree	39	53	60	−21
Difference	−35	−41	−24	−11
N	(87)	(307)	(261)	(655)

expanded more rapidly than the rate of growth of industrial output or total industrial employment. Presumably, the growth of the management corps reflects the increased complexity of industrial operations.

The managers' association encompasses 50,000 individuals with the same legal title, people who enjoy a similar high social status and have in common a minimum of wage and fringe benefits, granted by the common contract. But the title *dirigente* covers a range of functions which differ in responsibilities and decision-making power. Practically, the title is applicable from the level just above foremen and supervisors, almost to the very top of the hierarchy (it excludes the president and chairman of the board). Thus the general and the lieutenant wear the same label, but by no means do they identify with each other.[12] This is why the managers' union has never had the cohesion and the militancy that characterize workers' unions.

As we show in the pages that follow, the Italian manager is truly the man in the middle.

2

The Power
of the Managers

2.1. Power in industry

An understanding of managerial power is important because of the economic might that people in this profession can wield.[1] The manager is important by virtue of what he stands for: his power is of a structural nature, deriving from the organization and, more specifically, from the role that he performs.[2]

The economic power of the corporation has as its base the many people and institutions that it influences in a great variety of ways (its employees, suppliers, clients, and people in the communities in which it operates), its relations with other manufacturers or financial organizations, its use of lobbies in government, and its links to other power centers. Such power provides the opportunity to determine the products to be manufactured, their prices (and cost-price relationships), the investments to be made, the location of plants, the scope of scientific research, and the standard of living of its employees.[3]

Corporate power also extends beyond the economic realm, into the firm's cultural, social, and political environments.

Corporations and the nation's culture

Researchers focusing on industrial society have extensively described the impact of industrialization on attitudes and individual values. On the one hand, new modes of production have transformed the social system, family and informal relations, and the content of the educational system. They have promoted urbanization and infused society with a dynamism unknown to agricultural societies; in the process they have introduced profound psychological and cultural changes. On the other hand, industrial growth has introduced products that promote new life-styles and encourage imitation. "Business influence on taste ranges from the direct effects through the design of material goods to the indirect and more subtle effects of the style of language and thought purveyed through the mass media . . . Further . . . business leaders are dominant social models in our society; their achievements and their values are to a large extent the type of the excellent."[4]

Not all scholars consider these changes positive,[5] but all seem to consider them inevitable. The aggregate of large corporations' day-to-day decisions influences the life of the individual and the community. "They build or shift or direct frameworks of human experience within which great masses of men live."[6]

These values, in turn, reinforce the importance of business's social role, for business appears uniquely able to satisfy the community's aspirations for consumption and for its material well-being. Consequently, while there is often tension between business standards and societal values, there is also much complementarity and interdependence between them.[7]

Corporations and social structure

Corporate decisions that appear to be solely matters of internal concern, such as those concerning production and financial affairs, in fact extend their effects far beyond company walls. Even though decisions concerning investment, the location of new plants, and technological innovation are supposedly only related to productive growth, they clearly influence the structure of the job market, the geographic distribution of the population, and related economic activities. That is, they determine not only the economic structure but also the social structure of a country as well as its internal mobility and the effects of such mobility.

Society itself grants a certain power to industry by considering economic development as a collective goal and identifying industrialization as the most efficient means for attaining it. Community attitudes have often passed from mere tolerance of business to a belief that the production of material goods has a predominant role in the community: "Since the fruit of [businessmen's] activities slopped over in taxes, wages, and dividends, it was manifestly contributing to general welfare."[8]

An industry is often considered to have positive effects even when it is a monopoly and consequently has the power to determine prices and keep them high. The belief is that even if large corporations are free from competitive pressures and therefore enjoy large profits and increased liquidity, society will benefit because they will increase investments in new plant and equipment and in research and development, and finance scientific research and higher education.[9]

This consideration fosters the attitude that "anything which interferes with the orderly economic processes is an evil."[10]

Corporations and politics

The extension of corporate power into the political realm derives from certain characteristics that big business has acquired over time.

a. *The large corporation is an autonomous decision-making center.* It operates in an environment in which most market conditions are flexible, and the margin of choice left to management is great.[11]

b. *Corporate power is largely independent of government control.* The fragmented nature of public power, in contrast to the unifying tendencies of industrial development (concentration of production) and the growing complexity of technology, prevent effective government control of corporations.[12]

c. However, *the large corporation engages in an on-going relationship with the state*, which adopts various roles vis-à-vis the corporation: client, competitor, and regulator.[13]

d. *Industry-government relations are mutually supportive* because government rarely serves as an opposing force, given that its goals coincide with those of industry: after all, economic stability and expansion are in the interest of the community.[14] The two parties are symbiotic. Industrial growth has reinforced their mutual dependence and made it more visible: ". . . more and more [business] needs the state as active ally; and the national state, in turn, having delivered itself over by accepting the definition of its welfare as synonymous with the welfare of its business system, needs increasingly the utmost of aggressive efficiency from its business-men. . . ."[15]

In order to grow, industry requires a "climate of security." It requires appropriate institutions and above all, a stable social system.[16] A corporation's dependence on the environment is extensive: the loss of a market, the emergence of bold and successful competition, the intervention of restrictive legislation can all threaten its existence. This vulnerability, deriving from the necessity of long-term investments and the establishment of a plant in a specific geographic location at considerable installation cost, explains how vital it is for industry to control external factors or at least to reduce their potentially harmful effects. Projects involving long-term planning require that the largest possible number of relevant environmental variables be controlled. National political systems have proven to be the most controllable of the company's environmental variables, while international competition and scientific innovation are not readily controllable.[17]

e. *The close relationship with the state brings many advantages to industry.* Of all forces external to the company, government appears to be not only the most manipulable, but also the most benevolent. "The interaction between government and business has often been clearly very profitable for business. Much of the entrepreneurial skill displayed by business in the prosperous period dating from the end of World War II has been dedicated to making imaginative and inventive use of the opportunities afforded by government subsidies, tax reduction, contracts and investments in such things as airports, roads, schools and research. . . ."[18]

f. Finally, *big corporations often wield direct political power*, in that they are able to impose policy at both the national and international levels.[19]

The pursuit of legitimacy by industrial power

The state represents only one of the social forces interacting with business. Other groups may be antagonistic and conflicts may develop. Business's search for legitimacy is stimulated by the presence of other interest groups, some of which business itself may have fostered (like the working class and the labor unions). Although not always dealing directly with business, many such groups have come to harbor ambivalent feelings toward it: on the one hand, the positive results of business-generated economic wealth encourage the social acceptance of business; on the other hand, fear persists concerning business's having excessive political and economic power. A rift between business and society is a continuing threat.

For some time, business representatives have been concerned with their image in public opinion. For them legitimization means converting the situation from one that relies on coercive *power* into one that is based on recognized *authority*.[20] The desire to attain such a status has produced the search for "respectability" and for a "creed."[21]

In its search for legitimacy, business has followed multiple strategies:

a. Business presents itself as the socially *indispensable* producer of benefits in the form of necessary goods and services, and the generator of employment and income. Therefore, business argues that there should be no conflict between corporate goals and societal goals; indeed, they say, business and society both strive to foster the citizens' well-being through the creation of wealth;

b. Business presents itself as a *responsible* force and as respectful of the public interest. From this position emerges the doctrine of "social responsibilities."[22]

When the above two strategies fail, business can still try to:

c. Highlight business's inability to influence the social and political environment. The corporation's role is presented as being *circumscribed* by the corporation's own responsibilities, which are spent in the production of goods and services that satisfy society's material needs. Manipulation of social processes and social values is, according to business leaders, extraneous to business's duties; therefore its social obligations are limited to paying taxes;

d. Present itself as a *dependent* variable and not an independent force, i.e., as subject to, not a mover of, economic and social events. The picture then is that of an institution that is subordinated to and imprisoned by social controls.[23] As the president of a large U.S. firm said, "The corporation is a creature of society. . . . The social responsibility of business is to create material abundance, but to do so on the basis of the groundrules that society sets. We are hired guns. It is simply a matter of someone pointing us in the right direction."[24]

It is probable that the choice among the above strategies depends on a specific firm's size and resultant degree of visibility, on the amount of power it can exercise, and finally, on the overall framework created by the level of state interference or by the whims of public opinion.[25] Whichever strategy it adopts, business's efforts to demonstrate its social usefulness will make use of the culture's current myths: until the 1940s when it latched onto the "creed" of social responsibilities, industry was the champion of "free enterprise," which was then considered the backbone of economic development.

These images created by business about itself contrast with another image, advanced by critics, which stresses the breadth of industry's power as evidenced by the fundamental economic role it plays in a nation and by the political leverage gained from that role. Industrial power is further broadened by the absence of: counterbalancing forces[26]; social criteria suitable for evaluating economic policies[27]; and an authentic doctrine assigning its social responsibilities.[28]

Since productive organizations are perceived as impersonal entities, it is helpful to discern which individuals are actually able to exercise the power of the corporation. Management is important to examine in this regard, because many identify it as the seat of industrial power and the repository of the firm's social responsibilities.

As we will see later, one of the ways the corporation attempts to legitimize its power is to shift the firm's social responsibilities from its owners to its management.

2.2. Management as the seat of industrial power: The theory of managerial supremacy

Our research began with an examination of the widely held premise that today industrial power is held by the manager and no longer by the capitalist owner.[29] The manager is viewed as the person entrusted not only with technical, financial, and commercial operations but also with determining the company's relations with external institutions.

Underlying this view is the assumption that economic development transforms the structure of the society in which it takes place and that each stage of industrial growth is controlled by a different social and professional group. Yet, in Italy we found little evidence to support this theory of the "managerial revolution," which holds that industrial development brings an eclipse of the role of owners and the shift of decision-making power in industry to a group called "professional" managers.

Let us examine the individual factors that have been considered responsible for the shift of power from owners to managers.

The separation of ownership from control

A major development in the history of industrialization was the appearance of the large corporation, i.e., the genuine joint stock company, which was no longer a legal fiction but an expression of real distribution of stock.

The growth in company size, necessary to obtain economies of scale and to attain a position of dominance if not of monopoly in the market, carries with it the need for larger amounts of capital investment. Faced with insufficient capital to finance their expanding operations, owners need to resort to outside suppliers of capital, surrendering in return shares of stock. By doing so they may lose control of the company.[30]

Some students of modern industry argue that the birth of the large corporation, characteristic of modern industrialization, brought about the disappearance of the entrepreneur-owner described by Schumpeter. No longer the head of the enterprise, the corporate owner is said to have been reduced to the now passive role of stockholder.[31] Directing the large firm is a task of such complexity as to prevent any single individual, however gifted, from accomplishing it alone. Increased size and requirements for long-term planning produced this transformation: ". . . when an enterprise had grown large enough or the period of operation extended long enough so that the head of the unit had to share his duties of observation, planning, and execution with one or more other persons, he was in effect sharing his entrepreneurial function. . . ."[32]

The main actor in the development of modern industry is no longer the individual but the organization, conceived as a complex system of intertwined specialized functions.

The entrepreneur, the prototypical figure in the early phase of industrialization, was destined to disappear when the process of industrial development reached maturity. John K. Galbraith describes the transition:

> The great entrepreneur must, in fact, be compared in life with the male *Apis mellifera*. He accomplishes his act of conception at the price of his own extinction. The older entrepreneurs combined firms that were not yet technologically complex. . . . But the act of combination added new plants and products and therewith the need for specialization by function and knowledge. Sooner or later came more complex tasks of planning and control. Technology, with its own dynamic, later added its de-

mand for capital and specialized talent with need for yet more comprehensive planning. Thus what the entrepreneur created passed inexorably beyond the scope of his authority. . . . What the entrepreneur created, only a group of men sharing specialized information could ultimately operate.[33]

Before Galbraith, Thorstein Veblen noted in 1923 that the captain of industry, one of the major institutions of the nineteenth century, had since become a holdover of the past, essentially a "superstition." [34]

The decline of the family enterprise

Along with the entrepreneur's disappearance these writers highlight the decline of the family enterprise and of the system of nepotism and hereditary transmission of managerial positions. According to Daniel Bell, the end of family capitalism occurred when rapid industrial expansion required bank intervention.[35] Thus began the era of "financial capitalism" that at a later time was to give way to "managerial capitalism." This phenomenon assumes considerable social significance because it severed a thousand-year relationship between the two institutions that were at the foundation of society—ownership and family. This was an important turning point in the history of industrialization, because the birth of industry was not so much the result of individual initiative as it was of family solidarity: the family in fact provided the source of early capital, and technicians and managers were initially recruited from within the family.[36]

Already manifest in advanced industrialized countries, this process is now thought to be under way in the newly industrialized nations which, as a result, are witnessing the same conditions: the need for external capital deprives the old family dynasties of authority, and technological complexity discourages appointments based on kinship. Because the two phenomena result from growth in the size of the enterprise, the decline of the family firm is bound to follow the process of economic and financial concentration that seems to be an inevitable feature of industrialization's advanced phase. In each nation the state of affairs of the family firm would depend on the stage of technological and organizational complexity the country has reached, but its decline is considered inevitable.

The power of stockholders

According to managerialist writers, with the emergence of financial capitalism a new social group appeared on the industrial scene—the stockholders. Stockholders' ability to intervene in management, however, is limited by two constraints. The first consists of the diffusion of common stock itself, which impedes the formation of a powerful group; the second is the stockholders' lack of specialized knowledge and information about the company, which prevents them from exercising any real control over corporate management's decisions.

As early as 1929, Adolph Berle and Gardiner Means, in analyzing the 200 largest corporations, found that 65 percent of them were controlled by management or by the board of directors, with little participation by owners.[37] In Robert Gordon's 1937 study, the stockholdings in large corporations appeared widely distributed and dispersed. In that year, 88 percent of the holdings of common stock in the 200 largest corporations were of 100 shares or less. Gordon noted that it is precisely these small stockholders who foster the picture of corporate ownership without control. He concluded that the small stockholder cannot play a significant role because he does not actively and continually oversee the firm's leadership, nor does he have the power to exercise independent control over the executives. He is passive and impotent.[38]

By 1963, the process appears to have progressed. Comparing Berle's 1929 data with data gathered in 1963 in the same corporations (see Table 2.1), Robert Larner found the same trend and concluded that "... a corporation may reach a size so great that, with a few exceptions, its control is beyond the financial means of an individual or interest group."[39] Similar studies, like those conducted in Great Britain which compared 1936 and 1951 data, seem to confirm this trend outside the United States.[40]

In theory, small stockholders could unite by proxy, but in fact they are disorganized. Furthermore, since they tend to fragment their investments in order to reduce risk, when they are dissatisfied with the way a corporation is being managed they prefer to get rid of their shares rather than fight.[41] In any case, the isolated, disorganized, and weak group of stockholders faces the tight-knit group of managers who dominate meetings with a small majority of preestablished votes.[42]

Table 2.1

Ownership in the 200 Largest Nonfinancial
Corporations, 1929 and 1963 (Summary)

Characterization of enterprise	Degree of capital concentration (%)	As percent of total	
		1929	1963
Private ownership	80	6	0
Majority ownership	50-80	5	2.5
Minority control	20-50	23	9
Control by a legal device	variable	21	4
Management control	less than 5	44	84.5

Sources: For 1929, Adolph A. Berle and Gardiner C. Means, *The Modern Corporation and Private Property*, New York, Macmillan, 1932, p. 115. For 1963, Robert J. Larner, "Ownership and Control in the 200 Largest Non-financial Corporations, 1929-1963," *American Economic Review*, September 1966, p. 780.

Even if a proxy of small stockholders were to arise, the fact remains that to pass a judgment on a corporation's problems requires specialized knowledge which usually only management possesses. Galbraith emphasizes the stockholders' lack of information, which he calls a "failure of knowledge." He notes that it is natural that "power [go] to the factor which is hardest to obtain or hardest to replace." This factor is the "organized intelligence."[43]

Another kind of knowledge indispensable to decision making is familiarity with the specific and often unique problems of a particular enterprise. Only daily contact with the company's operations can furnish the information necessary for sound executive decisions. Thus the shareholders' lack of specialized knowledge is further compounded by their lack of familiarity with the corporation. "To manage a firm, it is necessary continually to exercise authority there. It is not enough to be the owner. In order to exercise continuous authority, the owner of the firm would have to become a manager; he has to 'enter' the firm."[44]

For its part, management deliberately withholds information to protect itself against interference from stockholders, especially when the latter attempt to unite through proxy.[45]

The manager's refusal to submit to outside control is in part a manifestation of the disdain that the "technician" harbors against the owner. The manager sees the latter's income as parasitic and prefers reinvesting profits to distributing them.[46] It would seem unavoidable that stockholders surrender the decision-making power that is their legal due to the experts operating within the organization—the only people who can authoritatively diagnose problems and design appropriate solutions.

The limits of the board of directors

When early theorists looked at the large corporation, they assumed that the locus of corporate decisions was the board of directors.[47] Today that institution appears outdated and inefficient. Formulated over a century ago, the rules of procedure of the board were presumed to apply to small local companies that had few stockholders and a few simple products. Today the large corporation caters to multiple markets with a variety of products and has developed a complex structure: managing it is a full-time profession.[48]

It is for reasons of professional competence that some top executives also sit in the board. Their influence on board decisions and the election of members diminishes the board's former characteristics of autonomy and superiority with respect to management. Furthermore, these overlapping functions allow management to perpetuate itself.[49]

In many cases the board of directors simply exists on paper for legal purposes and its activities at most consist of ratifying decisions made elsewhere.[50]

The development of a technostructure

According to the managerialists, control of the corporation has changed hands. Thanks to a "technocratic style of evolution,"[51] "capitalists lacking function" have been deprived of authority by "functionaries lacking capital." "Ownership management" has become "professional management."[52]

The divorce of ownership from control splits the role of the risk taker and the role of the decision maker. Initially the entrepreneur accomplished both functions; later both the capitalist and the manager determined the risk; today it is management who decides what risks to take, while it is the firm as an entity, as a social system, and finally the totality of owners, creditors, suppliers, and consumers who take the financial risks.[53]

Because of the divorce between ownership and control, a new elite is said to have emerged: the managerial group. Berle writes:

"... [the] concentration of economic power separate from ownership has, in fact, created economic empires, and has delivered these empires into the hands of a new form of absolutism relegating owners to the position of those who supply the means whereby the new princes may exercise their power."[54]

The most important aspect of this phenomenon is that today, along with control of the corporation, managers handle the social power deriving from it. Power, in fact, is in the hands of those who decide, that is, not in the hands of the people who possess wealth but of the people who manage it.[55] This power extends from within the organization out to the society because "the instruments of production are the seat of social domination; who controls them, in fact not in name, controls society for they are the means whereby society lives."[56] Thus we can refer to this group as the "dominant or ruling class ... Such a group has the power and privilege and wealth in the society, as against the remainder of society."[57]

The transformation that has occurred is much more than a transfer of economic power. The new protagonists in the history of the large corporation are those whom Daniel Bell labels "corporate organizers," "a special breed, often engineers, whose self-conscious task was to build a new economic form...."[58] The category of manager is different from that of owner because it is characterized by different goals and values, that is, by a new ideology. The criteria controlling business decisions have changed, as for example, in the matter of investments: "The managerial economy is no longer 'the profit system.' "[59] In fact, managers do not have an interest in increasing profits, of which they would enjoy only a small part[60]; rather, they "have an interest in maintaining and expanding their own power,[61] that is, in developing the enterprise and thus the breadth of direct and indirect influence that the enterprise exercises."[62] Having reached maturity, the large corporation is no longer forced merely to maximize earnings; rather its goals become to maximize growth and technical innovation.[63] These goals are interconnected since expansion depends on creative ability.

The values of the managerial group stress expertise together with a strong ethical sense and a sense of responsibility. The subjective nature of the traditional entrepreneur's decisions, his nepotism, and the intrusive effects of his personal idiosyncracies create an enormously different environment from that of the application of administrative rationality. The latter, which draws heavily on planning, formal organization systems, the application of mathematical methods, and the use of computers tends to highlight the objectivity of decisions.[64] New values governing the relationship between the corporation and society foster something akin to a "corporate conscience" which prevents the manager from acting solely in his own interest or in ways that are clearly socially irresponsible; they also lead to the search for public consensus. This requires a constant monitoring of public interests to which the manager will eventually have to respond.[65] These new values contrast with those of the old elite, the owner-entrepreneurs, who exalted individualism, property rights, and private initiative[66]; ostensibly the new elite is nonegocentric, responsible, and sensitive to social issues.

The new elite's values and behavior are important inasmuch as they have a tangible impact on the society surrounding the firm. Because of the complexity of the managerial role and the interconnections between the corporation and the environment, the consequences of managerial action go beyond the firm's walls. Thus, when an expert becomes a technocrat, he acquires influence in the making of decisions that have social and political implications. The technocrat's influence is "based on the fact that, although free from the bureaucracy's organizational and ideological ties, he 'speaks for' the organization. His competitive power vis-à-vis political forces derives not only from 'independence' with regard to everything which is political, but also from the fact that, at least in certain contexts, he can use the bureaucratic apparatus for political ends."[67]

According to Jean Meynaud, technocracy emerges from the possession of a competence that places the expert inside the decision-making apparatus; his role allows him to enter the political arena.[68] A change in the protagonists of economic life has thus brought about a change in the persons who possess political power.

Thanks to its growth, the modern corporation is today an economic entity of considerable might. Many writers have described business as free from the control of capital, guided by an enlightened elite whose behavior is rational and whose goals—inasmuch as they are aimed at achieving not profit but growth—are beneficial for the country's welfare and are pursued in congruence with social needs.

2.3. Is the manager a technocrat?

Once the new power holders are more clearly identified as members of the technocracy, their features still remain unclear. Some authors give them a very extensive definition, others a more restricted one. For Galbraith the technostructure is not limited to corporate executives, but also includes those experts, employees, and workers who contribute to decision making with their specialized knowledge, talent, and experience. This enlarged group constitutes "the guiding intelligence—the brain—of the enterprise."[69] Meynaud, however, does not think it possible to equate the expert with the technocrat. The transition from one role to the other occurs only when the expert "acquires the capacity to make or largely determine decisions as an empowered official."[70]

The manager's influence can both override the specialist's contribution and dispossess the traditional power holders. In transmitting important information, the expert serves the decision maker; but the technocrat deprives him of authority, because his knowledge is indispensable to the decision, and what appears as a suggestion on his part may in fact be the only possible option. When the expert is responsible for choosing among courses of action, he becomes a technocrat.[71]

In examining the managerial role one must not lose sight of the fact that the notion of technocracy implies proximity to political power—power external to the firm. However, a manager can exert influence of a political nature only after he has climbed to power in a large economic organization. For the manager to attain the political power needed to be defined as a "technocrat" two conditions must be met: the development of a managerial class in the leadership of the business enterprise, and the exercise of influence—via the enterprise—on political decisions.

Our analysis has been aimed primarily at measuring the presence of the first condition among managers; that is, at assessing the amount of power they enjoy within the corporation.

3

The Decision
Process

How can we measure the power of the managers? For this investigation we examined several alternative measures.[1] We rejected reliance on formal titles (i.e., identifying influential individuals as those who occupy high positions in the organizational hierarchy), because titles are not adequate proof of the presence of power.[2] We also rejected the use of hearsay (i.e., relying on the judgment of other organizational members)[3] because it is based on subjective perception. We elected instead to use an approach that focused on decisions—i.e., on actual behavior and its effects. Thus we decided to gather information on the types of decisions made by the executive and to analyze them from a qualitative point of view, that is, taking into account their impact on the organization.

Any analysis of decision making in large modern corporations confronts us immediately with the difficult problem of identifying who is really responsible for a decision.

3.1. Individual vs. collective decisions

Today corporate decisions are the result of an organizational process, not of an individual action. The complexity of the problems faced by a modern corporation requires the contribution of different kinds of expert knowledge and therefore the participation of persons having different functions. According to many of the people we interviewed, "Serious decisions are never made by a single person but always collectively. The corporation's real strength is precisely in the distribution of responsibility"; "All important decisions are made around a table."

In a large corporation, the cost of an error caused by a unilateral decision, which can be one-sided and influenced by idiosyncratic experience, is potentially very high. The organization protects itself against such a risk by creating a multistage decision-making system which provides a set of review procedures and controls. Thus the decision is the culmination of a process that involves different opinions meshing with, complementing, and displacing one another, permitting an exhaustive examination of a multifaceted problem. "An executive decision is a moment in a process. The growth of a decision, the accumulation of authority, not the final step, is what we need most to study."[4]

It follows that no single person "decides" anything: every important decision is the product of an intricate process of mediation involving individuals within and external to the organization. As one person interviewed commented, "In this corporation there are no major decisions for which any individual executive can boast of being responsible. Instead, decisions are made with the participation of various organizational levels, sometimes, in fact, without clear lines of demarcation between managers and technicians. Each proposal undergoes a set of checks." Other managers made the following remarks: "We have teamwork, and it is very unlikely that the responsibility for a decision would fall exclusively on one person"; "Decisions are always made with colleagues: one can share responsibility, but one cannot be solely responsible."

It follows that "decision making . . . is an organizational process. It is shaped as much by the pattern of interaction of managers as it is by the contemplation and cognitive processes of the individual."[5] The concept of final authority loses meaning and, as a result of the growing specialization of managers, responsibility becomes decentralized, shifting from the top of the organization to the group of those who are privy to specialized knowledge. When responsibility is parceled out, authority becomes pluralistic.[6] As Harlan Cleveland notes,". . . sheer size would produce a complex process of decision. For a large organization is a deliberately created system of tensions into which each individual is expected to bring work-ways, viewpoints, and outside relationships markedly different from those of his colleagues."[7]

To say that the corporate decision is more than an act of individual will, and that it is an organizational process, means that it is a kind of dynamic transaction. It can be divided into phases:

a. Someone in the organization identifies the existence of a problem.

b. The search for a solution activates a mechanism involving a varying number of people, according to the problem's complexity; the relevant information is conveyed through the channels of corporate communication and, at different points in the organization, reaches individuals with different specializations. In the case of a difficult problem, the search for a solution extends upward through the hierarchy, involving more than one executive level. This hierarchical ascent produces qualitative changes in the problem's definition, because it often causes the idea to be further generalized and to be placed in a longer time perspective.

c. Every individual makes contributions from his specialized point of view, based on his experience and personal acumen. From this process a variety of ideas, interpretations, and courses of action emerge.[8]

d. The initially confused and contradictory influx of ideas takes shape progressively and becomes a composite product: some proposals are reinforced by encountering other supportive ones, others are discarded following new critical input; different but complementary points of view become integrated.

e. In all phases of the process there is continual "negotiation" among interested parties aimed at solving interpersonal or interdepartmental tensions. These conflicts of interest and the compensating mechanisms necessary to smooth them over complicate the decision process and diminish its rationality—a rationality that is already limited by problem ambiguity and unclear objectives. The best solution is not necessarily the most technically accurate, but the one that has the greatest probability of being accepted by those who will have to implement it.[9]

f. When the alternative feasible solutions have been reduced in number, a point occurs when a particular decision becomes inevitable. From that moment anyone intervening in the decision-making process can only accept the suggestion and apply it.

When this stage has been reached, it is impossible to specify a single party who has been responsible for the decision, nor is it possible to roll back the decision's genesis to a specific temporal point or to a precise hierarchical level.[10] As one person interviewed confirmed, "If I have an idea, I propose it. Then, in discussing it with others, together we arrive at a decision. I do not feel, though, that I can say I have realized something of my own creation. Not even the one who implements an idea owns the decision."

The course of the decision-making process proceeds through different stages and different places. The place where the problem originates is often different from where the relevant information is obtained and where the information is finally translated into a set of executive orders. Typically the solution emerges at an intermediary point in the hierarchy, not where the problem originally emerged or at the hierarchical level that will announce the decision. The higher levels will receive an organized package of information that is internally consistent, already indicative of a determined line of action. Choosing among courses of action, elaborating and synthesizing proposals are the functions of the hierarchy, since the task of every organizational level is to diminish the degree of uncertainty. An executive interviewed noted, "Even the president and executive committee take as a matter of fact the decisions formulated by lower echelons; it is not difficult for a subordinate to present various courses of action in such a way as to condition decisions at the top."

Nonetheless there does exist a point in the corporate hierarchy where a decision crystallizes and a single individual or small group assumes responsibility for the idea, even if such an attribution, as we have seen, is spurious. Thus the high-level person who announces a policy statement or signs it becomes responsible for it in everyone's eyes. The very fact that he assumes responsibility for a decision's consequences means that he will tend to get credit for its creation as well.

This perception has a logical basis. At the beginning of the process the technical aspects of the firm's problem require the analysis of an expert; but once this diagnosis has been made, the problem is considered in the framework of medium- and long-term perspectives. In this way a solution can become a new guideline or a new policy, and as such it enters the top management's domain of competence. Furthermore, if it is true that top management's decisions are conditioned by lower management's information processing and progressive elimination of alternatives—a procedure of progressive filtering—it is also true that responsibility for the evaluation and acceptance of recommendations rests on top management's shoulders. Sometimes the critical evaluation is based not so much on the technical soundness of a proposal as on the competence and ability of the individual who proposed it. This judgment is itself a decision.

Accordingly, our research reveals a discrepancy: a complex decision-making process may be defined as collective, but there is often a widespread perception that a single person is responsible for each decision. While many executives interviewed stressed the practice of collegiality, only 1 percent of them, in describing important decisions, declined to ascribe responsibility to someone on the ground that the decision-making process in his firm was collective. Even in a cooperative system there are individuals who stand out from the group and influence it; furthermore, initiating a proposal and encouraging its adoption, sometimes against the opinion of one's superiors,[11] often shifts the responsibility from the executive who endorses the policy back to the person who started the process.

In fact a manager quite properly considers himself to have made a decision when one of his proposals is adopted by upper management; hence the sizable number of managers in staff positions who come to describe, as their own, important decisions that in fact they only proposed and supported. The endorser of a decision is presented as the carrier and not the author of the decision. The fertile seed is seen to have been sown by others. As one specialist put it, "I managed to 'insert' my idea into the minds of several executives."

In any case, there appears to be a deep-rooted tendency to attribute the authorship for a decision, sometimes unilaterally and erroneously, to a single individual. Such attribution is practiced by all parties—the one who believes he made the decision as well as the one who has to abide by it. In the first case, the explanation lies in the power gratification enjoyed by the one able to claim authorship for the decision; the fact that many managers are in fact "ghost decision makers"[12] is not always sufficient to confer upon them the mantle of power. For that, one's power must be visible to and recognizable by others. To participate anonymously is not enough; one must be perceived as one of the makers. Sometimes it is enough to be present at the "birth" of an important decision: the prestige of having been consulted and the precious knowledge of information unknown to others are indirect power indicators.

For the people whose relation to the decision is passive—that is, those who will have to abide by it—there is a compelling need to locate power. This need is both psychological and practical: the identification of "key" persons in an organization affords the member a clearer (if simplified) perception of the organization's operations and of the relationships that connect him to the other members; furthermore, having identified the focal points in which influence is concentrated, he is able to direct requests or pressures toward them. Protagonists and spectators alike therefore tend to identify individuals in a collective process which, were it to remain faceless, would elude comprehension and control.

The need to identify the locus of decision-making power is also strong in many people outside the enterprise. The community tends to personalize the corporation, since it is easier to hold responsible a person or group. In dealing with a legal body such as a corporation the only available instruments of communication are through formal and legal channels, while in dealing with an individual one can choose among a range of approaches, from informal manipulation to public pressure and even direct frontal attack, all more readily directed at a person than at his position.

Visibility and identification as a locus of power are also needed by the head of the organization when he has to deal with the outside environment. He must embody the enterprise and be able, if necessary, to impress external groups with the full weight of the firm's economic power and come to terms with them.

It is to the top person or to a narrow oligarchy that other political and economic leaders will turn by preference. Because external relations are managed by those at the top of the hierarchy, the intermediary levels that have contributed to decisions are at this moment excluded from the interaction. In fact they do not possess either the contacts or the necessary cloak of power to enable them to appear as responsible participants.

3.2. Characteristics and typology of decision making

Researchers have taken for granted the fact that decision making is the most important managerial function; choosing among alternative courses of action is a daily and significant event. Herbert Simon, who uses decision making to identify the managerial role, distinguishes three steps:
1. To single out problems requiring a decision.
2. To examine possible courses of action.
3. To choose among courses of action.[13]

To elaborate this classification, Simon points out that the organization operates on three layers, namely:

1. An underlying system of physical production and distribution processes;

2. A layer of programmed decision processes for governing the routine day-to-day operation of the physical system;

3. A layer of nonprogrammed decision processes for monitoring the first-level processes, redesigning them, and changing parameter values.[14]

It is important to distinguish the different types of decisions:

a. The *programmed* decision, which is repetitive and routine; it consists of applying a predefined procedure;

b. The *nonprogrammed* decision, which is innovative and not predefined.[15]

While the former decision solves problems that have occurred and been solved in the past, the latter tackles new problems or those of a sufficiently complex nature as to escape rigid rules and demand an appropriately new response. While the former follows a trail, the latter blazes it.

Simon's terminology is borrowed from computer language: a "program" is "a detailed prescription or strategy that governs the sequence of responses of a system to a complex task environment." While the body of procedural rules constitutes a "program," "nonprogrammed" describes the response to situations for which the system lacks specific procedures; the solution must spring from a "general capacity . . . for intelligent, adaptive, problem-oriented action."[16]

Simon points out that these two types of decision represent the poles of a continuum and that many cases are intermediate. Because of the repetitiveness of the productive process and the existence in the organization of a preestablished set of guidelines and procedures, the majority of decisions are of the programmed type. In fact, corporate life situations are predictable enough to permit people responsible at the highest levels to define in advance a set of behavioral rules. Company changes in response to new productive realities are more often smooth adjustments than dramatic episodes of innovation.

The effects of the two types of decision are different: while the programmed decision aims to keep the organization on its tracks, neutralize changes brought about by unforeseen obstacles, and maintain the *status quo*, the nonprogrammed decision opens the door to innovation and change. To abandon routine, i.e., the program, means modifying the existing situation sometimes permanently, and creating an array of new organizational procedures.[17]

Risk

An important component of the nonprogrammed decision is that it always entails a degree of risk. Innovation, by setting aside already tested and proven plans, is full of pitfalls. The consequences of a decision about new ideas or conditions are less predictable and the financial risk to a large corporation is often considerable.[18] In fact, we regard the considerable expenditure required by such an action as an indicator of decision-making power.[19]

Nor is risk necessarily only financial, even for the corporation (despite the fact that in the corporation's case all risks are ultimately translated into financial ones); there are cases in which the stakes are the firm's prestige or its industrial peace.[20] And there is the personal risk (involving his job or career) that the manager assumes when he makes a decision without having first sought higher endorsement, or worse, when he goes against his boss's judgment.[21]

Our analysis examined two types of managerial decisions:

a. The *routine* decision (i.e., Simon's "programmed decision"). Having been applied in the past, its effects are predictable. It involves a set of adjustments to cope with slightly changed situations; it does not involve creative or innovative activities and does not lead to substantial transformations in the work environment. Its function consists of keeping the organization on its tracks; the implicit risk is minimal (although sometimes choosing not to innovate is itself a source of negative outcomes).[22]

b. The *unusual* ("nonprogrammed") decision, which always has in some degree an innovative content. It involves a departure from beaten paths, and therefore brings about a greater degree of risk.

Clearly the exceptional character of nonprogrammed decisions makes them rare. The manager in his day-to-day activities engages in largely routine decisions falling within preestablished guidelines. Nevertheless there exists a substantial qualitative difference between a manager who *never* had the experience of confronting an innovative and risky decision, and a manager who has been challenged by the need to be inventive and has ended by modifying his own work environment, sometimes in a substantial and long-term way.

The managerial qualities required for the two types of decision making are different: while knowledge and respect for corporate policies and customs suffice for the routine decision, experience, insight, and intuition are required for the unusual decision.[23] Yet despite the special skills required by the nonprogrammed decision, its exercise does not depend on the personality of the manager but rather on the autonomy that the corporate system grants him.

By measuring the latitude of discretion bestowed on the individual manager we can focus on the qualitative aspects of the managerial role, well beyond those associated with rank. We can also distinguish the manager who makes decisions on the basis of already established programs and refers nonroutine problems to others, from the manager who may have formulated those programs and who has the authority to deal with nonroutine issues.

By applying these criteria we defined two categories of managers:

a. *The decision maker*, that is, the innovative manager whom the organization entrusts with the making of new and/or risky decisions, outside established plans;

b. *The routine executive*, who intelligently carries out others' decisions—by no means a limited task, as it sometimes implies overcoming sizable difficulties. Implementation of policies involves a continual process of short-term decisions, aimed not so much at adding new ideas as at smoothing over the difficulties of practical application. The routine executive translates into operational terms something that is abstract—the generic guideline, the objective. A manager comments, "To work is to choose. When one is working, one is continually making decisions."

The importance of this type of managerial activity should not be underestimated: to analyze the data, to evaluate the factors at play, to choose among alternative solutions is a process that implementation has in common with important initiatives. A certain degree of innovation and risk exists also in this case: the transformation of a policy into operational terms is often a creative act, not merely a rote application of experience and knowledge. A badly executed idea can produce harmful results and be costly to the firm. But inventiveness is exercised in a limited framework; the real agents of change, the persons responsible for major modifications, are to be found elsewhere.[24]

During our interviews, we asked managers to describe the most important decisions made in their present position and, as shown in chapter four, we rated these decisions according to their degree of innovation and risk.

Range and long-term outcomes of a
decision: The formulation of strategies

We also used another indicator of power, the manager's participation in the formulation of new company policies. This type of innovative decision covers the totality of organizational activities, has long-term consequences, and is closely linked to a firm's primary functions.[25] Examples are the formulation of new organizational goals or new strategies and procedures needed to attain the company's goals.[26] "The making of a policy . . . is at once a category of decision making, an aspect of organizational change, and perhaps the most significant expression of leadership."[27] It is characterized by its high level of generality or abstraction, the breadth of organizational scope it covers, and the length of time it affects.

Alfred D. Chandler distinguishes operational or "tactical" activities from "strategic" or entrepreneurial activities: the latter consist of the determination of the fundamental goals of the enterprise, the adoption of the rules of action and the allocation of resources suitable for achieving such goals. Examples are deciding on new investments, on expanding the volume of activity, on creating new establishments and branches, on taking on new economic functions, on diversifying productive output; all define new basic goals.[28]

Strategic decisions concern the future of the enterprise; tactical decisions concern the daily activities necessary for productive operations to be carried out efficiently and without hindrance. The strategic decision involves *long-term changes* (i.e., affecting the enterprise's structure), while the tactical decision introduces *short-term adjustments* (i.e., minor transformations of one of the structure's elements).[29] In short, the strategic decision has important implications for the future growth of the whole enterprise. It is distinguished by its *global* and *long-term* implications which are absent from the tactical decision.[30]

As noted earlier, most managerial decision making is routine and tactical, consisting of continual readjustments to general policies. The hierarchical structure plays a fundamental role in entrusting tactical decisions to low-level managers while directing the formulation of strategies to the top of the organization. Nonetheless it is possible for the low-level manager to participate in a consultant capacity and to become, if only occasionally, a policy maker.[31]

Thus for our study two types of managers were distinguished:

a. The *strategic* manager, who contributes to fixing the enterprise's long-term goals.

b. The *tactical* manager, who decides on the most appropriate means for realizing such objectives.

During the interviews, following questions about the most important policy changes in the firm, we inquired about the manager's participation in the formation of such new policies; those who had this experience were considered strategic managers.

3.3. The "internal" and "external" effects of corporate decisions

A decision can also be characterized according to the environment it affects: it can be "inner-directed," that is, it acts only within the organization (on employees, on technology); or "outer-directed," that is, it has effects on the social environment.

We therefore identified two additional classes of executive power:

a. *Internal power* which is exercised within the organization, affecting capital, tools of production, products, and its employees. It may also modify the corporation's structure and therefore the relations within it. For example, changes in the organization of production—e.g., the introduction of new work methods—change the type of expert knowledge required, the training requirements, the type of supervision, the interpersonal relations, and the communication process. The impact of technological and organizational changes on the social relations within the firm is sometimes considerable.

Internal decisions are usually linked to efficiency goals, such as increased productivity, market expansion, or cost reduction, and are strictly professional in nature. They lie well within the manager's realm of competence, and call for the application of his training and experience to the functions he must fulfill. Most executive decisions are of this type; that is, they have a technical character and usually are confined to one department and affect only a part of the organization.

b. *External power* exists when the manager can directly make or influence decisions that, while retaining a corporate character, generate an impact on the economic, social, and political environment external to the firm. They condition or transform the economic and social life of external groups of the community, and/or influence the economy of the nation (or of several nations, as in the case of the multinational corporation). Individuals holding this power affect, through the organization and albeit involuntarily, the society.

The long-term policies of the big corporations have consequences that may transcend corporate boundaries. They require a vision of the connections between the corporation and the industrial world (the firm's suppliers and buyers), the financial groups, the public institutions, and the labor unions. Certain company policies cannot help influencing these groups and therefore require more encompassing strategies.[32] Corporate decisions influencing development (expansions, new investments and their location, reduction of productive output and personnel, etc.) have tangible effects[33] on the firm's immediate surroundings; as a result the persons responsible for such decisions are singled out as holders of economic power and considered as the embodiment of the enterprise.

What we call "decision-makers" enjoy power *within* the organization, while "strategic" managers exert influence also on the world *outside* the corporation. The two types of power rarely overlap and, as we shall see, are in general exerted by different managers.

4

Limits and Conditions
on Managerial Power

Our research results run counter to the theory of the "managerial revolution." They show that a significant number of managers are excluded from major decisions and that the degree of autonomy they possess does not always correspond to that implied by their positions in the firm.

When asked to describe the most important decisions made while in their present positions, the majority of those interviewed described only routine decisions, that is, decisions that were simply the application of already established policies (see Table 4.1). In the picture that emerges the manager appears all too often as an actor playing a predetermined part, a player whose only choices are among lines from a scenario written by others.

Many managers are excluded even from decisions about problems that lie within their own area of competence and which, because of their professional qualifications and their years of experience, they would be well equipped to handle. It is little wonder then, that even more frequently they are excluded from consultation on the wide-ranging problems that involve more than their own department or have long-term effects. (See Table 4.2.)

Table 4.1

The Managers' Range of Decision
(in %, n = 653)

Routine	62
Innovation in one's own specialized area	28
Innovation in other departments or in the whole organization	10
	100

Table 4.2

The Managers' Participation in Policy Formulation
(in %, n = 618)

No participation	52
Preparation of data relevant to decision	22
Consultation about implementation of policies (once the decision has been made)	11
Participation in the act of policy making	15
	100

The managers' limited participation in policy making means that the basic issues, and thus the formulation of guidelines for a division or the whole organization, affecting it for years to come, are to a large extent settled by people who are outside management and may not even consult the managers. The judgment of an external consulting firm may carry more weight than that of a high-ranking executive.

While it is true that policy decisions belong to stockholders and their representatives on the board of directors, it nevertheless would seem reasonable to invite the managers most directly affected by a decision to participate, at least in an advisory capacity, in the discussions leading to it. Instead, the manager finds himself confronted with a *fait accompli*, the consequences of which he must bear even though it may profoundly alter his work methods and affect his career by establishing new rules and restructuring the organization. In addition, the manager is cut off from the complex network of contacts with the world outside the company. Investment decisions, for example, require that a relationship be established with the banking system, from which capital is acquired; with other companies, with whom alliances are formed; and with political agencies, in their dual role of regulating (as in zoning decisions, etc.) and assisting (as in providing financial backing). Such participation by the manager would enrich his role with political and economic responsibilities.

4.1. The gap between decision-making power and participation in policy making

Our study examines power as it shows up in the manager's decision making in an organization and in his participation in policy decisions. The instances where we encounter power and actual participation in policy making (which is rarer) seem to indicate that the manager's influence on the firm's decisions stems primarily from his specific professional knowledge and diminishes whenever nontechnical or long-term issues are the principal factors in the decision.

Our research devotes a good deal of attention to the relationship between decision making and participation in the policy-making process. The difference between these two functions is important; clearly, they involve two different types of managers. Our study shows that, of a total of over 600 managers, only 40—less than 7 percent—possess both types of power at the same time. These 40 persons represent only 17 percent of those classified as decision makers and are usually located at the highest hierarchical level. Thus it seems that the ability to make innovative or even risky decisions in one's own department does not necessarily enable one to participate in efforts to resolve the more general problems of the firm. But the reverse frequently occurs: 45 percent of the 89 managers we classified as policy makers report that they had the opportunity also to assume relevant responsibilities in their own department.

A decision maker's access to policy making is influenced, not surprisingly, by his position in the hierarchy: the higher he is, the more likely it is that he will be invited into the policy-making process (see Table 4.3a). But, curiously, the tendency to award more participation to the managers also varies according to the characteristics of the firm. It is least in multinational corporations (see Table 4.3b), which are the most generous, however, in granting decision-making power; in firms using advanced technology (see Table 4.3c); in decentralized firms (see Table 4.3d); and in large firms (see Table 4.3e and f).[1]

Certain firms appear to grant only one type of managerial responsibility, that is, they are inclined either to delegate specialized decisions to a manager or to invite him to consult in policy making. This aspect will be more closely analyzed in the following pages. Our first observation is that the least participation in policy making by managers is found in firms that have the greatest geographic, structural, or technological complexity. Because of their size, geographical dispersion, and product diversification, these

Table 4.3

Distribution of the Two Kinds of Power
(Decision-making and Policy-making) according to Company Characteristics

a. Percentage of power holders according to hierarchical level

	Hierarchical level		
	Upper	Middle	Lower
Decision makers	43	41	29
Strategists	33	11	6
Difference	10	30	23

b. Percentage of power holders according to corporate ownership

	Corporate ownership			
	State	Private	Multinational	
			Italian	Non-Italian
Decision makers	26	40	54	60
Strategists	30	40	20	32
Difference	−4	0	34	28

c. Percentage of power holders according to the type of technology

	Technology		
	Traditional	Intermediate	Advanced
Decision makers	37	38	39
Strategists	28	12	9
Difference	9	26	30

d. Percentage of power holders according to the organizational structure

	Structure	
	Centralized	Multidivisional
Decision makers	37	41
Strategists	18	7
Difference	19	34

e. Percentage of power holders according to corporate size (number of employees)

	Medium <2,500	Medium-large 2,500-5,000	Large 5,000-10,000	Very large >10,000
Decision makers	30	46	38	41
Strategists	20	29	11	8
Difference	10	17	27	33

f. Percentage of power holders according to corporate size (sales in billion lire)

	Medium <30 bill.	Medium-large 30-50 bill.	Large 50-100 bill.	Very large >100 bill.
Decision makers	34	39	44	36
Strategists	21	20	14	9
Difference	13	19	30	27

firms tend to specialize managerial functions to the greatest extent and the formulation of policies tends to be firmly centralized.[2]

4.2. The decisional space

Managers are not a homogeneous group: in their decision-making power and policy participation they enjoy different degrees of autonomy. The reasons for these differences are not immediately apparent; managerial power clearly depends on the interaction of several variables.

Many analyses of organizational behavior use the individual characteristics of a manager as a critical variable: the power enjoyed by an individual is considered a conquest achieved through personal ability. One cannot deny that in any social situation an individual tends to create around himself an area of autonomy that varies according to his motivation as well as his propensity to take risks and innovate or merely to manipulate his environment. Even in manual and repetitive jobs it is possible for a worker to widen or restrict the scope of his duties; the one who passes the buck is inclined to cut his work to the bone, while the ambitious worker tries to expand it by adding new operations.[3] If this phenomenon can occur at the workers' level, then it should be all the more possible at the managerial level where the individual enjoys more freedom to define his tasks and the procedures to carry them out. The diagram of these factors should therefore be simple (see Figure 4.1).

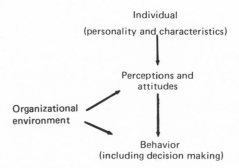

Figure 4.1

The individual is the independent variable; the environment, the intervening variable.

Figure 4.2

The environment is the independent variable; the individual, the intervening variable.

But an individual is not isolated: he acts in a context that cannot but affect his actions. In a work situation, in addition to individual traits—personality, attitudes, and motivation—we must add the impact of the organizational environment, the operating procedures, and the unique characteristics of each firm. The present research presupposed the causal framework shown in Figure 4.2.

Our main hypothesis is that the Italian executive's behavior is predominantly dependent on variables related to his role in the firm and on the firm's unique characteristics. That is, we assumed that the environment in which the manager is immersed is the most important factor in shaping his attitudes and actions. It is the firm's characteristics that determine the extent of his decision-making autonomy. The reason is that power does not reside in the individual but in the organization; it is the organization which has the economic might, the integrated knowledge, and the effective network of communication necessary to the exercise of power. The manager exercises power vicariously, through the organization.

The delegation process

Decision making is a prerogative of the firm's owners, or of those who are chosen by the owners to exercise it. This restricted group monopolizes the *entire* decision-making and policy-making capability. However, since complete centralization cannot be maintained, the top is forced to transmit a part of its functions and privileges to the lower echelons in the organization. Thus a portion of power changes hands; this transition repeats itself throughout the hierarchical ladder. The organization chart is a graphic representation of the process of distribution of functions and responsibilities, and of the decision-making power associated with them.

The organization can be considered a *sociophysical space*, made up of "regions" that are more or less related, peripheral or central, sometimes bordering and sometimes overlapping each other. Each region has a share of the delegated power. These regions are defined both by the hierarchical levels which create stratified horizontal spaces of decreasing importance toward the bottom, and by the different specialist categories which create vertically adjacent clusters. Every manager enjoys an area of autonomy defined by the simultaneous action of these two factors, that is, by the intersection of the hierarchical stratum with his functional area of specialization. He is simultaneously inserted at a particular organizational level and in a particular department. (See Figure 4.3.)

For the manager placed at the bottom of the hierarchical ladder, the levels having the right to interfere in his decisions become

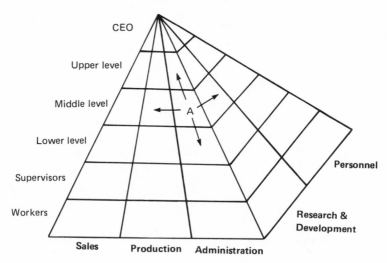

Figure 4.3

Decision-making realm. (Individual A is a middle-level manager in the administration department. His area of autonomy is defined theoretically by both the hierarchical position he occupies and the function of the department to which he belongs.)

more numerous and his field of specialization more limited; these two factors narrow his area of autonomy. At the bottom of the organization, employees involved with substantially routine tasks have extremely narrow latitude for decision.

If one considers the entire organization as a *field of forces*,[4] the area of self-determination will be defined by the points at which external pressures cease to act, creating a space free of interference. Thus the individual's sphere of influence can be conceived not only as a zone unencumbered by external pressures, but also as a field of forces that the manager uses to direct or influence others' actions. It is necessary however to keep in mind that the area reserved to the individual manager is encased in a wider "region," and borders others' areas; there is an *ecology of power*—a set of forces continually challenging the breadth of one's decisional space—and the manager must continually protect his territory.

For some authors power is a constant figure. That is, there exists a definite amount of available power in an organization, and therefore its subdivision constitutes a zero-sum game: whoever manages to annex a share of power or to increase the power he already possesses always does so at the expense of others.[5]

However it may be parceled out by organizational rules, power distribution is not static; each actor's power expands or contracts according to circumstance. By using his position in the hierarchy and taking advantage of his professional competence, the manager can trespass into and interfere with bordering areas. (In the case of Manager A in Figure 4.3, as a finance middle manager he can condition the decisions of colleagues in other departments by controlling costs.) Since these infringements on power can be reciprocal, the danger of baronial struggles is ever present in any large organization.[6] For this reason the organization has been considered "a deliberately created system of tensions."[7] These tensions originate from various points in the organization: from the top, when centralization reduces managerial autonomy; from below, when subordinates refuse to recognize the legitimacy of their superiors' power (as happened in Italy during the labor strife of 1969); or from lateral sources, when colleagues interfere in a specific area of competence of a manager.

Other factors limiting the exercise of power appear when information is inadequate or ambiguous; when the cause-and-effect relationships are uncertain, making it difficult to predict a decision's outcomes; and when a time lapse occurs between the decision and its effects (with delayed feedback, it may be difficult to make the necessary adjustments). These conditions create uncertainty which prevents the manager from making use of all the powers accorded him. He may choose voluntarily to restrict the width of his autonomy and to transfer responsibility to others.

Yet personal inadequacy is usually less decisive as a limiting factor than the stronger external pressures which, in concentric waves, continually pose a threat to the scope of the manager's self-determination as allotted by the rules. It is also necessary to keep in mind that new situations outside the organization itself can cause pressures that modify the amount of available power and change its distribution. For example, the amount of power in a corporation can expand with the firm's growth[8] but can also contract as a result of labor-union struggles or increased government control.[9]

4.3. Role variables

Individual power is not so much wrested from others as it is granted by them: power is variable and subject to the interrelated action of a set of factors, most of which are external and often outside the individual's control. The present research has examined some of the factors affecting the managers' power, grouping them according to whether they are variables involving (a) organizational role (such as the hierarchical rank, department, and functions of the manager); (b) the type of organization (such as the firm's ownership, the sector of technology, size, structure, and growth of sales); (c) personal traits (such as the age, social class origins, education, training, and previous experience of the manager).

4.3.1. Hierarchical level

The most traditional factor influencing the distribution of power is the hierarchical level of the manager—his rank or position in the firm. Not surprisingly, our research reveals a progressive reduction in decision-making power as one descends the hierarchical ladder (see Figure 4.4).

It is nonetheless instructive to note that, even at the highest hierarchical level,[10] the percentage of decision makers (those who take innovative and risky decisions) is less than half (i.e., 43 per-

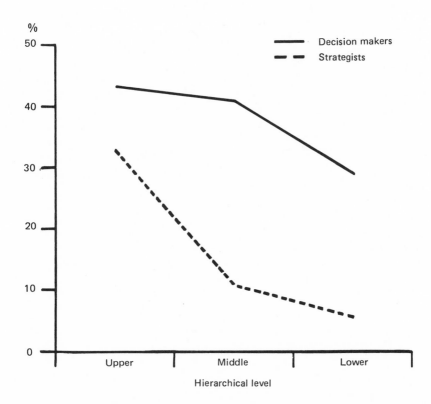

Figure 4.4

Percentage of decision-makers and strategic managers according to
hierarchical level.

cent) of those interviewed, and that at this level the percentage of
those who participate in policy formulation, if only in a consultant
role, is lower still (33 percent).

As we descend the hierarchy, a manager's exercise of power is
sharply reduced. Below the second level only 29 percent of the
junior managers have made innovative decisions, while participation in policy making is found in only 11 percent of cases.

Power assumes the form of an inverse pyramid, the opposite of
the organizational pyramid. The broadest scope of power is where
fewest people are in the organization structure (see Figure 4.5).
It would seem that the tendency to keep decision-making power
centralized is psychological as well as functional: people are reluctant to delegate authority because it represents the most impor-

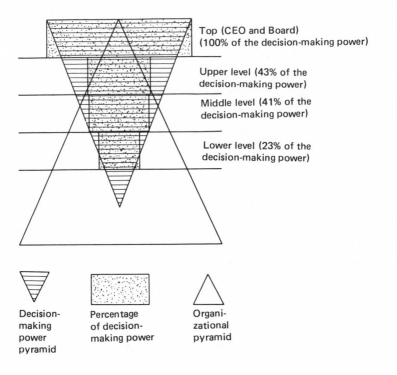

Top (CEO and Board)
(100% of the decision-making power)

Upper level (43% of the
decision-making power)

Middle level (41% of the
decision-making power)

Lower level (23% of the
decision-making power)

Decision-
making
power
pyramid

Percentage
of decision-
making power

Organi-
zational
pyramid

Figure 4.5

The power pyramid and the organizational pyramid.

tant privilege of their position and the most visible evidence of
their status.[11]

Degree of decentralization

Analysis of the distribution of decision-making power throughout
the hierarchical ladder permits us to assess the extent of decentralization in the firm and to define the organization's power structure.[12]

Hypothetically, the power structure of a firm could develop
over time—from a high degree of centralization in the hands of
the entrepreneur-owner of the small family business to a high
degree of decentralization resulting from the complexity and
breadth of the modern corporation. If this hypothesis is valid, the
degree of delegation observed in a firm should locate it at a definite stage of development. The last stage—that of "total decen-

tralization"—is purely theoretical, of course, even though it shows up in the literature on "corporate democracy" and in Yugoslavia's experiences of "self-management"; decision making occurs only after consulting all the organization's members, including subordinates. This last stage remains a theoretical concept. In the centralization-decentralization continuum, the Italian companies move from a situation of "absolute monarchy" to a limited oligarchy and finally to an increasingly broader oligarchy.

Our first attempt at measuring the degree of decentralization entailed estimating the share of power delegated to managers by the very top; this is the operational approach, described at the beginning of the chapter. As we noted, the fact that only 38 percent of the managers interviewed ever made an important decision indicates that decentralization had not progressed very far.

Another approach consisted of analyzing how the power of decision (delegated from above) is spread through the hierarchy. It is revealing to isolate the first stage of the decentralization process —that is, the transfer of power from the top to the next level— because it is here that the process of delegation begins, and here that the amount to be delegated is determined. (We hypothesize that the same criterion of granting or withholding power will come to be applied later by the upper level with respect to the following level, and so forth—delegation practices being a consistent company policy, i.e., a managerial "style.") One way of calculating the breadth of decentralization consists of measuring the gap in power between the upper and the bottom levels of the hierarchy. In the case of our firms, the gap is observable: 43 percent of the managers at the third level are decision makers compared to 29 percent at the bottom level.

On the hypothesis that a corporation's characteristics are responsible for the differences in the distribution of power shares, we grouped the corporations according to various organizational characteristics. For instance, we considered the form of corporate ownership (see Table 4.4).

The decision-making power held by managers is cut in half at the low hierarchical levels, except in the Italian multinationals where the bottom level keeps more than two-thirds. Visually, the structure of authority assumes the form of a funnel, gradually diminishing toward the bottom. In the two multinationals (which grant the largest amount of decision-making authority) the area of

Table 4.4

Percentage of Decision Makers according to Type of
Ownership and Hierarchical Level

| | Ownership | | | |
	State	Private	Italian multinational	Non-Italian multinational
Hierarchical level				
Upper	26	40	54	60
Lower	15	18	39	35
Difference	11	22	15	25

autonomy, although still contracting progressively, stays much higher at all levels than in the case of the state-owned firm, in which the slight autonomy accorded the upper level is consistently followed by the little authority accorded to the two lower hierarchical levels (see Figure 4.6a).

A more significant determinant of the distribution of power within the hierarchy is corporate size: the very large corporation, while the most generous with the upper level, drastically restricts authority below the second level (see Figure 4.6b).

The degree of decentralization is also a function of organizational structure[13]: a multidivisional structure, as expected, confers a greater degree of autonomy to all of the hierarchical levels than does a centralized one (see Figure 4.6c).

The middle manager

The state of affairs for those at the upper and lower managerial strata is fairly clearly defined: the former are partially inserted into the power structure and the latter, for the most part, are cut off. But managers of the intermediate level find themselves in an ambiguous situation: while they share with the upper level a similar autonomy in technical decisions, they are closer to the lower levels in their lack of participation in policy making (refer to Figure 4.4).

This situation may reflect the qualitative difference in functions; the middle level is composed primarily of specialists and efficiency experts whom the organization provides with specific decision-making power where technical issues are concerned but excludes from decisions on policy matters.

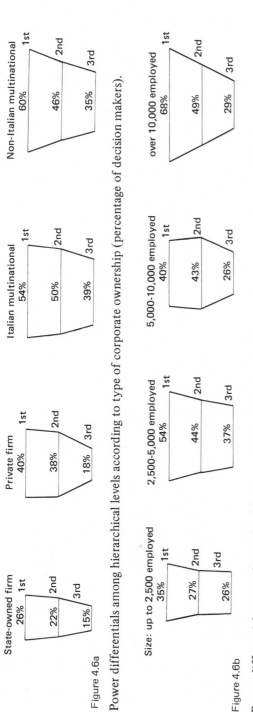

Figure 4.6a

Power differentials among hierarchical levels according to type of corporate ownership (percentage of decision makers).

Figure 4.6b

Power differentials among hierarchical levels according to corporate size (percentage of decision makers).

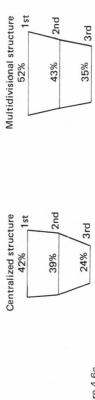

Figure 4.6c

Power differentials among hierarchical levels according to organizational structure (percentage of decision makers).

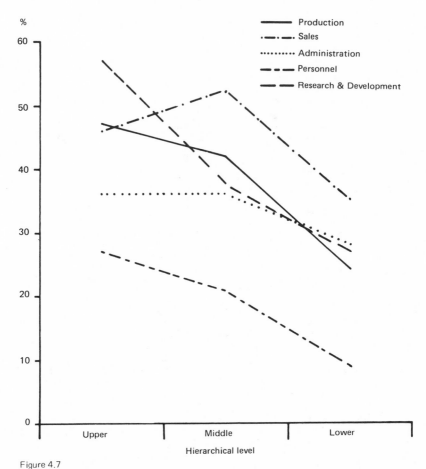

Figure 4.7

Percentage of decision makers according to departmental affiliation
and hierarchical level.

Further, even in the decision-making areas that would appear to
be under their jurisdiction, the middle managers are subjected to
restrictions in power, which vary according to each corporation's
unique characteristics (see, for example, the difference between
the Italian and the non-Italian multinationals in Figure 4.6a) and
by department (see Figure 4.7).[14]

The situation of the middle managers is therefore less predictable
than that of people immediately above and below. Climbing the
hierarchical ladder to attain the middle level does not automatically

guarantee the manager a wider sphere of influence, and his aspirations to take part in important decisions or to be consulted on new strategies are often thwarted.

4.3.2. The manager's own department

A second variable affecting the manager's power is the department to which he belongs. We hypothesized that in the process of distributing power, each of the sectors into which the firm is divided receives an amount of power related to its importance to the organization.

Thus the firm's "key" departments—so called not only because they are larger but because they carry out the major corporate functions—obtain a larger share of the power, which is lodged with the managers who work in them. We define the key sectors as those directly carrying out the goals for which the organization has been created. Historically, these are the line sectors, performing the vital functions of producing and selling; not surprisingly, these are also regarded as the most important in the managers' perception. (See Figure 4.8.) A staff sector such as the personnel department contains the least number of decision makers (see Figure 4.9).[15]

The actual situation is of course more complex than the simple model sketched here. For example, throughout a corporation's evolution, the traditional dominance of the productive function over the sales function tends to decline—and in fact many of the firms sampled recognize that they have switched from a productive orientation to a market orientation.[16] Our study shows that the sales departments had a larger percentage of decision makers than production departments (46 percent as against 36 percent). Further, in some firms the key sector is neither production nor sales; in many technologically advanced firms or firms marketing new products, R&D is seen as the key sector, being fundamental to the realization of the corporation's goals. (See Figure 4.10.)

It is clear that company traits, which give priority to some departments over others, are in part responsible for differences in the degree of power granted to certain managers. Thus production and sales, while dominant in traditional industry, decline in power and are superseded by R&D and administration in technologically advanced industry. (Production and sales departments' declining importance is also visible in the policy participation of managers in

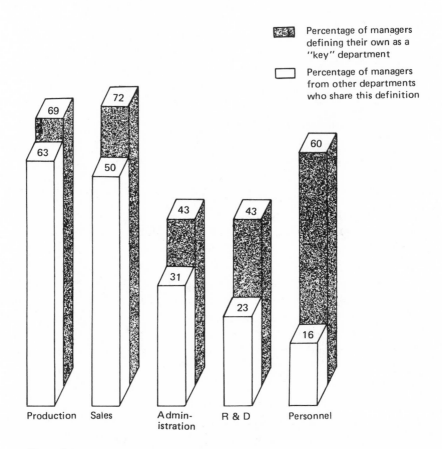

Figure 4.8

Managers' perception of the importance of the various departments.
The discrepancy between self-attributed prestige and actual prestige.

these departments.) The relative importance that a sector assumes within a given type of industry not only influences the distribution of decision-making power, it also affects managers' salaries; holding hierarchical level constant, managers in the key sectors usually receive higher pay.

As we mentioned, the managers' own judgments yielded a classification of departments by importance: production and sales were seen by most as the key sectors (Figure 4.8). But a considerable percentage of managers placed in the "minor" sectors tend to overrate the importance of their own departments. This tendency

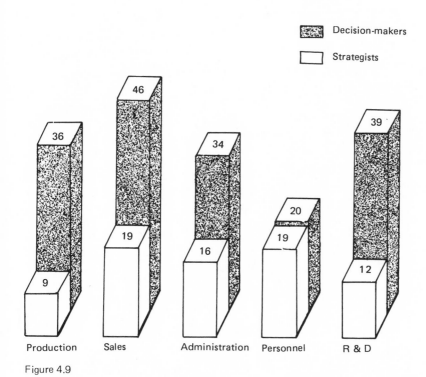

Figure 4.9

Percentages of decision makers and strategists in the various departments.

increases with the decline in the objective importance of a sector. While the managers in charge of production (the sector receiving the maximum recognition) were the most accurate in perceiving the importance of their own department, those in charge of personnel (which has the least prestige) appeared the least realistic.

This distorted perception, explicable in psychological terms, can also have a logical basis. Sales managers, for example, overestimated their department's importance and yet it is true that this sector is growing in importance in all companies; its members appeared to be aware of this, while the rest of the organization was still reluctant to admit it. The discrepancy between perceived and objective status, sometimes considerable in certain "minor" departments, could be interpreted in a similar way: those belonging to an "emerging" department (a typical example is R&D) are already aware of the major role they are bound to assume, while the rest the organization is clinging to the traditional perspective on the

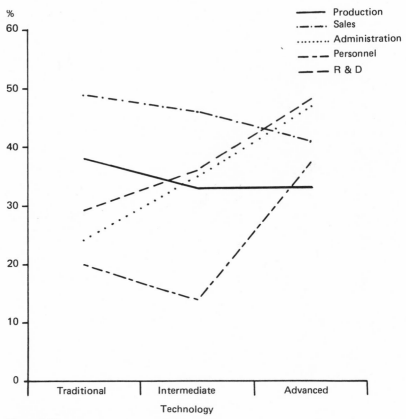

Figure 4.10

Percentage of decision makers according to departmental affiliation and type of technology.

productive and commercial functions. So also, the seriousness of industrial relations problems in Italy amplifies, in the eyes of personnel managers, the importance of personnel management and conflict resolution.

4.4. Organizational variables

The foregoing section focused on the role characteristics of the manager—his position in the hierarchy, his sector, and his staff or line function—characteristics that have the effect of changing the distribution of power *within* the firm itself. A second group of variables distinguishes instead the firm's unique characteristics as factors that also affect the range of possible management styles. Some of these characteristics are intrinsic to the firm and change little over time; these include the technological sector, geographic location, and size. Other features of importance depend on the policies of a given enterprise; they are the type of organizational structure, or a production versus a market orientation. Other characteristics may vary over time, such as the rate of a firm's growth in employees or in sales. Finally, a factor partly responsible for a firm's global behavior is its type of ownership, which can create different goals for the corporation and different concepts of leadership delegation.[17]

A difficulty encountered when measuring the effect of a corporation's characteristics on managerial authority stems from the likelihood that these characteristics have a joint impact which makes difficult a separate analysis. Therefore we examined also the interaction of some major variables—technology, size, structure, and ownership.

4.4.1. Technology

The type of technology a firm uses—classified here as traditional, intermediate, and advanced[18] —appears to influence the distribution of decision-making power throughout the hierarchy.

A firm using intermediate technology delegates the broadest decision-making responsibilities to the upper managerial level, and considerably less to the levels below it. Such a firm is characterized by the greatest inequality among hierarchical levels and the least decentralization compared to other firms. Firms using traditional or advanced technology delegate a smaller degree of power but maintain minor differences among hierarchical levels. In practice, the total amount of decision-making power divided among levels in each firm is identical[19] ; it is the distribution that varies. It appears more equitable and less influenced by hierarchy in firms using the two extremes of technology (see Figure 4.11).

The reasons for the above findings may be grounded in the diverse nature of these industries. In the traditional firm, decisions involve a modest financial risk, facilitating power delegation to lower levels; in advanced industry there is greater risk, but the technical content of problems fosters decentralization. Thus, with

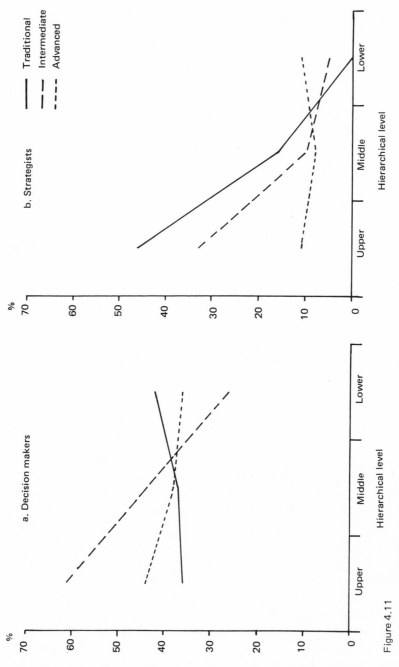

Figure 4.11

Percentage of decision makers and strategists according to type of technology and hierarchical level.

advanced technology, specialists at any level have a certain space for maneuver guaranteed them by the specialized nature of their knowledge. While different technologically, the two types of industry end up delegating power in the same way for different reasons—with the important difference being that in one financial risk is limited while in the other it can be high. Both types of firm have a flattened authority structure wherein each level has almost equal shares of power. One might ask why traditional firms under conditions of minor financial risk do not grant an even larger delegation of power to all levels. The reason is probably to be found again in the technology: in traditional industries decentralization is readily restricted by interference from the top because decisions do not require complex professional knowledge, a condition that does not obtain in technologically complex firms.

The importance of financial risk as a determinant of the distribution of decision-making power appears to be supported by the data on policy making in the various types of industry. In intermediate and especially in advanced firms, the heavy financial risk implicit in all long-term policy decisions seems to be the reason for limited consultation even with high-level managers (refer to Figure 4.11b). In general, as technological complexity increases, participation in policy making decreases (see Figure 4.12).

The unequal distribution of policy participation in firms based on advanced and intermediate technology confirms the separation between the upper level and the rest of management. Advanced industry once again exhibits a flattened authority structure but participation in policy making is very low at all levels, showing the tendency to centralize the handling of high-risk decisions when they do not require expert knowledge. In many cases long-term policies seem to be decided not so much on the basis of technical and scientific research as on financial considerations. In such cases the technologically skilled manager cannot count on his expertise to safeguard his decision-making power.

4.4.2. Size and type of organizational structure

One of the most important influences on the distribution of managerial power is the type of organizational structure in which the managers function.[20]

According to Alfred D. Chandler, the company structure repre-

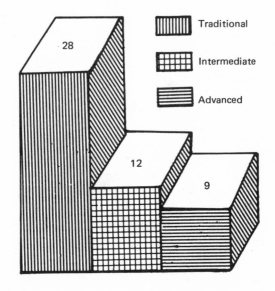

Figure 4.12

Managers' participation in policy making according to
type of technology (in %)

sents a strategic adjustment to a changing technological environment; for example, the decision to diversify production led to the
multidivisional structure.[21] It is logical that single-product firms
would tend to have a centralized structure and their managers a reduced autonomy. Indeed, this type of organization lends itself
better to simple routine production easily controlled from the center.[22]

When productive tasks are difficult, complex, and nonrepetitive,
a decentralized structure is necessary.[23] Another pressure toward
decentralization shows up in the rate of the enterprise's technological innovation: if it is rapid, the channels of communication
provided by the hierarchy are inadequate for conveying the increased flow of information. Thus rigid organizational rules are
barriers to an organization's smooth functioning, while a polycentric
system possesses larger information capacity and can more readily
adjust to technological changes.[24]

The diversity in structure produces two different corporate systems: a "mechanical" system, in which tasks are rigidly defined

and specialized, where interaction is vertical and control centralized; and an "organic" system, characterized by a less formal definition of tasks, by flexibility, and by communication which, even when conveyed through the line, takes the aspect more of informal consultation than of orders.[25]

Some writers believe, contrary to Chandler, that the primary determinant of the type of structure is company size. This variable is of particular interest because growth in size is an important goal of most modern organizations; growth permits the accumulation of resources and facilitates a greater rationality in the system.

Organizational size affects other corporate features. For example, large enterprises are more formal,[26] more bureaucratic,[27] and structurally more complex[28]; they tend to be geographically dispersed.[29]

Large size makes centralization difficult by preventing those at the top from controlling all the information relevant to decisions. Even when the increased importance and cost of decisions would call for centralization of responsibilities, the difficulty of achieving this forces some delegation of decision-making power.[30] Furthermore, growth in size carries with it greater vertical differentiation, that is, an increased number of organizational levels; the lines of communication are stretched, so that it takes more time to transmit information and the possibility for distortion is greater. The risk of inefficiency increases.[31] The large organization tends therefore to break up into small operational units having a measure of autonomy.

To exercise absolute power, top management needs the subordinates' consensus—a highly improbable situation. Large corporations in particular are plagued by internal conflicts.[32]

We begin, then, with two propositions. The first stresses the relationship between technology and type of organizational structure, the second sees structure as a function of organizational size. The apparent disagreement can probably be settled by considering the joint impact of the two characteristics. The interaction between technology and size is confirmed by American studies describing how organizational complexity (number of hierarchical levels) and formalization (which helps maintain centralization) only increase with size in technologically simple firms; by contrast, technologically complex firms employ technicians requiring little supervision and therefore less hierarchical control.[33]

When examining our fifty Italian firms in the light of these research results, the first thing we note is that in Italy there is only a weak link between structure and size and between structure and the level of the firm's technology. This weak relationship is found not only in Italy, but apparently in European firms in general.[34] Our analysis shows that while centralized structure is predominant in small firms (having fewer than 2,500 employees[35] and diminishes as size increases, only half of the very large firms (with more than 10,000 employees) have adopted a multidivisional structure.[36]

The fact that the majority of firms with multidivisional structure are in the intermediate sector of technology (steel and iron, machinery, and chemicals), and that only one firm in the traditional sector and one in the advanced technological sector had such a structure, makes it difficult to venture hypotheses. The multidivisional structure is most frequently found in multinationals, in particular the Italian ones (which are usually larger in size than non-Italian multinationals' branches), but not exclusively in them, nor in all of them. It is necessary to point out that this organizational setup is relatively new to Italy, so that for now, the type of structure may reflect above all the extent of top management's awareness of this organizational option.[37]

However, our research was concerned not so much with determining the causes of differences in company structure, but with checking the effect of structure on decision making and policy participation. For example, Blau and Meyer found that an increase in the number of organizational subunits ("horizontal differentiation") leads to centralization while an increase in the number of hierarchical levels ("vertical differentiation") fosters decentralization.[38] Our research aim was to identify the type of structure of a firm—centralized or multidivisional (according to Chandler's definition)—and to measure its effects on the decision-making power of managers. One of our questions then was whether the multidivisional structure would effectively include a broader distribution of power.

Our data reveals that the type of structure influences the distribution of both decision making and policy participation. But the most interesting fact is clearly visible in Figure 4.13, which shows that the effect of a multidivisional structure is to expand the realm of decision making and to shrink the realm of policy participation. The two effects are observable at all steps of the hierarchical ladder.[39]

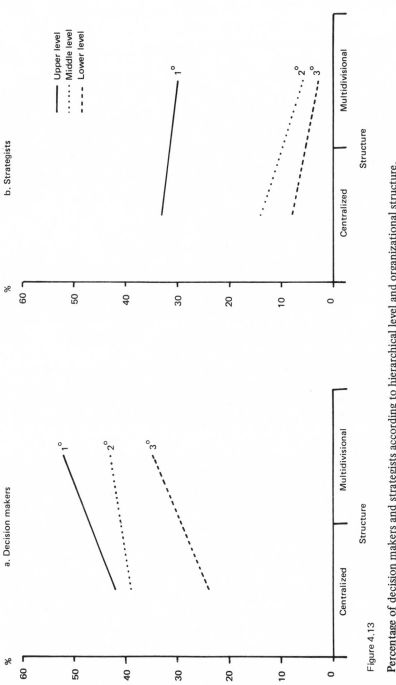

Figure 4.13

Percentage of decision makers and strategists according to hierarchical level and organizational structure.

However, this sharp distinction vanishes when other variables characterizing the firm are introduced; if, for example, we consider technology, we find that a multidivisional structure favors decentralization only in firms of the intermediate sector (steel and iron, machinery, and chemical firms) but depresses it sharply in technologically advanced firms (see Figure 4.14a).[40]

The most important variable in explaining these differences seems to be corporate size: only in very large corporations does a multidivisional structure broaden the decision-making realm of managers (see Figure 4.15a). It seems that the implications of a multidivisional structure—theoretically, its decentralizing effect on decision making—are illusory as long as an organization is small enough in size to permit centralized control over decisions. But when multidivisional structure and very large size are combined, centralized control over decisions becomes impossible because of the number of operational units and the complexity of functions. Multidivisional structure appears to be most functional for the very large firms and it is necessary if the organization must react swiftly and adjust to new situations requiring immediate feedback. The capability for solving problems where and when they emerge is crucial.[41]

Once a decentralization policy (expressed in a new organization chart) has been put into effect, the distance that develops between the top and the other layers tends to prevent a return to centralization, at least in large corporations. By then power has been diffused throughout the hierarchical ladder and every manager has acquired an area of autonomy which he is reluctant to relinquish. Once started, decentralization becomes a centrifugal process. Decision-making activity shifts toward the periphery which, in large corporations, is organizationally and geographically distant from the top: a diffused and complex polycentric system is created which functions to solve corporate problems and is likely to obstruct a return to centralization by the control and blockage of information.

Nonetheless there are situations in which the presence of numerous power centers does not increase the managers' role in the firm. For instance, managers' participation in policy making diminishes in firms with multidivisional structure, whatever their size (see Figure 4.15b). Decentralization, which is functional in dealing with technical problems, turns out to be counterproductive in

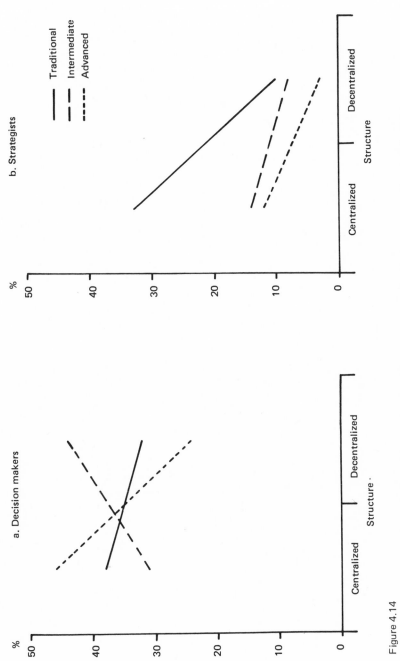

Figure 4.14

Percentage of decision makers and strategists according to type of technology and organizational structure.

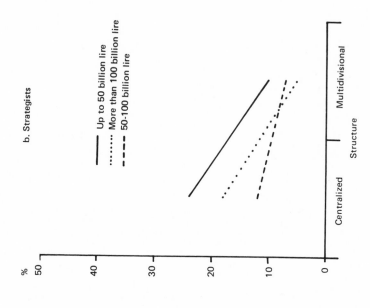

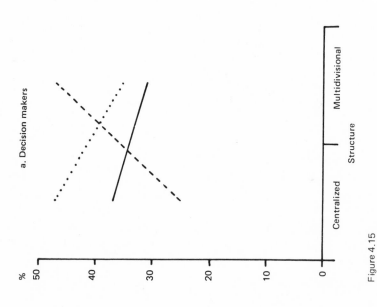

Figure 4.15

Percentage of decision makers and strategists according to corporate size (sales) and organizational structure.

handling global and nonspecialized problems; important corporate decisions are usually made by a tight, integrated group often acting in secret (as for example, when financial deals, mergers, and take-overs are considered). Only those executives physically and organizationally close to the top are selected as consultants.

The choice between centralization or delegation often depends on the nature of the problems to be tackled—specialized versus global, short and medium-term versus long-term. The periphery gets to deal with sectoral problems that concern only a part of the organization. These are objective problems of a concrete and immediate nature which therefore present few options. Whoever is put in charge—the top or the bottom—will in all likelihood reach the same solution. By contrast, corporate policies concern global and long-term operations and contain a high degree of uncertainty and many alternative courses of action. To shift the discussion of these policies to the periphery would risk provoking dissent and slowing the time it takes to put a decision into practice.[42]

Even if the corporation were willing to bear the cost of the time spent in consulting a greater number of managers and could take the risk of creating conflicting factions, there is no reason to believe that an enlarged discussion would lead to a better decision. The peripheral manager can provide a limited contribution to the solution of a global problem. He is deeply imbedded in his own department and oriented toward the pursuit of short-term and medium-length results (on the basis of which he knows he will be judged); he operates in a microcosm (the office or the plant), and his horizon is limited. But corporate policies must be examined in a broader framework and in an extended time frame.[43]

Extreme decentralization can create conflict between an enterprise's medium-term goals and a division's more narrow scope of action.[44] Because of the different perspectives of the two groups of managers (sectoral versus global), decentralization does not mean that the top rung relinquishes all its decision-making power; on the contrary, freed from operational responsibilities, the top concentrates on global objectives, on selecting the most appropriate means to attain them, and above all, on the control measures necessary to guarantee that the organization will move in the predetermined direction. Thus we arrive at the paradox implicit in delegating power: the more the top decentralizes its decision-making authority, the more it tends to centralize its control over global activities.[45] The result is a system of *decentralized management* and *centralized control*.

The growth in size of the firm brings about a division of work among managers, whose activities become specialized and differentiated. A portion of the managerial group devotes itself exclusively to functions vital to the enterprise: coordination (internal control) and handling of relations with the surrounding social milieu (external control). The remaining operational decisions are delegated to the second group of managers. This task division is

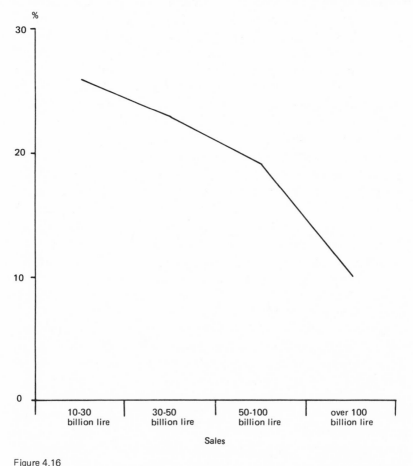

Figure 4.16

Percentage of decision makers who are also strategists, according to corporate size (sales).

sharper in very large corporations; the percentage of decision makers who are also strategists (i.e., policy makers) diminishes with the increase in a firm's size (see Figure 4.16).

The individuals in charge of global control have different characteristics from those engaged in operational activities: the decision maker operates on the basis of technical and scientific knowledge, the strategist on the basis of knowledge of goals. The former is primarily a technician, the latter a technocrat or a "politician." These different characteristics reflect different responsibilities and different organizational needs. The perspective of the operational manager is narrower: he is short-sighted and rightly so, while the policy maker is, or should be, far-sighted.

But, just as the increasing division in manual work is often criticized, would it not be also appropriate to consider the negative effects of excessive managerial specialization? Managers are rendered either "myopic" or "hyperopic" by the training they receive and by the type of problems they customarily handle. If each perspective derives from an organizational necessity, neither constitutes an advantage: the long-range view tends to ignore daily problems and to lack realism, while concentration on detailed activities outside the context of a larger framework is a limitation damaging to both the manager and the firm. Furthermore, management is divided according to whether its actions are based on short- or long-term objectives. When these come into conflict, the resultant tensions and misunderstandings damage group relations.

4.4.3. Managerial information and communication

Interdepartmental meetings

One way to broaden a manager's viewpoint is to expose him, if only in an advisory capacity, to a range of problems covering broader issues framed in longer time perspectives. This can be achieved by a system of collegial decisions. We therefore assessed the existence of interdepartmental meetings, viewing them as an influence on decentralization in a firm.

Such meetings are relatively new in Italian corporations. While meetings within each department are common practice, the problems discussed there are limited; also, participants are connected by formal relationships of subordination and supervision. Meetings among managers at the same hierarchical level—such as those of the management committee—are also a corporate custom. These meetings revolve around problems concerning more than one department or the entire firm but do not upset any hierarchical pattern (the participants being of equal rank).

Much less common are meetings in which managers from different departments as well as from different hierarchical levels exchange ideas. Here the nature of the problems discussed is necessarily broader—interdepartmental or global. Further, a low-level manager no longer finds himself in the presence of a superior to whom he reports, but with managers of higher levels who do not, however, have jurisdiction over him. The type of relationship established is different, primarily based on function, and freedom of expression is greater.

In this type of meeting, mixed in terms of departments and ranks, the emphasis shifts from hierarchy to functional considerations, from individual to collective decision making—perspectives that are new to Italian firms. The significance of such meetings lies in the changes they can bring to the system of internal relationships, to the company's management style, and, finally, to the allocation of power.

a. Organizational changes

The existence of interdepartmental meetings indicates first of all a different conception of the organization and its functioning and of the relations among its members. The classical organizational structure, purely hierarchical, provides a single channel of communication and relationship among members, based on authority relations and vertical in nature. Work relationships occur within the department, and the various departments are connected only through the top; a simple star structure illustrates the situation (see Figure 4.17).

The increase in complexity of tasks, the overlapping of areas of specialization, and the necessity to integrate activities at various levels (and not merely at the top) make new channels of communication and relationship necessary. Concern for the hierarchy gives way to concern for corporate needs.

The institutionalization of meetings formalizes a spontaneous process that even the most rigid organization cannot suppress. The star structure is replaced by a network of vertical and horizontal

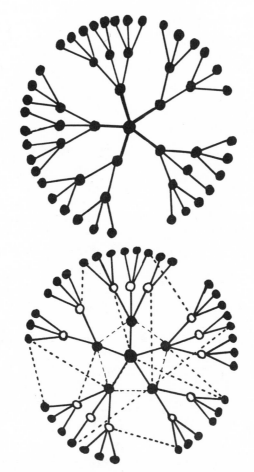

Figure 4.17

Figure 4.18

links (and, as we shall see, diagonal connections) (see Figure 4.18). This capillary-like system of information flows and relations enhances response time and efficiency.

b. Changes in the distribution of decision-making power

To change the information system means to change the distribution of power. Power is in fact connected to the control of information: whoever has this control has access to sources of data that are needed to carry out managerial functions.[46]

When centered primarily on general problems, the custom of interdepartmental meetings diminishes managers' degree of "uncertainty" and puts them in contact with raw information before it has been fully processed by the organization. At this stage it is still possible to check the validity of the information, to discuss its interpretation, and even to change it substantially. A decision can be reexamined, discussed, and changed.

c. Power equalization

The collegial decision shifts the emphasis from hierarchy to other factors; for example, rank is less important because an executive does not have direct authority over other participants, although he may belong to a higher level. Thus, in order to influence them he has to rely on his expertise and analytical skills, not on his position. The differences in power and status are reduced, the hierarchy is flattened and, most importantly, does not constitute the basis of all working relationships. The effect is to foster power equalization.[47]

d. Increases in the share of individual power

The collegial decision constitutes a unique form of leadership sharing; it permits the granting of power to an individual without necessarily subtracting it from another. The concept of power as a constant amount and of its distribution as a zero-sum game loses some of its validity. Sharing power has the effect of multiplying it: the volume of distributed power shares is larger than the total volume, or at least the managers think it is. If a modern firm's decisions spring from multiple actors, more than one manager can attribute to himself what is in fact a group action. And because they generate new informal relations and opportunities for further contacts—especially with the greatest source of organizational power, the chief executive officer—such meetings give a manager the opportunity to stretch his personal influence.[48]

Characteristics and effects of meetings

Throughout the interviews we gathered data on (1) managers' participation in meetings, (2) the nature of problems discussed, (3) the type of participants (departments and hierarchical levels), and (4) the influence the manager believes he exercised in that setting.

a. Focus of the meetings

Three types of meeting were identified and each has a different effect on the manager's perspective.

1. The *departmental meeting*: Hierarchical relations and an emphasis on problems internal to the department are maintained. The horizon of managers stays limited. The exchange, occurring among persons having similar professional background and sharing a common work environment, does not give rise to new perspectives. *The focus is departmental*, relates to a specific task, and is not usually framed in broad or long-term perspectives.

Two types of *interdepartmental meeting*:

2. One involves managers from more than one division; participants represent different functions, e.g., production, sales, R&D, and administration. The discussion centers on problems whose scope exceeds that of the department in which a single executive belongs, but it stresses the links between and among departments. *The focus is interdepartmental.*

3. The other is equally mixed, but the problems discussed concern the firm in its totality. While in the previous case, intervention may take the form of a manager interfering in another's department, here there exists no competition among participants; in fact, the group has the opportunity to have a say in activities that generally would fall within the sole province of top management. *The focus is on corporate-wide issues.*

b. Some effects of the meetings

Through such meetings, the middle or lower-level manager is offered opportunities for building new relationships within the company. He comes into contact with hierarchical levels from which he is normally separated.

In our research we looked at the hierarchical position of the manager being interviewed; we then determined whether his meeting with other participants tended to establish new organizational relationships in a *horizontal* or *vertical* direction.[49] Because of the psychological and practical implications, we took into account the possible presence at meetings of the chief executive. Figure 4.19 illustrates the situation. Both horizontal and vertical connections

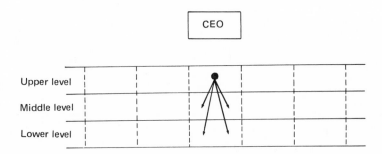

Figure 4.19a

Departmental meeting (vertical relationship).

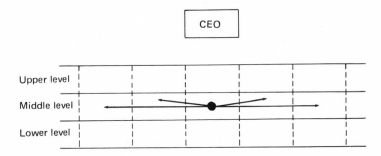

Figure 4.19b

Interdepartmental meeting (horizontal relationship).

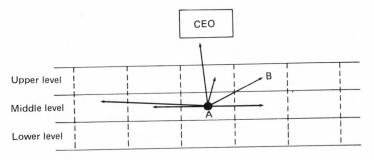

Figure 4.19c

Interdepartmental meeting at same and higher levels.

condition a manager's viewpoint on corporate activities. The fact that he belongs to a particular department often fosters a selective perception of problems, one that is unilateral and partial. To meet with managers of the same rank but who belong to other departments broadens the visual range by revealing the interrelation and complexity of corporate activities. To meet with managers superior in rank helps change the perspective too, since not only each department but also each hierarchical level develops its own special view of the company's problems; in moving up the hierarchy the need for specialized expertise diminishes, the visual field broadens, and the manager's time perspective is extended.

All the firms examined in our research had begun the practice of meetings only recently and in many cases these meetings were neither regular nor institutionalized.[50] Yet only 4 percent of the managers interviewed had never taken part in one. According to practically all managers, their presence at meetings, far from being a formality, was an enriching experience as it often meant that they had a greater chance for participation in decision making. The majority of managers believed that they, personally, made a significant contribution to discussions.[51]

Further, while consultation could appear to be a kind of interference in one's domain, it did not necessarily produce this effect; on the contrary, each manager had the impression that the occasions in which he intervened in other departments' problems were more numerous than those in which others intervened in his own.[52]

In most cases, the relationship established among participants at a company-wide discussion loses its hierarchical connotations. Here, the manager believes he exercises an influence stemming from his professional knowledge and not from his rank.[53]

The practice of *interdepartmental* meetings seems to enhance the distribution of decision-making power or at least creates this impression in the participants. But not all the managers are granted access to overall corporate problems: for a third of them discussion is limited to problems of their own department, and relationships are strictly of a horizontal or hierarchical nature.[54]

Although meetings may downplay hierarchical considerations in favor of professional competence, rank still clearly plays a determining role in selecting the participants. The percentage of managers excluded from general problem solving and limited to departmental meetings is largest at the bottom levels of the organization.

Thus, the new corporate practice of meetings does not always side-
step hierarchical considerations and sometimes reinforces the functional "myopia" of lower managers (who are admitted to discussions of company-wide problems in only 26 percent of cases). (See
Figure 4.20.) Even with this limitation, however, there is a positive
effect associated with meetings in that a number of middle and
low-level managers have a chance to approach large-scale problems
and that some of them come into contact with higher-ranking
managers, including in some cases the CEO (see Figure 4.21).[55]

Since they are not provided by the organizational structure, opportunities for broadening contacts would not exist were it not for
meetings. Furthermore, when low-level managers succeed in overcoming rank-related obstacles and take part in meetings that in-

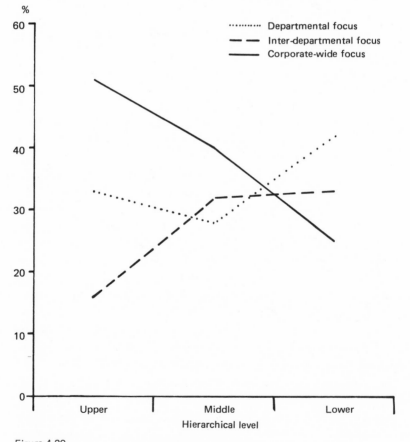

Figure 4.20.

Focus at meetings according to hierarchical level.

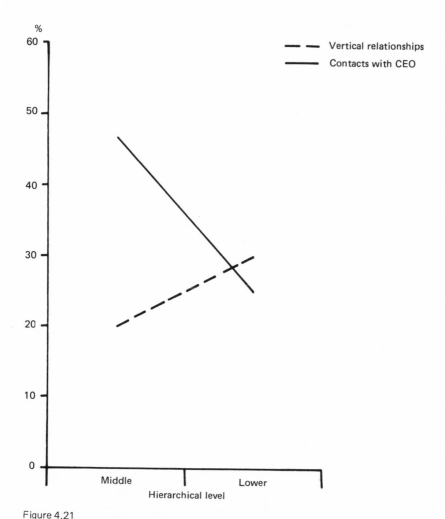

Figure 4.21

Vertical relationships and contacts with the CEO
according to hierarchical level.

clude the representatives of other departments, the possibility of
their making innovative decisions (or of contributing to them) increases considerably. The link between such meetings and the distribution of decision-making power was highlighted in our interviews of low-level managers. Among those who participate only in
departmental meetings only 18 percent have made an important
decision, but 44 percent of those who participate in company-
wide meetings have made important decisions (see Figure 4.22).

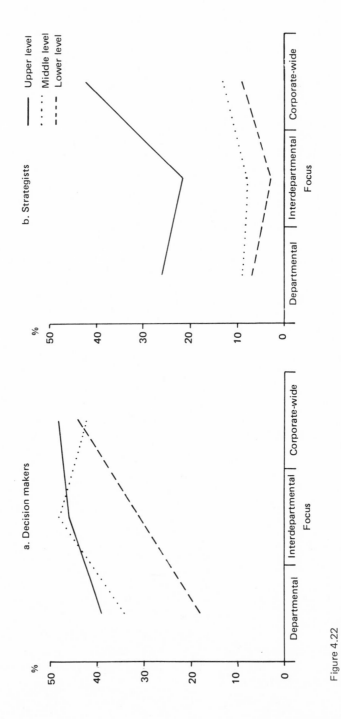

Figure 4.22

Percentage of decision makers and strategists according to level and focus of meetings.

The effect of power equalization is demonstrated by the fact that, for managers participating in company-wide decisions, the differences in rank fade: participating managers of different levels enjoy roughly the same decision-making power. However policy participation is not affected.[56] Better information and organizational connections reduce uncertainty and enable managers to take decisions that otherwise would involve too much risk. Consultation on policy matters, however, is not a manager's prerogative: it requires a definite policy from the organization's top.

4.4.4. Corporate ownership as an influence on decentralization

Not all factors shaping a firm's power distribution are as objective as size and technology. The decision to decentralize power is also contingent on a firm's "culture," on its tradition, and on the attitude of the organization's leaders.[57] It is usually not easy to determine the specific policies of a given firm in Italy, because they are rarely explicitly expressed. Furthermore, among all policies, the delegation of power is the most variable because it is contingent on the personality of the CEO or on the "philosophy" of the managing team at the top. It is primarily a matter of "style."

It is because of different philosophies of management that enterprises with the same size, technological focus, and other objective characteristics can differ greatly in their approach to decentralization. It seemed to us that a clue to these qualitative differences could be furnished by looking at the type of corporate ownership. The fifty corporations included in our research were private firms, state-owned enterprises, and Italian and non-Italian multinationals. It could be hypothesized that centralization would be more easily found in firms where financial interests were concentrated in the hands of an individual or one family. We could envisage a continuum, with the highly centralized private firms at one extreme, the highly decentralized state-owned firms at the opposite extreme, and the multinationals in an intermediate position. We considered the following continuum, which we shall call Hypothesis A.

Type of ownership	Private firms	Italian & non-Italian multinationals	State-owned firms
Delegation of authority	Least	Average	Most

Hypothesis A

It is also necessary to examine the differences between the degree of authority delegation (decentralization of decision making) and the degree of participation in policy making (consultation in the formulation of policies). It could be assumed that in the private firm the owner (entrepreneur or heir) would tend to centralize upon himself both the decision-making and policy-making powers, virtually excluding managers from both; that the geographic distance from the headquarters of the non-Italian multinationals would create the conditions for delegating the power to make technical decisions, but also for excluding managers from policy making (an activity carried out in the parent headquarters). On the other hand, the managers of Italian multinationals, who are located near the system's center, should enjoy both decision making and policy participation. Relations between the state-owned firm and the state should result in decision-making autonomy for managers on problems in which technical knowledge is more important than political knowledge, and their removal from authority in the case of policy formulation, which is influenced by sociopolitical factors and not simply by technical and productive factors. This gives us the diagram below, which we shall call Hypotheses B.

Delegation of decision-making power

		+	−
Participation in policy formulation	+	Italian multi-national	
	−	Non-Italian multinationals; State-owned firms	Private firms

Hypothesis B

Our data do in fact reveal strong variations in power distribution according to the type of corporate ownership, and great discrepancies between decision makers and policy participants (see

Figure 4.23). But our results do not confirm hypotheses A and B. In the decision-making power continuum the state-owned firm, which was expected to be the most liberal, instead turns out to have a very low percentage of managers who are decision makers, and is more highly centralized than all other firms, including private corporations (in which we had expected to find the greatest centralization). The Italian and non-Italian multinationals exceeded expectations by granting the most decision-making power to their managers, each practically to the same degree.[58]

Thus the centralization-decentralization continuum turned out as shown in Finding A.

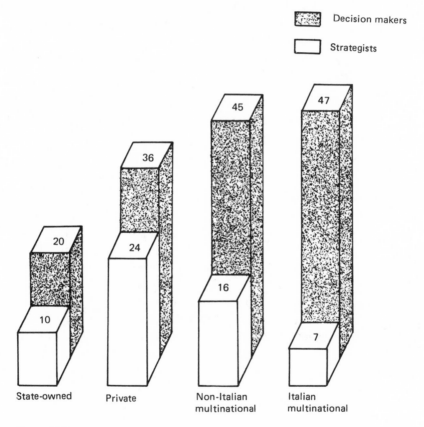

Figure 4.23

Percentage of decision makers and strategists according to type of corporate ownership.

Type of ownership	State-owned firms	Private firms	Italian & non-Italian multinationals
% of decision-makers	20%	34%	46%
Delegation of authority	Least	Average	Most

Finding A

Also the relationship found between the two kinds of power (decision making and policy participation) is peculiar and contradicts our expectations. The diagram turns out to be as follows:

Delegation of decision-making power

		+	−
Participation in policy making	+	Private firms	
	−	Italian & non-Italian multinationals	State-owned firms

Finding B

The Italian and non-Italian multinationals' managers have, as expected, a high proportion of managers who are decision makers. But all the multinationals are highly centralized in their policy making and, surprisingly, it is the Italian multinational that most tightly limits participation in policy decisions. Apparently, these two groups of advanced, modern firms both tend to specialize management in solving intraorganizational and technical problems, while reserving policy or planning decisions for the top—and geographical location seems to have little effect on these practices.[59]

The fact that both the Italian and non-Italian multinationals grant the greatest decision-making power and behave in the same way in spite of the different nationality is probably the result of their greater complexity (product diversification), geographic dispersion of their productive units, and international competition. These factors make a policy of decentralization economically rational, at least insofar as technical decisions are concerned.

In the first phase of industrialization both the decision-making and the policy-making functions were combined in the person of the entrepreneur; in the mature phase, represented by the multinational firm, they are entrusted to two groups of specialists, one oriented toward the solution of the firm's problems, the other toward external problems. The manager and the financier are two separate entities. The distinction is less sharp in private industry where the two responsibilities are the domain of a single individual who delegates them to others.

In state-owned firms, power is not only centralized but situated outside the firm; the separation between managers who are "technicians" and "politicians" is readily observed—but not the way we expected. Power rests in the hands of *real* politicians who are outside the firm yet take upon themselves many of the decisions usually left to the technicians (see Figure 4.24).

The data seem to confirm the common picture of the Italian state-owned firm, in which even strictly technical decisions are often influenced by political considerations and are removed from the regular managers' jurisdiction. The impact of external power groups on the firm, which exists for any corporation, is abnormally dominant in the state-owned firm and shapes all events occurring within it. While the private firm attempts to manipulate outside forces in order to pursue internal productive goals, the state-owned firm handles corporate affairs in order to achieve external—social and political—goals (such as maintaining or increasing employment levels or satisfying requests from political party factions) and is, more than any other firm, affected by external forces.

Theoretically, the state-owned firm constitutes the extreme case

Figure 4.24

Assignment of technical and "political" responsibilities according to type of corporate ownership.

of diffused ownership (inasmuch as it belongs to all citizens) and should be at the opposite side of the spectrum from a highly centralized firm. Yet it is also the best demonstration of the oft-described impotence of stockholder-citizens.[60]

But without technical knowledge and situated outside the firm, how can a political class, on whom the state-owned firm in fact depends, be capable of controlling technical decision making? (This question could be applied to the state bureaucrats as well.) Furthermore, in view of the fact that our data show that decision-making power in the state-owned firm does not reside with the managers, where then should we look for it? Power seems to be located at an intermediate point between the two different groups —the managers on one side, political parties on the other—in the person of the firm's chairman. The head of a state-owned firm is perhaps the single clearest example of the nonowner "technocrat" in Italian business.[61] Appointed by government, he cannot be identified with the group of managers who report to him, not only because he is usually not a technician but also because his career depends on the decisions of a political group rather than on the market or on the effectiveness of the firm. Unlike his counterpart in privately owned companies, the firm's profits and growth are not the most important measure of his performance.

In examining the effect of corporate ownership on the process of decentralization, the size of the firm shows up in unexpected ways: in both multinationals (Italian and non-Italian) managers' autonomy is greatest when the firm's size is not extremely large (i.e., annual sales under 50 billion lire); only in family firms does growth in size continually provoke an increase in the delegation of decision-making power, as if, beyond a certain size, total control by an individual becomes impossible. (See Figure 4.25.)

Perhaps product diversification and geographic dispersion, two characteristics of multinationals, make the influence of ownership on managerial power stronger than the variable of the type of technology. In technologically advanced corporations, in which managerial autonomy is usually reduced (refer to Figure 4.11), the two multinationals stand out for the broader decision-making latitude they grant to managers, a fact sharply distinguishing them from private and state-owned enterprises. (See Figure 4.26.)

Because of their dynamism, technologically advanced firms must both confront a larger number of decisions and make them

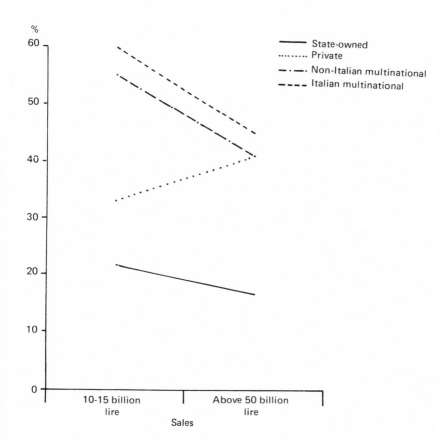

Figure 4.25

Percentage of decision makers according to type of
corporate ownership and size (sales).

on the spur of the moment; since the urgency of decision occurs in
the context of highly technical and diverse environments, it is in-
advisable to refer the problem to the central headquarters: the peripheral units of the company therefore take a considerable share
of decisions.

But policy formulation remains the most delicate area of decisional power and is not readily delegated where financial risk is
high, as in the case of investments for all firms, or any major
change in technologically complex firms (refer to Figures 4.11 and
4.14). Participation in policy making is low in all the technologically advanced firms we examined (see Figure 4.26b).

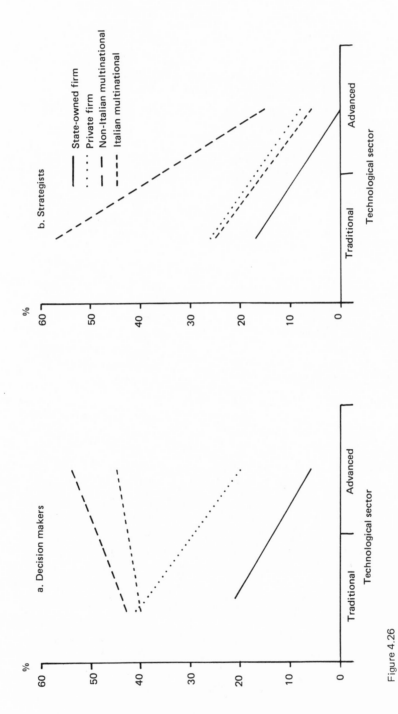

Figure 4.26

Percentage of decision makers and strategists according to type of corporate ownership and technological sector

4.4.5. Effects of corporate dynamism on
decision making and policy participation

Not only is delegation of authority shaped by factors external to the manager's will and beyond his influence, but its stability is precarious. For example, our study suggests that a growth in the corporation's sales[62] has the effect of reducing managerial autonomy (see Figure 4.27).

The different levels are affected by this phenomenon to a differing degree: primarily affected are the higher level (deprived of authority by the top which apparently resumes command) and the bottom level (subjected to more controls at least during the period in which new policies are implemented). The intermediate level maintains its position, probably because, as C. Wright Mills noted,[63] this level is made up of administrators and technicians representing the backbone of the organization, and its authority is difficult to challenge.

Expansion in sales does not change the lower hierarchical levels' already paltry participation in policy formulation,[64] but interestingly it does increase the influence of the higher level, which is called to participate in the solution of problems connected with growth, even though its decision-making power is diminished.

When the firm is small, a growth in its sales encourages the top to resume control over operational decisions and the percentage of decision makers diminishes. But in very large firms an increase in sales produces little change in managerial autonomy (see Figure 4.28).

According to the type of organizational structure, sales expansion may reverse the power situation: static and centralized firms grant the most autonomy to managers, as do decentralized firms during an expansion phase. The same occurs for policy making, though less visibly. Therefore, improved sales seem to penalize managers of certain firms and favor those of other firms (see Figure 4.29).

The restrictive effect of sales expansion on power distribution is unexpected; one would assume that during a growth period managers would have a freer hand, both because increased sales demonstrate the soundness of their decisions and because expanding corporate activities increase the number of decisions to be made. But apparently, growth, especially when rapid, creates a volatile

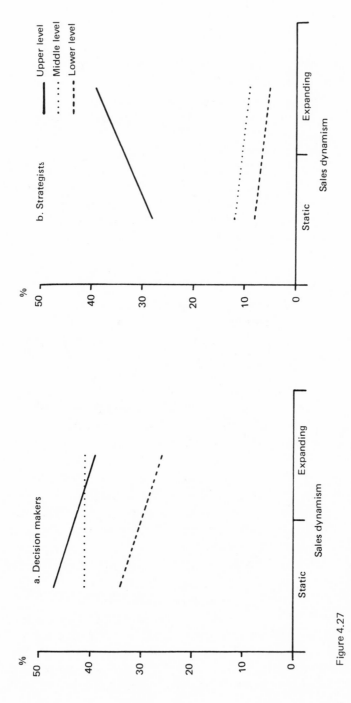

Figure 4.27

Percentage of decision makers and strategists according to hierarchical level and sales dynamism.

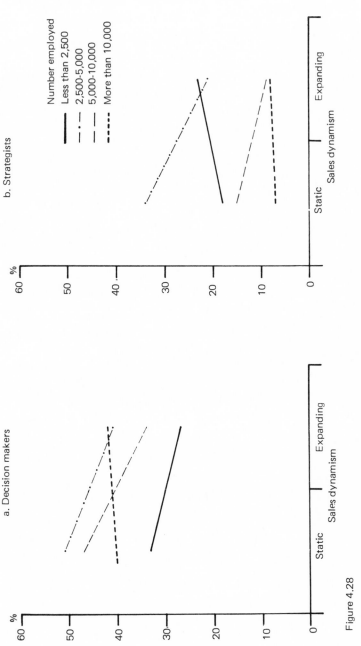

Figure 4.28

Percentage of decision makers and strategists according to corporate size (number employed) and sales dynamism.

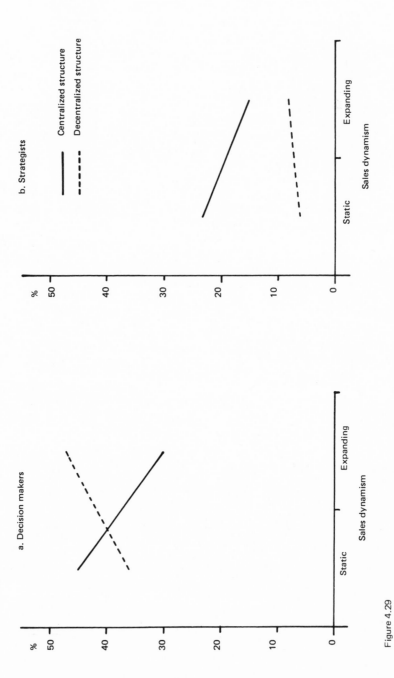

Figure 4.29

Percentage of decision makers and strategists according to organizational structure and sales dynamism.

and often imbalanced situation which forces the enterprise to adjust to changes in production and market. The expansion puts a stress on the corporate structure, a stress that is relieved in different ways in different firms.

When a corporation's structure is rigid, as in the case of the centralized firm, expansion poses a risk inasmuch as it constitutes a change. In this emergency situation the top tends to take over the reins of control. The ideal situation for the centralized organization is stability: only when roles are preestablished and clearly defined can control loosen up. While in the decentralized organization control is exerted on *results*, in the centralized organization control is exerted on the *practices* leading to results. Thus, each time new situations upset clear-cut rules and require organizational adjustments or demand more decisions, controls tighten as well.

The decentralized structure, on the other hand, has an inborn flexibility which makes it more receptive to change. Adjustment tends to be spontaneous as well as timely: as soon as the organization perceives new problems, each office, department, and manager adjusts to a new position without waiting for orders from above. It follows that in the decentralized, growing firm, the power of managers tends to grow together with the increase in the number of decisions (see Figure 4.29a).

Another factor revealed by the analysis is the different behaviors of the two types of multinational corporations: in the non-Italian firms expanding sales reduce the percentage of decision makers and policy participants, a phenomenon not found in the Italian multinationals (see Figure 4.30). In fact, the two multinationals are not always comparable, because the non-Italian firms represent but a branch of a much larger firm, the appendages of a body whose head and command centers are outside the country; further, they are smaller productive units than the mother company. Italian multinationals, however, have their "brain" (that is, their headquarters) as well as their largest productive units located within the country.

4.5 Effects of power on attitudes

Differentials in power are the most important differences within the managerial group, which is otherwise very homogeneous. They distinguish between the manager merely bearing a title and the one carrying on executive responsibilities.

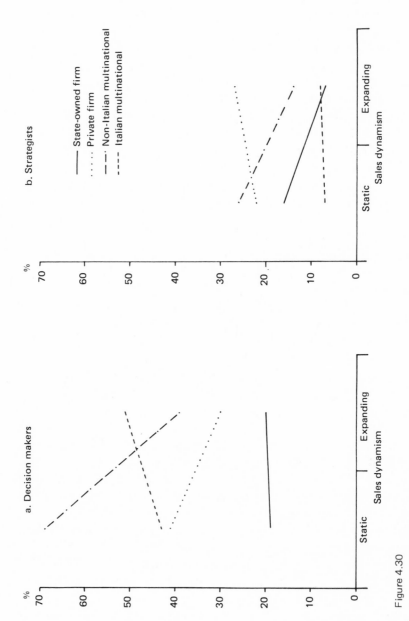

Figure 4.30

Percentage of decision makers and strategists according to type of corporate ownership and sales dynamism.

Different functions should ostensibly give birth to different attitudes. The perspective from which the decision maker and the strategist approach corporate problems should be different from that of the manager concerned with routine and tactical decisions.

Our research gathered data about managers' perceptions and judgments and grouped them in three categories: (1) the perception of the managerial role[65] ; (2) the perception of the prestige associated with the managerial profession[66] ; (3) the managers' evaluation of union-management conflicts and the firm's social responsibilities.

One would think that differences in function would lead to different perceptions of the requirements for the managerial job; that decision makers and strategists would expect promising career opportunities but at the same time would consider themselves more at the mercy of risks associated with faulty decisions (given the greater weight of problems with which they deal). Furthermore, we expected that decision makers and strategists would believe they enjoy greater social prestige than that accorded to tacticians and routine managers. Finally, since decision makers and, even more, strategists participate in important corporate decisions, we assumed that their attitudes toward union-management conflict and social responsibilities would again differ from those of the tacticians and routine managers.

However, none of these assumptions was borne out. The whole managerial group was generally homogeneous in its attitudes. Few differences in distribution were observed in the fifteen cross-tabulations attempted. Practically the only difference that emerges is the greater value that decision makers and strategists place on participation in planning as a motivating factor in their work.

Common class origins and common high educational levels, similarities in training before promotion, as well as psychological traits that led them to choose that profession could all help to explain the great homogeneity found in the managerial group.

Differentiations within the group appear when age and decisional power are jointly examined. We compared the two extreme groups—the new generation (aged 29-40) and the older group (over 50).

Young executives and decision and policy makers share some common attitudes. When the two variables of age and power are combined, the difference in attitudes increases. Two opposite groups emerge: on one hand, the young power holders; on the other, the older routine managers. For example, the aspiration to participate in policy decisions, greater among young managers in general (45 percent as against only 27 percent in the older routine executives), increases further in young managers who are also decision makers or strategists (respectively to 55 percent and 48 percent).

Some differences in perceptions among power holders seem attributable to age: while 30 percent of the older strategists believe that public opinion considers the management function important, only 8 percent of the youngest strategists share this opinion. Young power holders managers seem to look beyond corporate walls and to evaluate critically the importance of the economic function; they attribute instead more prestige to political action (see Figures 4.31 and 4.32).

The most important difference was found in suggestions on how to avoid repetition of union-management conflicts. While the majority of older executives, whether decision makers or strategists, favor solutions of a repressive nature (a halt to union activities, the recourse to force to maintain order, a "strong" government), younger executives of the same group favor "reformist" solutions (recognition of and dialogues with labor unions, fiscal and health reforms, a better state low-cost housing policy, etc.) (see Table 4.5).

Aside from these few differences, the managerial group is homogeneous: the values of the old managerial group are perpetuated in the new generation.

Table 4.5

Solutions Advanced for Union-Management Conflicts
(in %)

Solutions	Decision makers		Strategists	
	Younger	Older	Younger	Older
Repressive	35	52	28	67
Paternalistic*	30	32	22	22
Reformist	35	16	50	11
	100	100	100	100

*The easiest to code: includes proposals such as taking care of workers' health, bonuses, Christmas presents, loans, etc., granted without consultation with the parties affected.

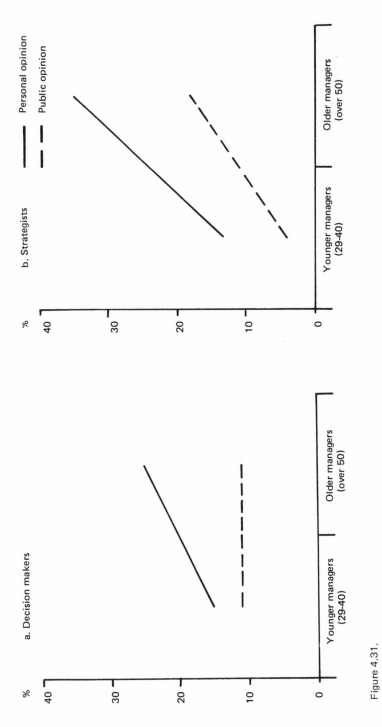

Figure 4.31.

Perception that decision makers and strategists have of economic activities (personal opinion and perception of public opinion), according to age.

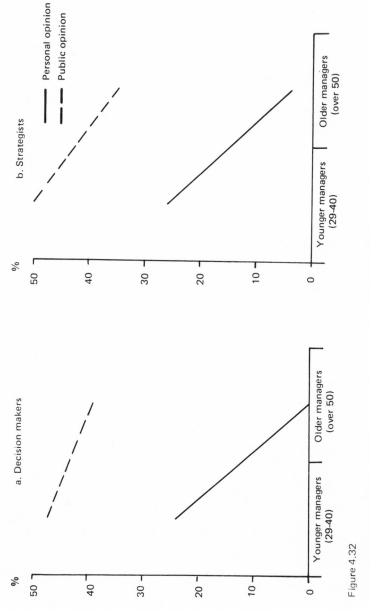

Figure 4.32

Perception that decision makers and strategists have of a politician's prestige (personal opinion and perception of public opinion) according to age.

5

The Crisis of
Managerial Authority

Although rarely consulted in the formulation of new company policies, and often deprived of responsibility for decisions in his own field, the Italian manager until a few years ago enjoyed one undisputed and gratifying form of power: he had full control over his subordinates. They were the only group he was allowed to shape. Cut off from lateral contacts with external groups in the industrial and financial worlds or in the community, weak in his rapport with the top of the organization, the manager exercised nonetheless a considerable influence when it came to his underlings in the organization. (See Figure 5.1.)

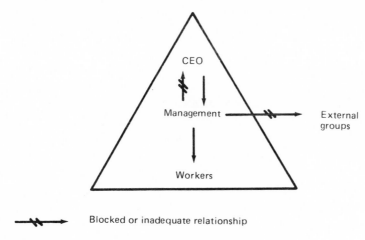

Figure 5.1

In his relations with subordinates, the manager was the administrator of the firm's system of rewards and punishments. This function entailed considerable power: first, to decide or influence the hiring, compensation, and work assignments of employees; then, to be the gate-keeper of their salaries and career advancement; and finally, to penalize and to dismiss them. The manager thus played a major conditioning role in the lives of his subordinates.

Rather than limit this power, the modern personnel office standardized the procedures for its exercise. The fact that power over subordinates is acquired through delegation and that the real authority rests at higher levels does not reduce its significance. The direct superior is the one who knows his subordinates best and can most accurately judge their efficiency; he works through them and is responsible for their performance. It seems appropriate therefore to let him play a determining role in the selection of his employees and the allocation of tasks, and to leave him free, if necessary, to eliminate unproductive employees.

Exercising authority over people can be most gratifying: it is an immediate and highly visible activity. And in a society as rigidly stratified as the Italian, this role of preeminence within an organization will be paralleled by other privileged situations in society. His whole experience, therefore, has socialized the manager to conceive of most relationships as essentially vertical—either subordination or command.

The most important socialization occurs when the individual is in a subordinate position: the young person in Italy is in an inferior position in the family, the school, the military service, and at least in the beginning of his work career. Later on the situation is reversed for some mature men: after long years of training, the manager has at last attained a position of privilege, and it is this which gives him much of the satisfaction he gains from his work.

The power the manager exercises over subordinates, inasmuch as it is instrumental to the pursuit of productive goals, is amply legitimated by the organization; even though he may have little opportunity to make or shape major company decisions, the formal recognition of his authority over subordinates is the main reason he calls himself a "manager."

5.1. The concept of authority in the organization

The need for authority[1] is amply defended in the writings of organizational theorists: "The logic of industrialization impels the employer to covet the role of rule maker. As a risk taker, he seeks control over any of the factors which must be coordinated in the planning-production-selling process. The specialization of functions which industrialization brings also requires, in management's eyes, that the work force accept tasks whose nature, time, and method of accomplishment are to be determined by management in its role of planner and order giver."[2]

Among the three types of behavior that management demands from the employees—subordination, loyalty, and productivity— "of necessity, subordination is the first objective of an employer in building a work force . . . The prerogative of management, as seen by its spokesmen, is to prescribe duties, assign tasks, and get satisfactory performance. To do this, it must maintain discipline; it cannot tolerate insubordination if it hopes to maintain its function as management."[3] "The efficiency of management as a resource is related not only to the individuals within the hierarchy but also to the system of authority which binds them together . . . The design of systems of authority is equally as important in the modern world as the development of technology."[4]

Authority appears as the pivot of organization. But, to be effective, authority must be accepted by those who will have to submit to it. "In joining the organization he [the employee] accepts an authority relation; i.e., he agrees that within some limits . . . he will accept as the premises of his behavior orders and instructions supplied to him by the organization."[5] The firm limits itself to requesting the subordinate's obedience, not his consensus or his acceptance.[6]

Those representing authority administer the system of rewards and punishments on which authority is based, applying them differentially, according to rank. In the supervisor-subordinate relation, both sides are aware of the inequality with which sanctions are administered, but both implicitly accept it.

The manager also is subject to authority, but unlike other workers, his intermediate position in the hierarchy induces him to willingly accept—or at least understand—a system that, while limiting him on the one hand, is advantageous on the other. He submits to the authority of those of higher rank, but in turn he exercises authority over others. Since he himself possesses authority, he is more inclined to justify it; he feels part of a larger system of authority within which he has some freedom to maneuver.[7] Corporate power and personal power are seen as inextricably intertwined.[8]

The manager's image of authority is therefore benevolent. He accepts it because the system of authority is at once a model for his actual performance and a projection of his future in the firm (in his career he expects to rise to increasingly important positions of command). Further, the manager is in a privileged position vis-à-vis all other workers and reaps a greater share of the rewards. Thus it is not difficult for him to follow the rules and to identify with an organization that can lavish these rewards on him.[9]

Attitudes toward authority in the firm probably originate from an individual's own experience of hierarchy in the society at large. The higher classes (to which most managers belong, thanks to their economic status and family origins) enjoy the most favorable treatment, which explains why managers more easily accept the concept of stratification.[10] The manager's perception of corporate authority is consistent with his experience in the external society.

5.2. The labor revolts of 1969 (The "Hot Autumn")

Managerial authority—impervious to attack from the organization, for which it is functional—has been challenged from below and from without.[11]

Until Italy's "Hot Autumn," employees had accepted the authority structure, the system of sanctions the firm had formulated to maintain it, and the disparities in their administration. The power exercised by the firm was not only "remunerative"—that is, based on rewards such as income, services, and career advancement—but "coercive,"[12] based on threats to block one's career, suspensions, fines, and dismissals. As long as this acceptance lasted, the conflict between employees and management was circumscribed, sporadic, and resolvable: the problems met by the manager in his relations with subordinates concerned mainly efficiency (training, performance appraisal, and motivation).

The new phenomenon during the union strife of the "Hot Autumn" was not, from the manager's point of view, the conflict itself, however violent it was, erupting after a long period of weak union activity; it was the fact that, for the first time in the history of union struggles, the manager himself was the target.[13] Even the managers of white-collar workers were brought into the dispute (before 1969 strikes mainly involved blue-collar workers).

Furthermore, the situation was more complex than a limited conflict between management and workers. Indeed, union action provided the channel through which organizational authority itself was directly challenged[14]; the challenge to authority, a broad social phenomenon, thus entered the corporation. Many managers did in fact perceive the workers' behavior as a manifestation of a wider unrest that had its roots outside the firm. The active participation of nonemployees in strikes (students as well as workers from other firms participated in picketing) led to the belief that the roots of the conflict were to be found in society at large. The virulence of public opinion vis-à-vis the corporation, the lack of police protection during the strikes, and the government's passivity were factors confirming the view that the entire social environment was hostile.

The managerial perception of the exogenous nature of the conflict is evident in many of the comments of those interviewed: "The center of the phenomenon is outside the firm"; "The situation is identical within and outside the firm: it is a general crisis of authority"; "All authority structures in the world have been severely shaken."

Management was not the only group to be challenged. In fact it was merely experiencing the fate of authority figures of all sorts: "They are protesting against the Pope, why shouldn't they protest against managers?" "The decline of managerial authority is similar to that experienced by all other forms of authority: from the head of the family to the state—all have lost it." "Everything has been shaken: a son no longer respects his father,[15] a worker no longer respects his supervisor or his superintendent, the respect of the white-collar worker for his superior has disappeared. This is not merely a corporate phenomenon, but an external one as well—occurring in the family and in society." Ninety percent of the managers believe that their authority has changed.[16] Managers see themselves as suffering from a crisis encompassing the entire society. "Protest involves the family, the school, the firm, and the army. The crisis stems from the changes occurring in the social structure."

For some managers this crisis of values was an unwelcome event. It represented the end to the Puritan conception of work: "There is more permissiveness; the only goals now are hedonistic ones. Nobody wants to make sacrifices, either to learn or to achieve a better position. A life of work is hard for everybody, but the workers demand automatic promotions without having done anything to deserve them. The most serious thing is the lack of a spirit of sacrifice." For others, it seemed inevitable: "Protests have shaken everything up. The times have changed." "The emancipation of the masses has wiped out social distance." The crisis was seen as the result of evolving customs ("there was a time when children kissed the hands of their parents"). "Humanity is in the process of dramatic evolution and the manager who remains hard-nosed will be swept away." An era of industrial history had ended: "The time is gone when one could summarily reject any request from workers; this type of authority could not survive because it had already been superseded in the world surrounding the firm."

A new society could emerge from this crisis: ". . . we witness today what could not be accomplished in the postwar period, when we tried in vain to bring democracy to our country."

Even the roots of union conflict and solutions to it were often said to be found outside the firm (the government was mentioned by 41 percent of those interviewed).[17]

Union conflict is an aspect of social change. But its perception varies according to individual experience and the climate existing in the firm before the strikes. Some firms continued to reject a dialogue with the unions while others changed their policies after the "Hot Autumn," showing a greater propensity to discuss matters with the opposition.[18] In the more flexible firms, employee-management relations changed suddenly and drastically, and had repercussions on personal relations between managers and their direct subordinates as well. In these firms we found the greatest number of managers who declared that they had undergone a psychological trauma and who feel there is a crisis in conventional corporate values.[19]

Protest against traditional authority was not aimed only at one group of managers. One might expect that those most exposed to the pressure would have been those in direct contact with the blue-collar workers (e.g., the managers in the production department) and those in line functions. We expected managers in staff positions (who usually have a smaller number of subordinates) as well as those managers in the lower ranks to experience less conflict. As far as the firms were concerned, the expectation was that greater pressure would fall on the managers of large firms; on firms in the most unionized sectors (such as steel and iron, and machinery); and on firms located in Northern Italy, which had a longer tradition of unionization. However, protest was generalized to all of industry and occurred on a national basis. It hit a sizable majority of managers and left them without shelter.

5.3. Effects of the "Hot Autumn"

The decrease in the power of the corporation

From the end of World War II until the autumn of 1969 Italian society perceived industry as an instrument of progress in the country, and in fact as the only real supporting structure. Other institutions such as government and the education system were judged obsolete if not actually obstacles to development. Until the "Hot Autumn," industry enjoyed a dominant position in its external environment, which it had shaped more than it itself had been shaped.

The goals of productive efficiency and economic progress at any cost have given way today to an increased appreciation of noneconomic factors which, though still not well defined, has raised community awareness of the social responsibilities of the firm. Criticism was leveled against industrialization, in particular its negative effects on communities (congestion, urban paralysis and structural decay) and at the national level (the increase in differences between industrially developed and backward areas within the country). This criticism attacked what appeared to be the country's only valid and vital structure. Managers' close identification with industry increased their sensitivity to the crisis. Unlike the independent professional, a manager can perform only within an organized structure; he is like a teacher, whose function is called into question the moment one disparages the school system, outside of which the teacher lacks identity and cannot perform.

Furthermore, the manager has been disappointed and rejected by the firm which once acted toward him as a nurturing mother. Many managers attribute the firm's inadequacy in dealing effectively with labor unrest to inefficiency and a long history of bad labor relations, which firms did not bother to improve, or even intentionally exacerbated.[20] Accustomed to being supported by the corporation's might, the manager discovered the firm's vulnerability and weakness. At the same time he felt forsaken by the firm which no longer provided shelter for his actions. In most cases top management was unprepared to face union pressures: it was unable to issue clear guidelines to its managers and left them in an ambiguous situation.[21] The managers found themselves without support in the midst of conflict, caught between two fires. In some cases, the managers were instructed to avoid open clashes, even at the cost of losing authority; they were thus forced to witness passively the attacks on their prestige. In other instances, the orders were to maintain discipline and the "hard line" at all costs, with the result that, when the firm was eventually forced to retreat to less drastic positions, the managers felt betrayed.[22] In any event, the substantial victory of the labor unions left all managers with the feeling that they had lost influence and status with their subordinates.

The loss of instruments of control

The existence of positive and negative sanctions (in the form of rewards and punishments) in a social group assures that its members will adopt the desired behavior. Negative sanctions are the simplest and also the most effective, because the impact of measures such as fines, suspensions, or dismissals is immediate. Positive sanctions require more skill and their effects are long-term. In making a choice concerning which tactics to use, the manager is inclined to rely mainly on negative sanctions, which in addition to their immediate character have the advantages of visibility and example.

The withdrawal of the right to administer punishment meant for many managers the loss of the main supporting instrument for carrying out their function: "The managers lack the means to get the work done; for instance, they no longer have the power to punish or reward." "The manager no longer has control—he no longer rewards or punishes." "The manager no longer has disciplinary authority." "Earlier, managers could give merit and salary increases in our firm; but no more. Now they can only make promotion proposals. Performance appraisal is no longer under our jurisdiction: it must be discussed with the unions. We have been almost completely deprived of authority." Therefore, "when the possibility for punishment is lost, there is no longer that submissiveness among the employees that stems from fear of losing the job."[23]

Managers seem to have lost yet another set of guiding instruments in their daily action. The rejection of authority engenders a crisis in the classical conception of the organization and, consequently, in its functioning. In addition to responsibilities and duties, organizational rules also determine each member's authority and status. The authority crisis endangers the legitimacy of the managerial role and diminishes the manager's self-image.[24]

The loss of professional prestige

Subordinates' changed attitudes turned union unrest and social protest into a personally felt wounding experience for many managers. In describing their loss of authority many interviewees recalled the frustrating facts that led to it; their depiction is colored by unresolved emotional tensions stirred by direct aggression (so much in contrast to the past "reverential fear" that some remember). Employees' aggressiveness was sometimes more than verbal: "The workers would enter the office and kick us out, amid insults. They would search our cars; they were violent and frightening." "I had to pass between two rows of women booing and cursing." "I was insulted and beaten." Sometimes it was symbolic: "They threw cherries and potatoes at me." "The boss's coffin was paraded amid red flags; it was not funny at all."

No wonder that the manager's function and self-image suffered; "The manager was attacked and wounded on the human plane and in his role." Above all, his function lost value: "In many cases, executive authority was not only shaken, but also defiled and humiliated." "We witnessed a desecration of the image of the manager." "My subordinates were present when the students came into my office, turned over my desk and pushed me out, booing; now they think they can demand everything." "I feel rejected, not so much as a man, but as a manager, as a person who fulfills a function that is not respected. Today the manager is a tragicomical figure, a kind of Don Quixote." "The manager is considered by the workforce as a boss and not an associate who breathes life into the firm; he is mistreated; he has lost authority and prestige. The managers were beaten up and nobody protected them. In order to compromise, the government bodies did not defend the victims of aggression; they let the guilty off the hook."[25] Since the

Table 5.1

Prestige Attributed to Professions
(First Choice) (in %, *n* = 627)

Profession	Personal opinion
University professor	37
Independent professional	30
High public official	8
Congressman	8
Bank director	2
Business manager	15
	100

attack on the role extended also to the person, it is not surprising to find feelings of shock, frustration, and insecurity; repeatedly we heard descriptions of "bewilderment," "dismay," and "panic."

The discomfort remains even well after the fact: "The oldest managers are in crisis, they feel tired and frustrated." "The manager is in the clutches of panic . . . today many managers assent to anything, out of fear." "I am afraid of the chaos we are up against." "Today we are dealing with a type of manager who lacks motivation. He earns a salary, he works and manages, without a deep conviction for what he does. He is insecure, emotionally unstable, and he feels detached from society. . . ."

A measure of the uncertainty in which the manager now finds himself is revealed by the limited social prestige that he attributes to his profession and, even more dramatically, by the discrepancy between his self-attributed prestige and the prestige he believes public opinion grants him. Presented with a list of six activities equivalent in terms of economic reward, only 15 percent of those interviewed put the job of manager in first place, with most giving priority to the university professor or to the independent professional instead (see Table 5.1).

Given that each person interviewed could make three choices in decreasing order, it is interesting to consider if managerial activity appears at all, even if in a secondary position; indeed, 73 percent of those interviewed attributed prestige to their job, mentioning it

Table 5.2

Manager's Position on the Prestige Scale

| | Opinion (%) | |
	Personal	Public
Manager in first place	15	3
Manager in second place	27	6
Manager in third place	31	13
Manager not mentioned	27	78
	100	100
	(n = 642)	(n = 636)

in one of the three choices (see Table 5.2). But a discrepancy is revealed when we compare self-attributed prestige with the prestige the manager believes public opinion grants him. We are dealing with perceptions and not with reality (since there has been no poll of the Italian population on this issue); but it is precisely the subjective evaluation that allows us to infer the ambiguity and the painful uncertainty felt by the manager about his own position, given his conviction that the importance he attributes to his occupation is shared only by his professional group and is not recognized by other groups in society. The percentage is very indicative: 78 percent of managers believe that the public does not include them among important professionals.

A similar discrepancy in perception is also found in the priority the manager gives to the intelligentsia (independent professionals and university teachers) versus the priority he believes that public opinion grants to activities of a political nature (government and high-level civil servants) (see Figure 5.2). The manager perceives himself as living in a society with whose system of values he disagrees. If we group the professions into intellectual, economic, and political categories, we see that the manager's scale of values puts intellectual activities first, followed by economic activities, while political activities are last. But the manager believes that public opinion gives top prestige to political occupations, then to the intellectual ones, placing economic activities last.

It is interesting to note that the differences in evaluation found among managers cannot be explained by any personal character-

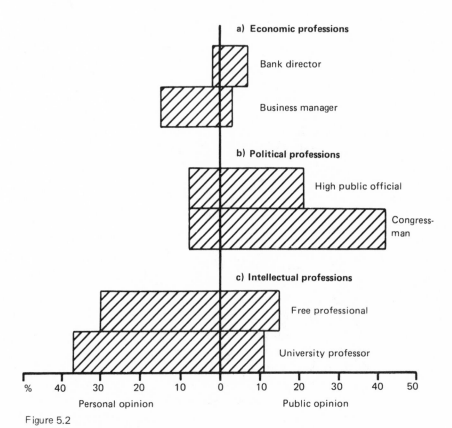

Figure 5.2

The prestige accorded professions.

istics such as age, level or type of education, social class background, hierarchical level,[26] or departmental location.[27] Nor are these differences affected by corporate variables such as size, type of product, or location of the firm (North or South). Differences within the group of managers appear to be explained only by a set of corporate variables connected with labor conflict—in particular, with the workers' degree of unionization in the firm, the amount of conflict and its variation over time, and the company's policies toward labor unions.

These data allow us to infer that the manager's view of the public prestige of his profession is closely linked to his contact with workers' protests. Unfortunately we do not possess any measure of managerial prestige before the labor unrest; however, it is possible to analyze the changes associated with variations in the intensity of protest. When the variables related to conflict—i.e., level of conflict, the firm's labor union policies, the degree of unionization—are considered jointly, the changes in the manager's view of his prestige are most pronounced.[28]

The variations are more visible in the manager's self-evaluation of prestige than in his perception of public opinion. This leads us to surmise that the real crisis was internal, and that the manager suffered a decrease in prestige not so much in the eyes of the public (a fact that he could choose to overlook) but in his own eyes (a more serious and demoralizing event).

Managers in firms with a tradition of hostility toward labor unions ("closed firms") and whose workers were heavily unionized, attribute the lowest prestige to their profession, both from their own standpoint and in their perception of public opinion. The perception of prestige is in turn connected to authority: 50 percent of those who believe the manager's job is highly regarded on the public-opinion prestige scale do not feel that their authority has diminished.

It is interesting also to examine the prestige accorded other professions. The manager's predilection for the independent professional could be interpreted as a yearning for another kind of work: the frustrated manager looks to the independent professional (with whom he shares the same high education level) as the image of someone he could have become or would like to become. While the free professionals have low prestige with managers in firms in which there were no changes in union policies and fewer strikes (that is, in "closed" firms with little conflict), their prestige is much greater with managers who have suffered intense union conflict. Similarly, in the "closed" firm with low conflict levels we find the greatest number of managers attributing prestige to jobs in the economic field (43 percent as compared to 23 percent). In firms with high conflict levels and "closed" to dialogue with labor unions, 79 percent of the managers believe that public opinion gives greater prestige to political activities. The "politician" (government representative, high-level civil servant) is probably seen as an individual endowed with greater power, whose intervention could change the internal corporate situation and succeed where the economic agent has failed.

5.4. The crisis in the managerial role

Involuntarily and without warning or preparation, the manager was forced in 1969 to reexamine critically his own role and seek out new modes of behavior. The required change in his social role was very different from the transformations in technical-organizational roles which frequently occur along with normal corporate development. These adjustments can create a state of stress.[29] The process can be synthesized in the following diagram:

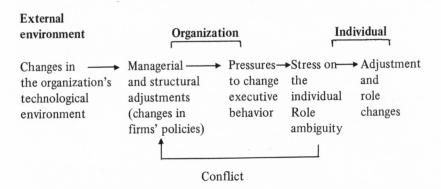

External environment	Organization		Individual	
Changes in the organization's technological environment →	Managerial and structural adjustments (changes in firms' policies) →	Pressures to change executive behavior →	Stress on the individual Role ambiguity →	Adjustment and role changes

Conflict

Our research shows that considerable changes in managerial tasks customarily follow important changes in corporate policies.[30] However, there was a set of factors helping adjustment: first of all, the changes in technical-organizational roles occurred in a dynamic milieu in which positive sanctions were abundant and firms were expanding. In this setting, the importance of the individual manager was increasing not only in terms of salary and career improvements but also in social prestige.

In bringing them increased importance and/or greater autonomy in decision making, technical-organizational change was generally beneficial for managers. The inevitable stress and conflict of change was overshadowed by the positive results and more readily handled.[31] Repetition of this experience tended to give managers a more positive view toward future changes.[32]

Furthermore, technical and organizational changes are usually the result of a logic of rationality to which the manager subscribes; as requisites for corporate development, they are ultimately accepted even by old timers torn between their desire to retain former work practices and their identification with the firm. For the new managerial recruits, more open to innovation, or at least not so rigidified by decades of habits, changes often mean the beginning of a career.

Similarly, the manager has always experienced power conflicts; moreover, even a personal defeat need not damage the importance of the executive function. When frustrated in his personal expectations the manager can still seek solace by identifying with the whole managerial group or with the firm, viewed as a power center. Power gratification is seen only as temporarily deferred; the hope of future opportunities remains.

Thus, organizational changes and conflicts in the managerial role are part of the work experience, and as such are acceptable. The manager is familiar with technical-organizational reasoning, and is willing to yield to its logic. He is inured to organizational conflict—among professional fields, hierarchical positions, and sectors—because his entire experience in the corporation is a balancing act between conflicting organizational demands and personal viewpoints; he must continually compromise between ideal goals and limits inherent in daily reality.

Further, the technical-organizational conflict does not necessarily question the executive function per se. But this function was precisely the object of the attacks of 1969. Hostility against the role was often transferred to the person, undermining the prestige of the individual occupying a managerial position. While in a technical-organizational conflict a manager can protect himself with the shield of professional competence, in the case of workers' protest he found himself unable to cope with forces he knew little about, which, moreover, were outside his control. The problem did not call for individual solutions—because the pressures placed on the manager were not caused by his individual behavior but had more complex and wider origins. It is not surprising that the impossibility of controlling and dispensing with tensions at their place of origin would engender a sense of powerlessness in so many managers.

A further frustrating factor was the manager's inability to escape the conflict. To reduce the tension he might have tried to decrease his area of contacts, confine his activity merely to technical functions, and curtail all communication. However, a strategy of "closure" proves impossible in situations in which a high degree of functional interdependence exists between the individual and the role-change factors. Interdependence requires continual coordination, which is not possible without constant interaction. Cutting communication undermines effective action. Isolated from his subordinates, the manager would be unable to carry out his function, even in a minimal way.

Without this organizational connection with subordinates, both labor-union protest and social protest would have remained remote for many managers, who could have shielded themselves from labor by answering only to their superiors, and from society with the barrier provided by the company walls.

Justifications for and acceptance of change

A large group of managers (30 percent) supported the workers' reasons for challenging authority; they believe the protests were legitimate. In fact they distinguish between *authoritarianism*, which should not survive in the firm or in modern society, and *authority*. The majority of them claim that they have never applied an authoritarian form of leadership and they did not consider themselves to be involved in what others termed a crisis.

For these managers the world is evolving: before there was "servility, fear and absolute obedience; the manager's authority served to preserve old and new privileges."[33] We are now witnessing, in the workers, the end of "reverential fear," and in the managers, the end to an authority derived from investiture, from a halo of infallibility, and in essence, from "charismatic power." The manager has been forced to open himself to new and broader considerations. "Earlier the manager was enclosed in a glass bubble." "He lived in his own world, which is small compared to the rest of society."

The new situation is the outcome of the "workers' greater consciousness," because "the working class has become aware of its own dignity." It is interesting to note that for some of those interviewed this process is intimately connected with technological evolution, and is a direct effect of the changes occurring within the firm itself. "Technology has increased professional and educational levels. Before, the worker was illiterate; today he is a frustrated technician." "The qualitative levels of jobs are higher than before. The organizational pyramid has been flattened because the bottom has raised itself."

For this group the introduction of more "democratic" relations did not substantially change the substance of the managerial role;

the workers' protest brought only the end of power based on hierarchy ("the old manager with the iron fist cannot and should not exist today"; "the image of the manager as a roaring lion is obsolete") but not the end of technical or moral influence. The comments expressed are interesting from many points of view, and not least for the managers' tendency to reassert their superiority over workers in new and distinctive terms.

Even in an increasingly democratic environment, managers have not lost their superior position; they are a better qualified elite who "once received from investiture a power that they must now retake with intellect." But the power issue remains. No longer able to base power on hierarchical position, the managers now must rely instead on two elite characteristics—professional knowledge and human skills.

a. *Technical superiority.* There were recurrent statements of the following type: "What declined was authority of a hierarchical nature, not authority based on knowledge." "Authority has been shaken for those who think of it as an absolute power, commanding servile obedience from subordinates, but not for those who conceive it as superior technical ability, professional training, and managerial sensitivity." "If authority means essentially skill in communication, expertise and the capacity to convey it to others, primarily to those who have to work with us, then the manager has not lost this type of authority."

Some interviewees proudly stress their technical superiority over their subordinates: "The manager gives orders because he knows more, not because he has a title." "I am tough, and get angry when I must lose so much time in convincing people of the validity of an order, but today we must use persuasion. I do not fear losing authority because my workers know that I know each task better than they do." As one interviewee sums it up, "Charismatic authority has been replaced with professional superiority."[34]

b. *Moral superiority.* A second type of authority derives from personality characteristics. While "the old sergeant" did not know how to carry on a discussion, the modern manager knows that "he must convince people, not force them," that "authority relations need to be based on esteem," and that "the only way to achieve full compliance is to set an example and be open to dialogue." For these interviewees, professional skill is less important than one's human qualities: "Prestige goes hand in hand with personality; the

respect goes to the man, not to the manager." "What is authority—to yell an order? That is no longer possible. If I give an order, my people obey because I have made them understand its reasons and because I enjoy prestige and influence. Authority has not
diminished: even before, a mediocre manager had little of it. Maybe he was obeyed out of fear, but that was not really authority."

Professional ability together with moral qualities help to recre-
ate an aura of influence and prestige around the manager, which
he needs to fulfill his tasks. "Even before, real authority was obtained with professional ability, with education, with communication skills, and with a superiority that speaks for itself." "It is a
challenge. Today the manager must earn his stripes. If subordinates
accept him, it is no longer out of fear of punishment but because
of his social skills." Therefore, "Today, to be obeyed is more satisfying than it was before."

c. *Authority based on consensus.* For the managers who based
their authority on professional superiority or personal skills, the
relationship with workers is nonetheless a vertical one, as it involves
a subordinate and a superior. But a small group of those interviewed
reported a change from a vertical to a horizontal relationship: they
stress teamwork and collective participation in decision making—
in sum, "consensus." These managers believe that what happened
in the wave of protests and strikes was not only a revolt against authoritarianism but also a revision in values because "The man of
today has a different conception of leadership and subordination."
"Before there were only a few people in a position to lead; today,
most people want to understand why an order is given before they
will follow it." "Today we can no longer pretend to be the bear-
ers of absolute truth; we must discuss problems, listen to other
people's opinions, and make them participate in the decision process. . . . It is better this way because managers need others' help
too."

Therefore "authority is a set of values that must be accepted by
both sides." A new image of the manager arises, different from
that of the traditional manager. "Before, the manager was the one
who gave orders; today he is the one with whom employees discuss work-related problems and who assumes responsibility for the
completed work." Once the practice of two-way communication
has been accepted, the concept of authority vanishes and is replaced with the concept of "collaboration among persons with dif-

fering responsibilities and with the same goal." For the managers who share this attitude, the problem is not so much one of changing the authority pattern but of creating a new type of relationship.

The various types of reactions to authority change helped us define different types of managers:

1. *The authoritarian*, who mourns the loss of the instruments of coercion and the end of his discretionary power over subordinates (and who, in some extreme cases, ultimately hopes for a return to high unemployment rates, which would bring back the employees' acquiescence);

2. *The frustrated manager*, who underwent the trauma of the "Hot Autumn" of 1969 and has not recovered from it;

3. *The technician*, who relies on his professional superiority;

4. *The leader*, who places the highest value on personal influence;

5. *The primus inter pares*, or "first among equals," who thinks of himself as a member of a work team that must reach collective decisions through discussions and consensus.

These types are like a ladder of rungs corresponding to phases in the transformation of the managerial role. This change must be understood in the framework of a drastic transformation in values— one that goes beyond the corporate walls to touch upon broad social relations.[35]

6

The Managers'
Dilemma

6.1. The crisis of the managerial role

Before the "Hot Autumn" of 1969 and the Employees' Bill of
Rights of 1971, the limitations on the decision-making power of
managers (especially at the bottom of the hierarchy) and their exclusion from consultations on new policies were compensated by
the authority they enjoyed over subordinates. Furthermore, the
manager was satisfied with his status in society and with the
prestige of his profession. His high income made him privileged
with respect to other employed people. For many individuals, promotion to an executive position also meant social advancement:
13 percent of the managers we interviewed were of working-class
origin and 46 percent were from lower-middle-class backgrounds
(i.e., from families of white-collar workers, school teachers, etc.).[1]
Thus, in almost two-thirds of our cases, becoming a manager meant
the individual had achieved a social and economic status superior
to his father's—this in a society with little vertical mobility.

The authority over subordinates, the awareness of the status
achieved, and the satisfactory income until recently amply compensated for the manager's narrow area of decision making and his
lack of participation in long-term corporate policy decisions. As a
leader of men, the manager could forgo the roles of corporate
strategist and politician. The power he exercised at the bottom of
the organization counterbalanced his weakness at the top.

The manager's situation until a few years ago could be summarized as in Figure 6.1. The manager was subjected to one-sided
demands from above—that is, he had to implement decisions in
which he had not participated. In turn, he would transmit orders

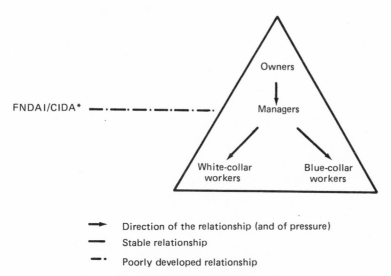

Direction of the relationship (and of pressure)
Stable relationship
Poorly developed relationship

*CIDA (Italian Confederation of Corporate Managers) was created in 1946. It is divided into six federations according to the type of enterprise: industrial (FNDAI), commercial, credit, insurance, agricultural and state-owned firms. The federations in turn have regional and provincial offices. FNDAI is tied to the institutions of social security (INPDAI), medical assistance (FASDAI), and a comprehensive insurance fund (FIPDI).

Figure 6.1

Direction and types of past relationships.

in an equally unilateral manner, to the bottom of the organization.

In the closed system of the firm, the manager lacked contacts with external groups such as labor unions, financial institutions, or those government agencies in charge of economic activities (e.g. with Planning, or with the Secretary of Work and Industry); his relations with his own professional association and his union were formal and passive.

Today the situation is different, as seen in Figure 6.2. The amount of pressure, some of it indirect, that is placed on managers has increased without a corresponding development, on their part, of new abilities to establish contacts or to exert pressure. Yet there are many factors that give the manager a sense of action. There is the increased awareness that henceforth he will never again be "out of the action" because none of the pressures exercised on the firm—and consequently on the managers, its representatives—is likely to diminish. Remaining passive in the hope of restoring the past situation would mean accepting a serious reduc-

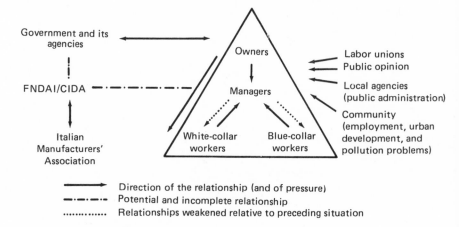

Figure 6.2

Direction and types of current relationships.

tion in one's role. Managers are responsible for corporate affairs in society's eyes and, like it or not, they are already involved in the country's economic events.

Furthermore, the manager's already small share of power is still decreasing. It is being eroded by the top because important decisions influencing corporate survival and development, at least in large firms, tend more and more to be made externally to the management, by agencies with which the managers do not have formal ties (such as the boards of directors of large financial institutions, the headquarters of non-Italian multinationals, or political and government agencies). Where power is still localized internally, its centralization—the persistance of ownership control—bars managers from decisions. The erosion of authority from below on the part of subordinates is already a *fait accompli*.

And, to make matters worse, managers are no longer able to take advantage of increases in the total economic power of the corporation. During periods of growth, career opportunities open up even if no vacancies occur at higher levels. The firm's expansion creates new positions, increases the number of subordinates, the complexity of managerial functions, and the amount of money administered; new products and markets are added. As a result, the power of the individual manager expands. This is one of the reasons why managers' efforts have been oriented for years toward corporate expansion. Expansion usually translated into advantages for the entire managerial body. But since the late 1960s a condition of economic recession or stagnation has blocked many firms' development and therefore the managers' access to expanded power.

6.2. Aspirations for power

The desire for a greater share of power, both in their own departments and in the realm of long-term company-wide decisions, is very much alive among managers. As is shown by the data about the incentives that motivate managers (see Figure 6.3), salary and career are rarely considered alone (salary never, career in only 4 percent of cases). Instead the greatest motivation, "responsibility" (seen as increased decision-making and policy participation), snows up alone in 41 percent of the managers' responses and together with other issues in 90 percent of the cases.

This explains why the managers believe, for example, that "The

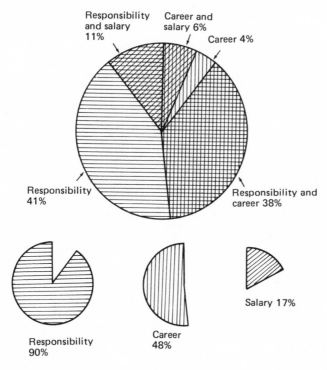

Figure 6.3

Managerial incentives.

manager should be part of the general staff that steers corporate policy and thus be able to exercise the responsibilities that have been given him." "Managers should sit on the board of directors." "The manager must take part in policy making. I cannot accept the opinion of those who still doggedly believe that the most important decisions belong to the representatives of capital. These people invest and risk only their money, but we invest our knowledge and our very lives in the firm. . . ."

The desire to participate in the formulation of corporate policies is more frequently found among young executives.[2] Comparison by age groups shows a difference in the generations of managers: the expectations of the younger group indicate that the future generation of managers is likely to be less tolerant of and less resigned to being excluded from important corporate decisions.

Even when the groups having different power are kept distinct, the age variable dominates (see Figure 6.4). In whichever group they are found, the young managers show a stronger desire for power, valuing personal recognition much less than do the older managers (see Figure 6.5).

Which type of power?

Given that aspirations toward greater responsibility are increasing, in what direction should managers steer their efforts? Toward attaining autonomy in one's professional field (decision making), or toward securing a voice in determining the company's long-term goals (policy making)? This choice is important because it governs both the strategies the manager will adopt and the personal characteristics he will try to develop. Also, the types of personal gratification derived from each orientation are different.

To participate in policy formulation provides a higher visibility in the firm. But such participation is infrequent because the big decisions are made only rarely in a firm's history, after which long stages of implementation and organizational readjustment follow. Feedback on the soundness of a policy is diluted over time (its effects being long-term) and responsibility for it is shared with others. If the manager is interested not only in influencing a firm's vital processes but also in getting immediate feedback on the soundness of his diagnoses, he will not be satisfied.

Decisions in one's professional field are much more frequent but they concern a narrower area. Decision-making power has a

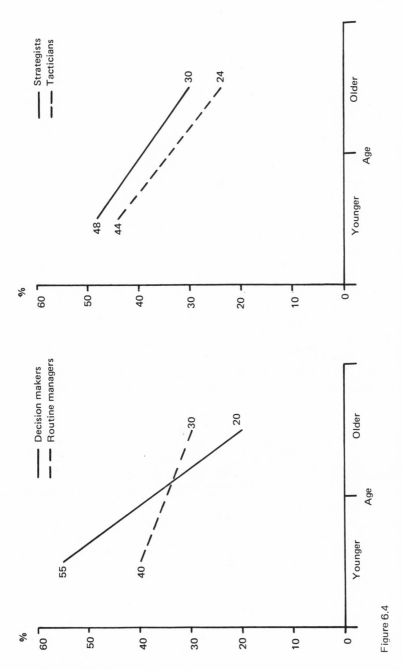

Figure 6.4

Frequency with which participation in policy making is considered the most important work incentive.

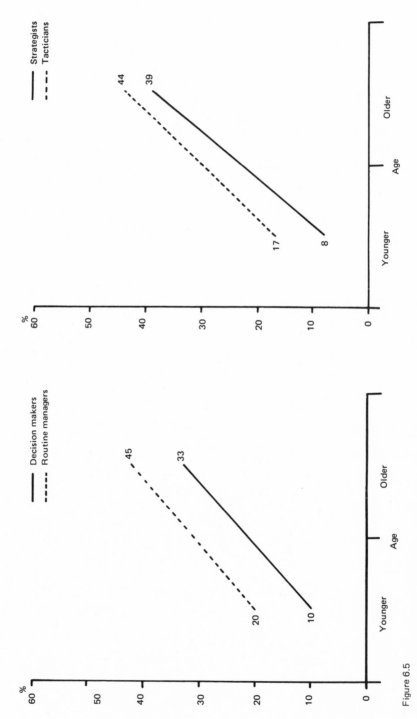

Figure 6.5

Frequency with which recognition of ability is considered the most important work incentive.

different kind of visibility; i.e., colleagues and subordinates perceive it. It concerns the people who are at the manager's own level or below, while policy making puts him in touch with the upper echelons. Making decisions in one's own professional domain is often an individual act, while defining a new policy is usually the fruit of collective activity. In the first case, the manager assumes direct responsibility; in the second case, he is only a consultant. Those who have a taste for visible power will prefer decisions whose authorship is clearly identifiable. While the strategist can only assert "I was there too," as would a participant in a famous battle, the decision maker can instead say with good reason, "This is my creation." (See Table 6.1.)

The new elements in corporate life—the firms' opening toward the external world, awareness of the need for continuous relations between corporations and other economic and political groups—impart a greater importance to policy formulation. It is difficult for the manager to represent the firm in the eyes of its employees and to be judged as responsible for its policies if he has not participated in their formation. The most recent trade-union struggles, in which the manager was involved and made accountable, have made him sensitive to this aspect of power.

6.3. The managers' strategies

Managers have reacted to the loss of authority either by adjusting to it as to an unavoidable phenomenon or by acting to modify the situation so as to regain some of their lost privileges.

Table 6.1

Characteristics of Decision-Making Power and Participation in Policy Making

Characteristic	Decision-making	Policy making
Initiative	individual	collective
Area	departmental	company-wide
Frequency	frequent	rare
Responsibility	direct	indirect
Power	internal	external
Feedback	short- or medium-term	long-term

Adjustment reactions

The managers who tend to accept the loss of influence have generally sought compensations at the individual level.

a. *Deferred gratification* ("Time will take care of things . . ."). Attainment of power is projected into the future, in the anticipation of promotion and the greater authority associated with a higher rank. The manager's attention is focused on the long-run possibilities of his career. But, given the firm's pyramidal structure and the very low Italian turnover, not everyone can reach his goal. The resulting competition creates "lateral" conflicts with colleagues. The fact that Italian firms are no longer expanding, and, worse, are actually contracting, makes this perspective illusory for many managers.

b. *Identification with the group at the top* ("We, the management . . ."). The manager recognizes that he lacks power but feels he belongs to the group that holds it and experiences a vicarious satisfaction from that fact. This identification is helped by the similarity that members of the group have in personal characteristics (education, social class) and in their roles (because even low-level executives carry on some leadership functions) as well as by common elite attitudes.

c. *Exalting professionalism* ("We are important because of what we know . . ."). In a nation where only 2 percent of the adult population have a university degree and where 70 percent of citizens have not finished mandatory schooling (as reported in the 1971 census), managers, with their high educational level and technical-organizational knowledge, represent a highly qualified professional group. Their greater cultural and technical training foster consciousness of a distinct professional identity. His specialized skills reinforce the manager's perception of himself as an "independent professional," "the owner's economic collaborator," or "special consultant to the firm." Due to his specialization the manager distinguishes himself both from the corporate owners to whom he sells a service and from other, less qualified employees.

By giving him an indispensable attribute, the manager's technical knowledge provides him with contractual strength and the basis for his security vis-à-vis both entrepreneurs and employees. It makes him aware of his capacity for fulfilling a unique function which puts him in an independent and intermediate position.

"In the firm, managers are the 'Third Estate.' On one side are the masses of workers and white-collar employees; on the other, the board of directors and the stockholders. We are the result of a selection; we were carefully chosen out of a mass of subordinates. ... We understand the problems of the two other groups and yet we do not belong to either side. We are in an objective position: we can be the connecting link. The employer sees things from a biased standpoint but we understand both his objectives and the workers' demands."

Strategies of change

Other managers aim their strategy toward a reconstruction of the manager's autonomy, through either individual or collective action.

a. Individual strategies

Above we stated that many scholars see power as a constant sum, whose shares are distributed unequally. If we imagine an individual's area of autonomy as a zone within a larger region, limited by other individuals' influence zones, the only way to increase this zone is at the expense of neighboring areas, either above or at the same level. In order to expand his autonomy, and with it his influence and importance in the corporate context, the individual must exert pressure in other directions.

Horizontal pressures. The regions beneath the manager's are not available, because they have already taken their share of power from the manager (employees are now able to interfere with management decisions). The remaining areas are situated at the same hierarchical level or at higher levels. It would seem logical that attempts would be directed toward that part of the firm in which power is found in the highest degree, that is, toward the top. But in practice this strategy is the least feasible, given the risk entailed in challenging the higher ranks. The superior may indeed be a protector when he plays a supporting role in the fulfillment of a manager's career expectations, but he can also become a "career wrecker." The community of feeling born of shared problems and similar professional backgrounds, as well as a more intense identification with one's own department than with the firm, can foster the creation of tacit alliances. The superior, rather than being a competitor for power can prove to be an ally, united to the lower-level manager by their common interest in the advancement of the department to which both belong.[3]

It follows that horizontal conflicts over domains of competence —that is, intrusion into a colleague's functions and rejection of other departments' interference in one's own—are more frequent than requests for delegation from above. Some of a manager's activities are directed at protecting his own "territory" (which in extreme cases can mean a breakdown into feuding camps) and attempting to enlarge it at the expense of colleagues. The fact that tensions within the managerial group are not manifested openly (as would be the case in a strike) reduces the visibility of conflict at the same hierarchical level, within the same department or among different departments.

Vertical pressures—the broadening of the oligarchy. If the manager were to receive greater authority by delegation from above, he could compensate in part for his loss of influence over subordinates and rebuild for himself a satisfactory area of autonomy. A process of redistribution of authority is already taking place as owners progressively retreat from management because the growing complexity of problems demands the use of specialists. Qualities such as professional competence and specialized knowledge, which modern managers of large firms abundantly possess, favor a spreading of the process.

In addition to individual action, the manager can increase his power by engaging in a complex game of interactions and trade-offs. Inserting oneself into cliques or factions is not an infrequent strategy. The familism of the traditional enterprise has given way to a kind of ideological nepotism, in which blood ties have been replaced with social connections that are not related to one's function, rank, or department, but stem instead from personal factors— e.g., friendships (sometimes predating association with the firm), common enemies, the same social and regional background ideology, etc. In this system of alliances, the quota of power is administered by the group, which then allocates it among its members.

The desire to "wrench" ever larger shares of power from the organization's top echelons stems not merely from the manager's effort to indemnify his recent loss of authority. It also stems from the manager's incessant search for an identity, which would be fulfilled if he could ally himself with the firm's owners or even take their place (as in the old dream of the "managerial revolution"). Many comments explaining the rejection of the managers' union focus on one of these two interpretations of the managerial role. (a) On identifying with the entrepreneur: "Above a certain level, a manager must consider himself an employer and not an employee." "When I work, I use the same standards as the entrepreneur." "I cannot conceive of a managers' union just as I cannot conceive of a union for Presidents of the Republic." (b) On replacing the entrepreneur: "Today managers *are* the firm—there no longer is an owner." "Now stockholders no longer have a voice; the firm is in the hands of the technocrats." "The character of the owner is bound to disappear. Agnelli and Pirelli are exceptions in an irreversible process. Managers have already in part assumed entrepreneurial functions and it is for this reason that employees consider them responsible for the firm's overall operations. . . ."

The conquest of greater responsibility can be realized without serious conflict since decision making is already an accepted feature of the managerial role. The problem is to extend it to the entire managerial group, for until now power has been confined to a narrow oligarchy. Instead, the changes in managerial authority which occurred because of workers' pressure originate from a situation of conflict and only create further internal conflict (see Figure 6.6).

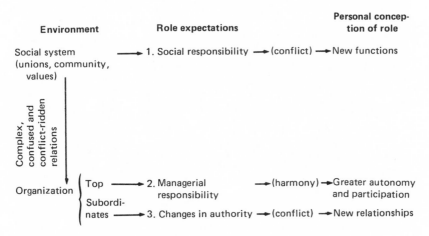

Figure 6.6

Effects of social pressure on the managerial role.

b. Collective strategies

Segregation of the managerial group: divorce from ownership and the creation of a pressure group. The managers' consciousness of themselves as a distinct professional group is fostered by a number of factors: their growing number (managers were only 6,000 in 1938 but are over 50,000 today), their greater professional training (leading the manager to identify more with the profession than with the firm employing him), and finally the recognition that restructuring the managerial role—a necessity after the 1969 workers' protest—cannot be achieved individually but requires collective action.

Unlike their counterparts in other industrial nations, Italian managers have long possessed a representative body and a union. However, their participation in these associations has generally been slack and essentially passive.[4] Further, almost half of our interviewees declared they were not interested in or are dubious about the role of their union.

A professional association could accomplish the goal of cementing the group by stimulating an awareness of the role's common aspects and by creating communication channels between the managers and the external world. The managers' problem is not only to acquire a collective consciousness but to become a responsible national elite, an elite that should have a say in the handling of national economic affairs because it is already considered responsible for many of their beneficial and harmful effects.

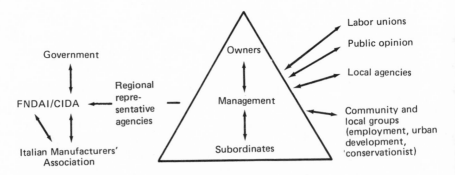

Figure 6.7

Direction and types of relationships desired.

Managers' perception of the need to establish relations with the larger community stems from their knowledge that the roots of the events that upset industry not only during the "Hot Autumn" but thereafter originated outside the firm. Communicating with other social groups represents an essential part of the managerial role. The need for these relations is acknowledged in the CIDA (Italian Confederation of Corporate Managers) Statute, and already there have been some attempts to establish them, although still in embryo form.[5] The new network of relationships required could be conceived as in Figure 6.7.

6.4 Success of individual and collective strategies

Defining the managerial role: the limits of professionalism

The adjustment of many managers implicitly entails the acceptance of their impotence, and succeeds largely by reducing the individual's level of frustration. When the adjustment leads the individual to stress his professionalism, the manager's intention is to outline the peculiar characteristics of the managerial function, to smooth the conflict with subordinates and to highlight his importance vis-à-vis the owners. But can management be considered a profession?

Characteristics of a profession are, first of all, autonomy—that is, independence from an employer and a direct relationship with a client; and second, public usefulness—the service offered by the independent professional must be "altruistic," available to all, and beneficial to the community. A manager's activities, which involve subordination and unilateral subjection, do not fit this definition.[6]

Nonetheless some authors propose a more extensive definition of professionalism, emphasizing the high degree of systematic theoretical knowledge,[7] the autonomy in organizing one's work, expertise, and a sense of responsibility and commitment,[8] all of which are elements found in the managerial jobs.

The assertion that a professional's activities must be primarily oriented toward the community interest means that, by definition, the profession must largely be pursued for the benefit of others and not merely for egoistic goals, and that the material advantage deriving from practice of a profession should not represent the only measure of success.[9] Yet there exist other aspects to professionalism that are not currently found in management: a professional group should be characterized by a strong sense of identity that unites its members, a common language, a shared system of values, and agreement on the definition of its functions. In this sense the professional group is like "a community within a community."[10] From this strong identification stems the impetus to associate with one another. But our research reveals that managers are unable to identify with one another; every hierarchical level feels it is different, and each individual finds refuge in his own uniqueness, exalting the unique characteristics of his task with little regard for its similarities with the tasks of colleagues dealing with other realms of expertise. Further, managers communicate very little among themselves, except for reasons relating to work, and even in that case they usually do so in a narrow context. Each remains locked in his professional domain, as in a fortress.

But, above all, the entire group lacks a distinct and common system of values. Managers have been unable to formulate a group ideology, even under the pressure of social and worker protests— events which, after the first shock, could have proven stimulating. Their culture is limited to reflecting the value system of the social class where they were placed by their birth and their economic status, and their largely urban, high class culture.

The development of a managerial ethic cannot take place as long as the manager's horizon remains confined to the enterprise: it presupposes an understanding of the problems of a society with which the firm continually interacts. A close relationship to the community would make social action an integral part of the executive function. The solution to the dilemma of the managerial role does not seem possible without revising the role the manager plays in society.

Another trait distinguishing managers from other professionals is the fact that managers are the only professional group that "habitually employs for gain another group whose function, economic interests, and social position are entirely distinct from its own.[11] The result is a conflict of interests not found in other professions, which are able to establish clearer relations with the rest of society.

Finally, every profession sets rules of behavior for the job as well as for relations with other social groups; these rules reflect a higher standard than those legally mandated. The code of professional ethics describes the behavior that is suitable in dealings with the community and its representatives, and with individuals such as colleagues and clients.[12] While, as in other professions, there can be instances in which the manager's professional interest clashes with that of another individual or a group, managers lack the guidelines of a code of ethics based on considerations that transcend both the personal interest and the minimum requirements of the law.

While other professional communities have power over their members, whom they can punish or expel in cases of ethics violations, a similarly empowered association does not exist for managers. The activity of the managers' association is mainly union-related, aimed at improving financial and fringe benefits.

So far the manager's professional requirements and rules of conduct have been defined by industry, or more accurately, by the individual employer. These rules are confined to a specification of responsibilities within the firm. In fact, industry still lacks a definition of its own social responsibilities; in the interim, it is up to the manager to define his role vis-à-vis owners, workers, and other groups.[13] In the absence of a code of ethics his function remains uncertain and ambiguous, and he will be unable to establish a clearly defined and harmonious relationship with the rest of society.

Unlike independent professionals or consultants, the manager is deeply embedded within the organization and he cannot remain "out of the action." To define himself as a specialist is to seek refuge in an ivory tower from which he would continuously be pulled by his need for frequent contacts with other members of the organization. These contacts cannot be mediated (only the consultant can limit himself to written reports) but must take the form of face-to-face, daily communication. Unlike the consultant, the manager is more than a formulator of new decisions: he is responsible for translating those decisions into action, using the firm's facilities and personnel. The consultant is judged on the validity of his suggestions; the manager on the results he obtains (production, cost decreases, and so forth). Thus, both the people at the top and those at the bottom of the organization prevent the manager from limiting his role to that of a consultant.

In short, the concept of the manager as a professional is but a variation of the concept of the manager as a pure expert, something that the daily reality of corporate life denies. The ivory tower does not exist, the manager is indeed involved in the day-to-day affairs of the enterprise. He is exposed to the elements and sometimes finds himself in the eye of the hurricane.

The fact remains that in Italy there is no clear definition of the manager's role. The development of the new professional identity of managers occurred simultaneously with the crisis in the managerial role. In industrially more advanced countries the managerial class had time to emerge and define itself; but in Italy, the crisis relating to the managerial function was violently superimposed on the managers' slowly emerging awareness of their professional role. This role was challenged before it was firmly established.

Defining this role constituted one of the objectives in the 1975 managers' national contract. The managers' union thought it necessary to reformulate the definition of the managerial function given by the Civil Code and to insert it as the opening clause of the contract.[14] The new definition lends itself to various interpretations; the official stance taken by the managers' journal seems to emphasize subordination more than professionalism.[15] Under this interpretation, the new definition states, for the managers, the divorce of their responsibility from that of the entrepreneur; for the firm it makes the manager similar to the other employees, by extending to him provisions that previously were limited to workers and white-collar employees.

During the contract negotiations, the managerial journal *Realtà* underlined the need to "define the managerial position as having executive status in the firm, but without confusing it with the firm's ownership."[16] After the contract was signed, the same journal stated that managers are "employees" and that "the managerial position is a position of subordinated work," adding, "The entrepreneurial position is very different and distinct. We mean by entrepreneur the owner of the firm, that is, the person who controls it and who is the only one who can overcome subordination by delegating authority. . . ."[17]

By voluntarily relinquishing responsibilities of an entrepreneurial nature, the managers risk the creation of an unnecessary limitation on their tasks. It is doubtful that it will serve the purpose of protecting them (since employees and public opinion will continue to view the managers as responsible for the firm). Rather, it ratifies the managers' exclusion from most important decisions, which, according to the contract, the manager would not formulate but only implement. He is only an "executor of entrepreneurial will."[18]

The emphasis on professionalism in the contract is always accompanied by a recognition of the subordinate position of the managers; we are therefore a long way from the image of the independent professional. The new objective pursued by the contract is not autonomy but *security*. This aim is achieved by (a) the guarantee of the job; (b) greater protection in criminal and civil matters; and (c) the separation from entrepreneurial responsibilities, to which we alluded.

In 1975 the managerial union presented, this time successfully, a request for "just cause," that is, a firm's obligation to justify dismissals in writing (article 20); moreover, the contract established a system of arbitration[19] to which the manager can appeal (article 17). However, unlike the other employees, the manager cannot count on being reinstated in his job and function but only on a potentially significant financial compensation.[20]

Job security is important in the context of the present economic crisis. Article 12 aims at the same goal, guaranteeing the rights already acquired by the managers in the case of ownership transfers, concentration, mergers, and divestiture (these events, according to our survey, have sometimes drastically interfered with the careers of the managers involved).

Article 14 of the contract—concerning civil responsibility or criminal liability connected with job performance—extends the manager's protection to cases involving law violations (all civil responsibility and all legal costs for criminal proceedings must be borne by the firm). In addition, the manager under investigation retains the right to his job and salary.

But the price for this greater security is a limiting definition of the executive function. The new contract seems to ratify the end of the managers' pretense that they are members of the technostructure. In the Italian setting, the replacement of entrepreneurs or owners with managers seems to be still a long way off. For the managers it has now ceased even to be an aspiration.

It would be inaccurate, however, to interpret the new contract as a sign of the proletarianization of the managerial class: the emphasis on professionalism, just as it distinguishes the manager from the entrepreneur, also distinguishes him from the less qualified employees. But because managers are distinct from employers and from other workers, they remain isolated and lose the advantage of coalition with either of the two groups. Furthermore, they are caught between two powerful forces who subject them to demands, albeit differently, and both hold them responsible for corporate matters.

Thus the problem of decision-making power presents itself anew. It is the logical consequence of the responsibility placed on the managers and the need to become a separate and distinct group— a third force.

The conquest of power through delegation

Increasing one's area of competence is the strategy that should have the greatest chance of success, because it reinforces a process of delegation already taking place.[21] The managers must carve out a place in a small oligarchical group, which has already brought some of them into the fold. In pursuing this end, however, managers encounter two relatively new phenomena: first of all, the total amount of power to share has diminished because of external groups' interference in decisions that were once exclusively in the firm's domain. Further, they find themselves acting in a competitive situation: before they were able to conquer a greater share of power from above, the bottom of the hierarchy beat them to the punch and made itself a participant in the decision-making process. Even when specific problems of his own department are at stake, the manager now meets competitors for power among his own subordinates or external groups of various types. After the limitations and frustrations suffered within his own area of competence, the manager may be induced to consider intervening in activities of a wider nature, that is, in the formulation of company policies. But here, competence and technical expertise, which justify and encourage requests for greater decision-making responsibility, are less decisive factors. The obstacles to managers' participation in policy formulation are not to be found in the managers, who requested that this right be inserted in their 1975 contract, but rather in the owners, who through their own Manufacturers' Association have repeatedly turned down this request.[22]

Participation in policy formulation remains difficult to achieve. It seems to be an occasional gift bestowed by the power holders (as in family enterprises), or a specialized activity that is increasingly moving out of managers' reach (as in the Italian and non-

Italian multinationals). This power is the most difficult to secure because it is the last entrepreneurial function to be decentralized. Since policy making has been rendered vitally important by the challenge of the times (economic crisis, political instability, union aggressiveness), the top echelons of the organizations are currently concentrating on it. But even if the top were favorably disposed to extending the managers' participation, the organizational tools to realize it are still in the embryonic stage. It is not unrealistic, however, to imagine a broadening of the executive committees to include managers of lower levels, or the insertion of managers on the board of directors, or the institution of union representation for managers.[23]

The managers' union representation in the plant

Of the above-mentioned alternatives, the one that has been implemented is managers' union representation (RSA). Its function is justified both by the separation of managers from ownership and by their belief that they are a distinct professional group. One manager commented: "Until yesterday the manager identified with the firm because of tradition, now he is no longer inclined to do that; he wants to express a power of his own because he considers himself as a worker like any other. He therefore has the right to his own representation in controversial matters."

Limited to a few large firms, the managers' RSA may introduce divisions among managers, both according to the size of a firm and according to hierarchical level. As the great majority of Italian firms are below 500 employees, the number of managers (usually 1.5–2 percent of total payroll) is also small. Union representation makes sense only in the few very large companies with over a hundred managers. The function of the RSA is to secure for the managers the access to information and the advisory capacities that the very nature of their function and their status in the organization should naturally grant them. While the workers' RSA represents a victory, because for the first time the worker is let into the "control room," the managers' RSA is primarily an acknowledgement of their painful exclusion from that right.[24] It therefore risks exacerbating the division between those managers who, as participants in the decision process, do not need a representation, and those who are excluded from it, creating a split between the oligarchy and the cast-offs.

Given that this division exists already in fact, the real problem is elsewhere: it resides mainly in the uncertainty of the managers' RSA functions, an uncertainty that is not only due to the lack of contractual agreement between the managers' union and the Industrialists' Association, but also to the fact that the spectrum of the RSA's interests ranges from narrow issues of a corporative nature (i.e., privileges accorded by the contract) [25] to problems of substance. [26] Even in the latter case, the RSA is sometimes not exempt from the suspicion that it pursues narrow group interests. For instance, it is difficult to interpret some positions taken by the managers' RSA in state-owned firms: sometimes they appear to be simple expressions of a desire for greater participation in policy making, sometimes they touch on problems that interest all workers; but other times they appear to serve a self-protecting goal or to be instrumental in a partisan political game. [27]

A second problem is the uncertainty of relations between the managerial RSAs and other RSAs or other expressions of the workers' movement (from labor unions to workers' production conferences). For example, the managers' RSA has not tried to connect itself with the plant committees. [28] The problem is two-sided because while it is necessary for the managers' RSA to establish relations and communication channels with other groups, it is also necessary for it to win recognition and acceptance from workers' representatives. [29]

If the RSA's primary objective is to establish a relationship with the top of the hierarchy independently from the other groups in the organization, it will have limited scope. If the RSA's goal is to extend participation, then this objective should be pursued together with the representatives of the other groups of employees. Otherwise the goal of the managers' representation will be mainly to enlarge the oligarchy.

However, the managers' union representation in the plant is a new phenomenon, both because it is the collective expression of a professional group that was previously fragmented and because it establishes communication channels along two avenues. For now it is used by leadership groups, but it represents a new resource capable of further development.

The greatest obstacle to the establishment of a managerial group strategy is to be found in the individual manager who conceives his tie with the firm as primarily between a professional (himself) and an organization, or, even more narrowly, as an extraprofessional relationship built on trust. Very often a group spirit is lacking, along with any inclination to identify, organize, and act collectively with colleagues. (See Table 6.2.)

The professionalist attitude, which could theoretically constitute a rallying point, is usually accompanied by a heightened individualism preventing the development of a sense of community of interests and thus of any collective action. Paradoxically, the awareness of his professional ability leads the manager to refuse to identify with the group. A great many responses justifying refusal to join the managers' union are based on heightened individualism: "I do not like being considered a number." "Managers are not part of the masses."[30]

Professional consciousness is so individualistic as to induce many managers to refuse even comparisons or a rapprochement with colleagues bearing the same title: "The manager's work is individual, unique; the relationship with the employer is based on trust, therefore the contract has to be personal. The manager is an independent professional." "The manager must maintain his individuality, both to his and his employer's advantage. I do not feel that I belong to a group." "I would welcome unionization as long as it did not call for identification with a group, be it the managerial group or, even worse, the company."

A competitive spirit vis-à-vis one's colleagues emerges in some

---

Table 6.2

Opinions on Union Representation for Managers
(in %, $n = 655$)

No opinion	11
Against	
—because ours is a relationship based on trust, or because each case must be handled individually	18 ⎫
—because we identify with the firm or the owner	8 ⎬ 34
—on general principle	8 ⎭
In favor	
—only for large firms	9 ⎫
—on behalf of team spirit	21 ⎬ 55
—on general principle	25 ⎭

responses: "I like the idea of free competition among managers." Some express the desire to safeguard hierarchical distances: "I have managers working under me, and I do not wish to align myself with them since occasionally I find myself on the other side of the table and it would be embarassing. . . ."

Other comments reveal an extreme elitism and a refusal to allow managers to be compared to the employees they supervise: "If they unionized, managers would be like laborers, clerks, and bookkeepers." "Union representation would debase the position of manager. It is all right for all other categories of employees but not for the managers, who must and can protect their interests alone." "Workers' unions have a specific function because they represent masses who have low education. . . . Managers have a higher cultural background and representation would constitute a loss in prestige. If the manager is one whom the firm harnesses to protect its interests, he should not need a mediator: otherwise he would be a manager in name only and not in fact."[31] Others are against union representation because they reject the concept of unionization in general: "Whatever the system of representation, it ends up belittling the individual." "I disdain any union contract. I have a personal relationship with the boss and when I want something, I approach him directly. I do not accept any intermediary."

Only a very few managers criticized this extreme sort of individualism: "While the worker has a class consciousness, the white-collar employee does not, so you can imagine how much the manager has." One manager interviewed commented bitterly, "Managers do not have a professional consciousness. Together with whores they are the only workers who never have and never will go on strike."

The conception that the manager has of himself as an independent professional is a nineteenth-century view based more on the status achieved and personal ability than on a specific function. The manager seems to be the equivalent of the family doctor, a role that is disappearing in the medical profession. But the modern professional, to whom the manager attributes so much prestige,[32] can count on very aggressive professional associations; the fact that professions like medicine, law, and architecture are often conducted on a private basis does not prevent their members from organizing. These professionals have long been aware that to carry out their activities effectively they must face many problems that are not strictly professional. The physician has become interested in hospital management and national health reform, the lawyer in code reform and the reorganization of judicial administration; the architect cannot avoid considering urban and regional planning. These professionals not only have active organizations they can use, they are also endowed with a broader conception of their activity, in which the professional role is framed in the context of the society in which they work.

Managers as a pressure group

Until now managers have made limited use of CIDA (Italian Confederation of Corporate Managers) as a pressure group. Many seem to consider it with the same mistrust Italians apply to all representative institutions, which are often considered self-serving, inefficient bureaucracies, the personal fiefdom of a politician, or the hidden mouthpiece of a particular interest group.

As one manager phrased it, CIDA appears like "a large head with no body" because it lacks the support of the ranks, a support which is the strength of workers' unions. Furthermore, CIDA is the expression of various professional groups that are not homogeneous in problems and attitudes (in addition to business managers, CIDA represents managers in banking, insurance, commerce, and agriculture)[33] and seldom can agree with one another.[34]

Interestingly, managers' participation in regional associations is more active and seems spontaneous. These associations are less bureaucratized and closer to the manager; via their press and meetings they have provided a platform for many interesting proposals and debates.[35] It is probably through the activity of the flexible and more representative local organizations that the managerial group could "take over" CIDA and influence its action at the national political level.

However, the development of a group spirit among managers, were it to occur, would not necessarily in itself constitute a positive achievement. Some professional associations hold rigidly to traditional and conservative views and pursue narrow self-interests. A group search for greater power could have as its aim power for power's sake; in this case the rise of a technocracy could mean little more for the firm than a change of bosses; a professional group would supplant the financial group, without necessarily changing the objectives or the philosophy of management action. It would bring about a change of bodies but not a change in the type of the organizational relations, nor a change in the relations between the firm and the society.

Thus we come full circle to the problem of the need for a managerial set of values and the means to make the managers become attuned to and acceptable to other social groups.

The identity crisis: A rift in the managerial group

But if managers are in fact incapable of recognizing themselves as a group and behaving as such, and if the stress on professionalism proves insufficient to provide identity and security, with whom can they identify? (See Table 6.3.)

We described earlier the managers' growing awareness of their intermediate position, halfway between workers and owners. One person interviewed stated: "The manager is undergoing a crisis. Once he was very close to ownership and embodied it; today he is like a bridge, the link between capital and labor. But he has not yet chosen a precise role, that is, he does not know whether to stay close to the owners whose problems he knows in depth or to approach the workers, or still yet whether to become a mediating factor. . . . The manager is in an intermediate position between capital and labor; upon considering both points of view, he still does not know which to embrace."

The two possibilities that are open—identification with owners

---

Table 6.3

Types of identification and relationships:
Alternative choices for managers

Identification with	Type of relationship	Power	Perception of managerial status
1. The firm (or the owners)	based on trust	personal influence	upper class
2. The profession	individual contractual	derived from technical-organizational knowledge	"intelligentsia"
3. Management	collective contractual	union-based	technostructure
4. Workers	collective contractual	union-based	proletarianized

or identification with workers—imply the potential for a rift within the managerial group: a horizontal split along the levels of the hierarchy could occur. This presumably would separate the managers of the upper level (coopted by owners and often sharing their power) from managers of middle and low levels, who are deprived of power.

The nonhomogeneous character of the managerial group is recognized by the interested parties themselves, and informally by their representative body. The subdivision of managers into groups according to their rank has been considered by CIDA. This solution would probably be attractive to the corporations' top echelons, who could more easily delegate power to a narrow group. It would also not necessarily arouse negative reactions from the middle managers, who could consider their inferiority temporary as they await promotions. Nonetheless, the effect would be to destroy the fragile solidarity of the managerial group.

Recognizing their marginal status vis-à-vis organizational power centers, some middle and low level managers readily identify with the bottom of the organization: "We have almost the same problems as the working class and the white-collar workers." [36] Identification with the top is seen as illusory: "The manager is still unaware of the fact that he is a subordinate. He still thinks of himself as a businessman." "The idea of the manager as an employer has been left behind: he is in fact a salaried employee with relatively great responsibility. . . ." "Our work is subordinated work: we do not influence corporate policies."

For some, this proletarianization is the consequence of the top echelon's attitude: "The firm treats us as illegitimate children. We are often denied the recognition we deserve"; or of protest: "The manager has lost his status; he is neither more nor less than an employee." For others it is a way to extricate oneself from an ambiguous situation: "Unionization is the first step toward recognition as subordinates; it ends the uncertainty of our relationship with the owners and other employees. We managers have always been caught between two fires: on one side there is the board of directors, on the other the workers; we are the buffer between them and we take our punches when it is convenient for management."

For many it is a matter of acknowledging a state of fact. Together with a decrease in authority, union victories have reduced the distance between managers and employees. For managers delegating from above is slow and unable to remedy a situation which is the result of rapid change and cannot be reversed. The prospect of acquiring greater power is far away, especially for low-level managers, some of whom commented: "The distance between managers and white-collar employees is fading from every standpoint (normative, economic, social); the same thing already occurred between white-collar and blue-collar workers. . . ." "Managers have understood that there are three categories of subordinates: workers, white-collar employees, and managers." "On the normative level the difference between managers and white-collar employees should disappear. The distinction between them is blurred and there remains only a difference in function. The manager's status is an anachronism." "The manager is simply a particularly qualified worker, with rights and duties."

These comments could signal a different view of organizational relations; the tendency enforced by labor unions to level out job qualifications is reducing the previous extreme vertical nature of the firm and its rigid stratification: the emphasis is now on function and no longer on hierarchy. Some managers believe that, for this reason, all the employees should band together and build a common front. But the "proletarianization" of the managers will not occur without affecting attitudes: "The relationship of trust between the firm and the manager will disappear, and maybe that is just as well." "At one time the relationship was based on reciprocal trust . . . today it is simply a matter of selling professional knowledge." Managers' loyalty to the firm will diminish as a consequence: "The company once tolerated disaffection from the workers but not from the white-collar employees; later it had to accept the lack of loyalty also of the white-collar workers; now it's the manager's turn." The new attitude takes into account conflict with ownership: "When we become organized, we will be able to enforce our demands. The manager can go on strike for the same reasons that induce other groups to do so. . . ." "As subordinate workers, managers should not give up the economic and normative rights due them as a result of their new status. They too can be protected by the Employees' Bill of Rights."

Identification with the bottom of the organization can take the form of:

a. *A partial proletarianization*: a portion of managers will join the occupational group of the white-collar employees, from whose ranks they emerged and from whom they are distinguished only by their exercise of authority; often both possess the same educational level and professional competence. A more feasible alternative would be to follow the example of other European managers and join the *cadres* (supervisors and superintendents without managerial titles), similar to the managers in terms of the nature of their responsibilities. A joint association with the cadres would have the advantage of numerically reinforcing the managerial group, and increasing its strength in exerting pressure. (In France, La Confederation des Quadres has a million members, and it is calculated that the currently scarcely unionized Italian cadres number about 900,000. The Italian managers are 100,000.) While the Italian bank managers have invited the bank cadres into their union, and the managers in commercial firms are considering this option, the managers have turned this opportunity down. On this issue, industrial and commercial managers' representatives clashed earnestly at a 1977 CIDA meeting.[37]

b. *A complete proletarianization*, by which the manager would accept a self-definition as worker, in the wake of the white-collar employees' rapprochement with workers. This solution is not without problems. The split with ownership could assume the form of a conflict, an unusual situation for the manager. Also the identification with a lower social class would carry with it a painful feeling of demotion. Even that minority of managers which emerged from a working-class background have already psychologically distanced themselves from it.

A rapprochement by one or the other group does not seem to stem from a spontaneous choice. Rather, one has the impression that the manager, in finding himself between two conflicting groups of equal strength and unable to build his own pressure group, attempts to escape by taking refuge in one of the two camps. Choosing to identify with the entrepreneur or with the workers often seems to stem more from an attitude of withdrawal from the other group than a willful choice. Being drawn toward workers seems to grow out of some managers' bitter acknowledgement that they have been rejected by the top, while rapprochement with top executive levels in other managers seems to stem from resentment caused by employees' attitudes toward them. In both cases, it is a reaction based more on spite than on actual inclination.

For this reason, managers are increasingly aware that they must become a third force; the development of managers' union representation is an attempt to give institutional backing to their group. Autonomy need not be synonymous with isolation and withdrawal; on the contrary, it could confer sufficient security to permit the establishment of relations with other social groups. Distinct from both entrepreneurs and workers, the manager can enter into dialogue with both, and still maintain his individuality. To accept the workers' world does not necessarily mean to identify with them. However, some managers argue that the manager's point of reference must be furnished by the situation and evolution of the workers' world.[38]

6.5. Choosing among courses of action

The group's lack of uniformity with respect to decision-making and policy-making powers does not help predict which strategies will actually be adopted.

Identification with owners has diminished, and identification with the working class is rendered difficult by conflict and class differences. There remains an intermediate position, represented by two separate lines of action, one on the individual plane (identification with the profession), the other on the collective plane.

The choice of strategy will be dictated more by characteristics of the work environment (degree of decentralization, size, type of ownership, conflict levels in the firm) and by role characteristics (hierarchical level, breadth of power) than by the individual manager's personal characteristics.

Despite the safeguard of managers' separation from entrepreneurial responsibilities, those who are excluded from decision making and policy participation will be following an inadequate strategy if they choose to lock themselves in the profession. If this strategy is adopted, the only advantage for the manager is the pecuniary reward he receives in comparison to other salaried groups.[39]

Robin Marris notes that in a society in which the manager's institutional role is not clearly defined, he will tend, more than the independent professional, to concentrate on the pecuniary aspects of his job. Whenever a society, because of its imperfectly integrated structure, subjects the individual to incompatible demands, the most frequent response is to search for personal interest conceived in its most material form.[40]

In a general situation of insecurity, economic compensation provides not merely the only gratification possible but also the only motivation and goal in one's work.

The opposite position stems from a larger and more realistic consideration of the managerial role. Were the manager to choose to wear the subordinate's uniform, he still could not remove himself from the "scuffle": in the eyes of workers and public opinion he is responsible for corporate affairs, even if he did not shape them. The strategy of avoidance cannot help him escape responsibility in the eyes of a public which becomes every day more attentive to business behavior.

To this recognition we must add the managers' aspirations for greater responsibility and participation, which are mainly manifest in the new managerial recruits. Evidence is found in the beginning politicization of the group,[41] in the renewed interest in their professional association, and in the organization of the managers' union representation in the firm.

Although undoubtedly the managerial class is gaining awareness, its expression is still in the embryonic stage.[42] The few instances of autonomous action are taken by a small group of politically oriented, aggressive managers, usually located in the very big corporations. It is still difficult to judge whether this elite within an elite really represents the vanguard of a group movement, just as it is premature and unrealistic for now to regard Italian managers as full-fledged technocrats.

7

The Powerless
Elite

The Italian manager is revealed in the preceding chapters as a socially isolated, professionally underdeveloped, and psychologically conflicted individual. He lives in an occupational world in which his superiors, subordinates, and colleagues seem all too ready to undermine his role and vitality. And for the most part he is personally blameless; he is simply a product of the social, economic, and historical forces that have made modern Italian industry.

Italian managers have virtually all of the sociological characteristics of an elite group. Yet they are stymied in their quest for status and power. The forces that constrain them are many, and they are all played out within the firm. Some stem from the way Italian companies are organized or their ownership patterns, some reflect the interaction between the managerial ethic and the internal dynamic of contemporary firms, and some stem from the imperatives of the Italian society. All together, they are the forces that have created this "powerless elite."

7.1. The environment of the manager

The manager works within his firm, which is itself a part of a larger economic and social structure. He is guided by a set of beliefs or assumptions which give a kind of ideological coherence to his role in the firm and the system. And he lives within a social network that shapes his performance and capabilities. We now review these elements of his environment.

The structure and goals of the firm

The unequal distribution of power stems from the type of vertical structure that is found in all firms: the emphasis is on hierarchy. The organizational pyramid can be flattened more or less (with few or many levels, few or many persons at the top), but it is always a pyramid. The distribution of power is therefore unequal, creating a situation in which individuals compete for it in an "economy of scarcity."[1]

As noted earlier, in a hierarchical structure power appears to be a zero-sum game and can be increased only at the expense of others. Consultation—that is, the introduction of other individuals into the decision process—seems to threaten the power holders; further, power needs to be continually confirmed by use, and making decisions is a way for the manager to reaffirm it.

We can, of course, conceive of organizations structured in nonhierarchical (functional) and participatory ways. But firms are built on models offered by the external society. The authority system is not a product of industrialization; it is not fundamental or paramount to the productive process, which could take place as well in nonhierarchical organizations. The differentiation of functions does not necessarily imply their hierarchicalization according to importance.[2] The authority system is a social product.

The pursuit of efficiency. The centralization of power within an organization, at least regarding new policy decisions, seems to respond to an objective need for efficiency, timing, and consistency.

In competitive situations on the national and international levels, the productive organization must be able to move swiftly toward new strategic positions required by changing situations. Market competition demands continual control and adjustment of price strategies, costs, and distribution. The introduction of technological innovations and new products must be timed correctly.

Many corporate decisions are therefore taken under urgent pressures that leave little time for broad consultation. The stress thus exerted on the organization justifies authoritarianism; one of the factors determining the choice of type of leadership (authoritarian or democratic) is the degree of urgency of decisions.[3] Among conditions limiting participation are: the availability of time; economic rationality (the cost of consultation[4]); the intercorporate strategy (sometimes secrecy is necessary); the extracorporate strategy (technological secrecy) together with the preexisting lack of adequate communication channels and lack of training of possible collaborators.[5] Geographic decentralization and size of organizational units are other variables.[6]

However, even within a hierarchical structure, decentralization of decision-making power can be realized through:

1. a broader participation, made possible by systems of collegial consultation (by including part or all of the management group and possibly employees' representatives);

2. delegation of functions that once were the sole domain of top management.

From the point of view of corporate effectiveness, collegial decision making presents some disadvantages compared to the centralized decision-making system, whether it is individual or oligarchical. The group involved in a collective decision often tends to take on a bureaucratic structure and act in a conservative way; further, consideration of a great variety of viewpoints and alternative courses of action often produces compromise solutions that attempt to reflect disparate views and take all objections into account. The group may also tend to reduce the risk to a minimum by choosing a "logical" process of decision making, based exclusively on the available facts, often showing little inclination to tackle the uncertainties implicit in innovation. Thus in long-term or global decisions, in which rationality is always imperfect, collectively discussed solutions may lose some of the important elements of imagination, intuition, optimism, and nonrational characteristics linked to personality.

The adventurous and daring nature of decision making under conditions of uncertainty is the most unique and peculiar characteristic of the classical entrepreneur, whose role was considered by some to be precisely that of "gap-filler" or "input-completer."[7] The entrepreneurial type of decision is one that cannot be delegated to a computer precisely because of the insufficient data available. Unorganized figures and facts must be integrated with personal judgment, which stems more often from intuition than from logical analysis.

In fact group decisions really cannot necessarily be defined as rational or as more rational than individual decisions. The corporate decision is strongly conditioned by uncertainty and by the human mind's difficulty of picturing and solving complex problems; the need to simplify them gives way to a "bounded rationality."[8]

Furthermore, in the process of making collegial decisions, rationality is blurred by a number of factors: the fight for the control of resources within the managerial group often causes the methods applied to the search for the solution to be particularistic —connected, that is, to the goals and prospects of rival groups— and not company-oriented.[9] Organizations are coalitions of interests and corporate decisions are primarily the product of negotiation; they are influenced by the desire to reduce organizational conflicts resulting from the presence of differing goals.[10] For this reason, the collegial decision has a rationality of its own, a rationality the nature of which is not technical but social, producing solutions that are acceptable to the organization's members and which they are willing to put into practice.

A second mode of decentralization consists of delegating to individuals functions that were once in the domain of the organization's top echelons. This is the most common form of power distribution, but the delegation is seldom complete. It is important to identify which functions are delegated and the criteria by which the top of the organization decides which activities must remain within its exclusive domain.

One of the criteria applied seems to be that of uncertainty: the organization's top reserves for itself the right to intervene where the degree of uncertainty is the greatest because of insufficient data, the unknown elements implicit in any long time-frame, or the variability and fluctuations of external situations. Thus, not surprisingly, decisions in the area of production are the first to be decentralized, and certain long-range financial decisions (distribution of profits, investments, search for new capital) are practically never delegated.[11] It is not by coincidence that the organization chart of the majority of Italian firms lacks some managerial positions that are found in the organization chart of U.S. enterprises. Such positions are those of "controller" and finance manager, representing not the administration of balance sheets and budgets but the functions of planning and control of operational and financial management (relative to sources of financing, negotiations with credit institutions, etc.). Another position often missing in the organization charts of many, even big, Italian corporations is the one in charge of long-term planning. This does not mean that these functions are not carried out, but only that they are not delegated to middle and lower management and remain the prerogative of the top. The head of the firm also tends further to maintain final control over decisions concerning the organizational structure, whose changes he often initiates himself.[12]

Relations with the unions, with the community and with government are activities that are seldom delegated. "Labor, the public, and the government are three of the most important groups affected by the large corporation. Whenever a powerful interest group exists, the company executive is likely to reserve for himself the direction of relations of the firm with that group. This holds for bankers and other financial interests, large minority stockholders, important customers or competitors, and so on."[13]

If we examine the role of the big financier we find it multiform. This new entrepreneur is no longer oriented toward the firm's internal affairs; he long ago delegated the organization's "maintenance" functions. Today the financier is primarily a politician in a broad sense, that is, an individual who is continually relating with the environment, which he attempts to interpret, to manipulate, and with which he establishes compromises and alliances. The interaction occurs primarily with the outside environment: with union representatives, with other businessmen, with the large private or state-owned banks, with the state, and last but not least, with the public, whose opinion is shaped through the mass media.[14]

The entrepreneur-financier is usually better qualified to maintain these relations than the professional manager. The latter lacks a skill that universities do not develop: the creation and maintenance of economic and political alliances; further, he also lacks the network of social relations that the owner has inherited or has succeeded in developing beforehand.

The shortage of nontechnical, social and political skills is not the only reason for justifying the managers' exclusion from the interaction with the external environment. Relations with power groups and the creation of a network of alliances are more important than is pure economic power deriving from ownership. These relations constitute the bases of the exercise of social influence, and therefore they cannot be delegated, or could be only at the risk of being cut off from the political game. It is the exercise of this responsibility that characterizes the technocracy.

The ideology of the manager

The importance of status. We said that hierarchical structure creates a system based on power inequality, placing certain individuals in more favorable strategic situations than others. A high position in the organization chart provides many advantages: in addition to the greater economic rewards accompanying greater responsibility, there is the psychological gratification derived from the exercise of authority.

In a society that emphasizes the importance of both economic and social status, it is understandable that power holders wish to perpetuate their privileged state and if possible strengthen it.[15] Hence the importance of protecting the prerogative justifying this privileged position—the decision-making function. According to some authors, consultation erodes power; therefore, for a group or individual to extend participation to others means losing a strategic advantage: ". . . the real source of power is not the superior but the subordinate. Men can only exercise power which they are allowed by other men. . . ."[16]

Consultation not only involves participation in decision making but also in sharing the vital information that is necessary to reach a decision. Whoever occupies a privileged position possesses resources that others lack, one element of which is information. We have already noted that the importance of a decision derives from its being made in a situation of uncertainty; whoever can diminish uncertainty for others thereby legitimizes his own function.[17] One way of protecting one's own position is to create artificial situations of uncertainty, for example by blocking the transmission of the very information that could eliminate it.[18]

Ideological cooptation. Nevertheless, the strategy of blocking information is a double-edged weapon and could effectively be used by the bottom of the organization as well: by blocking or distorting communication essential to decision making, the lower level managers can make themselves indispensable and insert themselves by force into the decision process.[19] The fact that managers rarely make use of this tactic has been explained by their reluctance to set themselves against owners; indeed they do not even attempt to distinguish themselves from the owners. Both Mills and Meynaud point out that so far managers have not adopted an opposite stance vis-à-vis owners. Although such a stance would not necessarily represent conflict, it would at least demonstrate a different ideological basis. However, "managers have not been known to act intentionally against the property interests of the large owners."[20]

For some authors, managers' acquiescence derives from their

having adopted the goals and ideology of owners and therefore having no reason to revolt against them; for other authors, the acquiescence derives from being a subordinated class that does not dare rebel.

The acceptance of the hierarchical structure, even when it is strongly centralized, seems to occur without serious conflict. The manager usually behaves uncritically toward the firm and tends to adopt positions taken by the corporation's top leadership. In part this attitude existed before he was promoted in the firm and even before he was hired. To assure the pursuit of corporate goals over time, homogeneity in the managerial group is considered indispensable. Therefore, together with professional knowledge and technical ability the selection and training of new managers also takes behavioral conformity into account: "What is required from technicians is not so much productive rhythm as it is ideological consent, the identification with the values and goals of the firm."[21]

Acceptance of corporate values is also facilitated by social mechanisms in society: ". . . consumerism, the ideology of career, status symbols . . . all strongly condition the individual long before his entrance into the world of work. . . . Indeed, the two value systems—that of the corporation and that of society—overlap and partly complement each other. . . ."[22] Thus cultural and social training and corporate conditioning reinforce one another.[23]

The profit-making ideology. An example of how managerial ideology is not detached (leaving formal and nonsubstantive distinctions aside) from capitalist ideology is shown by the attitudes managers have toward corporate profits.

The managerialist writers have often asserted that the manager, contrary to the owner, rejects the ideology of profit. Other authors believe instead that, even if it is true that the professionalization and bureaucratization of management creates values and orientations different from those of the entrepreneur, these still cannot concretely influence the enterprise's goals.[24] In fact the pursuit of profit is not a psychological motivation but an economic prerequisite, and therefore it survives even if the responsibility for running the firm shifts from the capitalists to the managers. Managers operate in a capitalist market and are forced to orient themselves toward the traditional capitalist goal of profit, just as owners are.[25] Profit maximization is an objective necessity in firms because it is essential to their survival.[26]

Pursuing society's goals can be costly and can directly threaten a firm's existence. Even in companies led by managers and not by owners, there has been opposition to the reductions in working hours, to salary increases, and recently to the introduction of anti-pollution devices—all factors that decrease profits and, in turn, capital investment and market competitiveness. The corporation does not survive or develop because it has satisfied the demands of its workers and the community, but more often because it has ignored them as long as possible. Most social innovations have been introduced in firms from external sources and by force, often after long and bitter struggles.

Past high profits allow a company to withstand union pressure, and, when it has to give in to demands for higher wages, not to incur damaging losses. On the other hand, when corporate profits are used to grant wages higher than average, the firm's (and its management's) standing in the community is enhanced and so is its influence.[27]

In his comparison of firms controlled by management and firms controlled by owners, Larner found that the rate of profit was practically identical: the two types of firm—manager-controlled and owner-controlled—were both oriented toward profit in the same way.[28]

Indeed, the advent of the professional manager and the introduction of scientific management reinforces rather than weakens the tendency toward profit maximization.[29] There are other objective reasons that confirm the importance of profits. Together with corporate growth, to which they are tied, profits are in managers' eyes the test of the validity of their decisions and the indicator of success. For the manager, aware of his lack of wide social approval, success as measured by the firm's profitability is the prerequisite for prestige; he must earn the right to a high status and justify his own high salary by the results he procures for the corporation.[30]

In the view of some scholars, the importance of profits lies in the personal economic advantage that they directly imply for managers. In the United States, managers are often themselves stockholders whose shares are usually minimal for the firm in percentages but substantial from the standpoint of personal property.[31] The amount of stock in the firm held by managers usually does not allow them to exercise control of the firm but has the effect of making managers identify the fate of the firm with their own. Management shareholding is an effect both of the stock option plan adopted by a large majority of the firms quoted on the New York Stock Exchange and of managers' tendency to invest in stocks the savings derived from their substantial salaries. In fact, corporate managers are the professional group most represented among stockholders: 48 percent of them possess industrial stock.[32]

Sociological influences on the manager

Social background. One of the reasons for managers' close identification with owners is their similar social background and the characteristics derived from it. Studies of the class origin of corporate managers and entrepreneurs have all stressed the fragile linkage to the working classes: the 13–14 percent of managers coming from the workers' strata is a steady figure throughout time, both in industrially advanced countries and in the developing countries.[33]

The managerial group in Italy is the product in equal measure of the upper and middle classes. What is equally important is the fact that his income automatically situates the manager in a high socioeconomic stratum and grants him a situation of privilege. It is therefore natural that "he does feel in unity, politically and status-wise as well as economically, with his class and its source of wealth."[34]

A corollary of social origin is the educational level, which in Italy still largely remains a class privilege. When elites in a society are largely recruited from a superior class that has precise economic and cultural interests, it is likely that their background would inspire, on the basis of a common model, the goals and types of action they will adopt.[35] The values of the new group, therefore, will most probably be similar to those of the social strata from which the group originates and with which it identifies.

Lack of alternative models in industrial societies. On the other hand, how could one not assume an identity of values and goals between managers and owners of capital? In order for differences to exist the manager would have to have a model of the firm's management, organization, and social functions, different from that of the capitalist. This model could be found outside the individual firm, possibly in other countries, or else, ideally, be formulated by the manager himself.

However, industrial reality does not abound with new examples;

the earliest industrialized countries were those with an Anglo-Saxon culture and their model has fashioned the industrialization of the European countries, which are also similar from the cultural standpoint. In late-developing countries industrialization was not born of their local culture but was acquired as an external fact that often conflicted with their culture in spite of its contribution to the physical survival of their population. Socialist countries have given us an example of a state capitalism in which types of organization, management, wage and salary administration, etc., are not distinct from the Anglo-Saxon model, other than for reasons of lesser productivity. When the USSR commissioned the design of the Togliattigrad plant from FIAT, it also implicitly accepted the underlying ideology, together with the productive methodology (division of labor, technology). China still remains a little-known territory whose new approaches to work organization clearly have not produced efficiency. Within some industrialized capitalist countries a different model could be furnished by the state-owned industry, and yet its system of management is not dissimilar from that of private industry; the differences felt by the manager are more in the field of company policies (less oriented toward profit) than in organizational styles or management.[36]

The firm is not very different in its internal structure from the surrounding society. Industry reproduces some of the social experiences that influenced the individual's earlier socialization: in industry as in society there is a vertical thrust to relations, with predominance of superior levels over others, etc. Further, in the actual social and industrial structure, the manager is a privileged person and is naturally aware of it. Thus the incentive for him to conceive or realize a new model of the firm (for example, one without a hierarchical structure and more open to external control) is minimal.

The absence of a spirit of association and of ties with other elites. C. Wright Mills notes that the effective exercise of power on the part of a group depends on its internal cohesion and its alliances with other, similar elites, in a community and continuity of interests.[37]

In the case of managers it is unrealistic to expect that their power automatically derives only from skills of a technical nature, that is, from the indispensable role that they perform in society.[38] The conquest of power by a group requires group solidarity, internal coordination, an organization aimed at pursuing common goals and establishing ties with the outside, and effective representation and leadership—all factors that the Italian managers lack.

Compared to other elites—the owners in particular—management is not only isolated from contact with other social groups but internally disintegrated, divided by conflicts, scarcely aware of its goals, lacking effective internal and external communication channels, and scarcely able to form coalitions. Its limited spirit of association with respect both to its own representative group and to other groups bears witness to this social disarray.[39]

The attitude toward its own professional association and union is usually one of distrust which translates into indifference. Even for the acquisition of advantages that could derive from union activity—salary increases, a minimum wage, job security—the manager seems to prefer to make use of his personal relation with the employer. It is likely that the competitive situation in which he often finds himself vis-à-vis his colleagues prevents him not only from taking part in organized activity but also from identification with his own group. The stress on hierarchy divides managers by stratifying them according to rank. Personal power is pursued by using one's technical competence and occasionally one's friendships or temporary coalitions.

The manager further lacks the opportunity and the will to play a role in different social groups, which would have the effect of broadening his range of influence.

Mills considered the central region of power as that occupied by individuals who, simultaneously or successively, are in a position of leadership in certain important social institutions (military, economic, political). Nothing could be further from the manager's situation; when we inquired about the associations the managers join, we found a poor contact network, and above all a passive kind of involvement when indeed it existed at all. A typical example is membership in the managerial association (CIDA, to which 52 percent of interviewees belonged) which was mostly limited to paying registration dues (active participation occurred in only 6% of cases). Thirty-eight percent reported they did not belong to any association at all (see Table 7.1).

We also examined associations not connected to professional activity—e.g., cultural, charity-related, and recreational groups—not only because they can reveal a manager's interest in expres-

Table 7.1

Associations to Which the Managers Belong
(in %, n = 647)

None	38
Only professional associations (CIDA, Engineers Association, etc.)	37
Cultural, sports, philanthropic, and religious associations	11
Professional and cultural associations	10
Political parties and professional and cultural associations	4
	100

sions and problems of the society in which he lives, but also because they could represent a manager's indirect way of establishing contacts with other groups that could later be used to professional advantage.

It is not a coincidence that a community's most influential individuals, in addition to belonging to their professional association, join various other representative groups. The chief executive of a business often sits on other firms' boards of directors; he plays an active role in industrial associations and participates in groups that do not have a direct connection to activities related to production, as in the case of those having charitable, cultural, and social goals, such as hospitals, schools, and clubs.

Membership in nonprofessional groups is generally justified by the desire to participate responsibly in solutions to social problems. In fact it permits one to establish relationships with representatives of various pressure groups. Moreover, the less direct its usefulness is, the more easily it can serve "political" ends. An example can be found in clubs (such as Rotary, Lions, etc.) whose statutory goal is to bring different professions together or to "serve" (one presumes the community), or is purely recreational. Their meetings provide a useful informal setting in which mutual solidarity and alliances are established and reinforced.[40]

Membership in certain associations, in large part justified by the homogeneous life-style of a class of people that have many things in common (Mills labeled it "the fraternity of the successful"),[41] also plays a cohesive role because it reinforces the common ideology.

Table 7.2

The Affiliations of an Italian Industrialist*

Professional roles		Social roles		
Industry & commerce	Professional associations	Cultural & philanthropic	Clubs and recreational activities	Miscellaneous
	Chamber of Commerce	Hospital	Rotary	Trade fairs association
Food		School	Regional club	
Textiles	Industrialists Union			Honorary Consul
a. cotton mill				Local
b. wool mill				tourism
c. spinning				association
Publishing				
Machinery				
Steel				
Construction Corp.				
Subway Corp.				

*In all these groups, the industrialist held executive positions (President or Vice-President) or responsible positions (auditor, director).

The little time left at one's disposal after handling work-related problems and the need to keep oneself up-to-date professionally —factors that managers often mention to justify their limited proclivity to join associations—are characteristic also of businessmen (bankers or industrialists), who nevertheless have developed a rich network of extracurricular contacts.

In this connection it is interesting to examine the network of associations of a typical Italian industrialist, obtained from his recent obituary notice (see Table 7.2). The list of the leadership roles he occupied in various organizations shows a number of dissimilar and unconnected associations. Yet on closer analysis, a pattern emerges: his position in different manufacturing firms could be due to the wish to diversify his personal investments; his membership in the two unions (Industrialists Union and Chamber of Commerce) is directly functional to good business management.

Belonging to the trade fairs and technical exhibitions associations is not only functional to the sale of goods produced by the firms owned, but also means participating in a pressure group at the regional level. The two clubs are the informal equivalent of professional associations. Contacts with the local public administration occur through membership on the boards of directors of a hospital, a government tourism corporation, and several schools. Some of the honorary appointments are a direct consequence of filling important professional roles, others are probably a consequence of personal prestige, yet others are probably functional to a steady network of contacts with persons in key positions. The various roles, although dissimilar, reinforce one another.

Note, by way of contrast, the degree of participation in associations of five managers, selected from among those who declared the greatest number of affiliations (see Table 7.3).

The limited participation in social groups is not compensated for by political activity—which moreover, usually did not exist before joining the firm either, and is reported by only 4 percent of interviewees.[42] The managers' indifference also shows in their limited roles in public affairs, even in roles that could be rather compatible professionally. Only 8 percent of managers had ever held positions in community administration or in public agencies. Like the businessmen, managers abstain from direct political participation, as represented by party militancy. Yet, in the businessman's case, this hardly means he is isolated from political power.[43]

If nothing else, one can say that the proclivity to join associations, which the businessman use as an instrument in a parapolitical game, is spontaneous and genuine in the manager when it occurs; i.e., it is not tied to the pursuit of a career. But this having been said, there remains the depressing observation of the Italian managers' widespread lack of interest in professional and nonprofessional groups.

The manager is clearly isolated both within his professional group and vis-à-vis other social groups. Within the corporate microcosm the manager is often in competition with his colleagues; even when this is not the case, he still does not closely identify with them. Each hierarchical level is a separate stratum, every department a foreign region. Outside the firm, the managers do not attempt to take part even in the leadership of their own union. No formal contacts with other groups are established, and there-

Table 7.3

Affiliations of the Five Most Active Managers

| Manager | Political roles | | Professional roles | | Social roles | Clubs and recreational activities |
	Party	Public administration	Industry & finance	Managerial associations	Cultural & philanthropic	
1	Member of the regional council	Local official	State-owned firm* a. Vice-President b. Banking Institute (board member)*		Hospital (board member)*	—
2	—	—	—	CIDA (member) Engineers association (member) Electrical-technical Association (vice-president)	Archeological society (member)	Rotary (member) Association for the elderly
3	Enrolled	—	—	CIDA (member)	Parents-Teachers Association	Lions (member)
4	Enrolled	—	—	CIDA (member)		Lions (member)
5	—	—	—	CIDA (member) Managerial union (board member)		Lions (member)

*Appointed by his political party.

fore there are no alliances or coalitions with them.

The consequence of isolation is that managers are at the mercy of other groups who manipulate them, as in the case of the owner-elite, or oppose them, as in the case of workers' unions.

7.2. Who sits in the seat of power?

Inasmuch as the majority of Italian managers are excluded from making innovative and risky decisions, and even more from participating in policy formulation, where is industrial power located? The real power holders do not belong to the managerial ranks. Managers often locate the powerful outside the firm, and thus wholly out of their range, since the organizational links necessary to establish communication with them are absent.[44]

In our research we asked managers to identify the people who were responsible for recent policy changes in their firms. Though based on the managers' perceptions, these findings are interesting since the organizational position of the interviewees makes them reliable informants. On the hypothesis that the locus of decisional power affects the opportunity to participate in the exercise of power, we considered four situations (see Table 7.4).

1. *The locus of power is external to the firm and outside the range of the managers*; managers have no organizational contact with stockholders nor with the Board of Directors that represents them[45];

2. *The locus of power is both internal and external*; power is shared between representatives of stockholders, external to the firm, and the head of the firm (CEO), who acts as a link between the board of directors and the hierarchical organization. The organizational connection with the head of the firm theoretically permits the manager to be in contact with one of the seats of power;

3. *The locus of corporate power is within the organization* and thus theoretically accessible. Nonetheless, decisional power is strongly centered in only one individual and this reduces the actual possibility of managers' participation;

4. *Power is distributed within a small oligarchy*. A process of collegial consultation permits managers in the highest hierarchical levels to participate in decision making.

One-fourth of the managers believe that corporate policies are

Table 7.4

Managers' Perceptions of the Locus of Decision-making Power
(in %, $n = 663$)

Outside the firm or unknown to interviewee—out of reach	26
Intermediate (Board of Directors and CEO)—partially out of reach	21
Centralized in a single individual	33
Collegial power with participation of upper-level managers	15
Collegial power with participation of middle-level managers	5
	100

decided outside the firm; the fact that the seat of power is external to the organization makes it "out of range," because managers lack the organizational channels necessary to enter into relation with the power-holding group. In a third of cases power is described as being centered in a single individual. The process of consulting managers appears in a fifth of responses: participation is limited to the upper managerial level and only in minimal part reaches the middle management.[46]

The type of corporate ownership seems to influence the location of power (see Table 7.5). Very strong concentration of power in a single individual appears in family businesses and in Italian multinationals, firms under the control of an individual or a family. In firms owned by financial groups or those that are branches of non-Italian multinationals, the seat of power is perceived as being external to the firm (as localized in the board of directors in firms belonging to financial groups; in the headquarters, abroad, for the multinationals).

Thus three different situations prevail, which could be interpreted as stages in the firm's historical development:

1. In firms in which shareholding is still concentrated, power is located within the firm but strongly centralized in an individual; he may disseminate it throughout a restricted group of collaborators.

2. With the dispersion of stock ownership, power escapes the individual, but the seat of power shifts externally beyond the organization and outside managers' control. As noted above, this situa-

Table 7.5

Managers' Perceptions of the Locus of Decision-Making Power,
by Type of Firm Ownership (in %)

Perceived locus of decision-making power	Ownership of Firm				
	Family-owned	Large financial group	Italian multinational	Non-Italian multinational	State-owned
External location	13	38	20	46	23
Intermediate (CEO and Board)	7	24	19	26	27
Single individual at top	54	14	47	11	27
Consultation with upper management	20	17	11	11	16
Consultation with middle management	6	7	3	6	7
Total %	100	100	100	100	100
N = 642	(136)	(29)	(168)	(167)	(142)

tion is frequent in non-Italian multinationals and firms owned by financial groups.

3. Finally, managerial participation is beginning to show up in all kinds of firms. This new tendency could increase in the future.

A number of managers (14%), after having described the policy changes they have witnessed in the firm, are unable to state who is responsible for them. This is surprising, because these are not simple employees but people in charge, for whom such changes are likely to have repercussions. Uncertainty about the locus of power is greater at the bottom of the hierarchical ladder (it practically doubles below the first managerial level)[47] and is greatest in large firms.[48]

A manager's inability to identify the seat of power means he does not know where to turn when he disapproves of decisions, nor where to exert pressure, nor with whom he could possibly form a coalition; he is thus unable to formulate any strategy and is a passive recipient of changes thrust on him.

A critical analysis of the theory of managerial supremacy

The description of modern industry—that is, the scattered shareholding, the disappearance of the entrepreneur and owners, the emergence of a new "class" of corporate managers—has been uncritically accepted not only by the interested parties (whom it largely flattered) but by society as well. The concept of managerial supremacy developed by Burnham and Berle has been widely accepted and has been restated and further developed by prestigious scholars[49]; above all, this concept has also been applied to the analysis of the industrial situations in other countries.

The theory of the managerial revolution is based on the analysis of a well-defined social reality, that of the Unites States, in which the characteristics and consequences of advanced industrialization are more visible. The scholars who applied this theory to the reality of other, less developed countries accept the premise that the industrial process implies fixed characteristics that will inevitably occur in any society undergoing industrialization. Thus the analysis of countries in the process of development, or of countries such as Italy which are less intensively industrialized, would benefit from the perspective furnished by a more advanced nation. That is, the assumption is that a country at the beginning of its industrial development will go through the obligatory stages through which the more advanced nations have already passed. Differences among countries are mainly temporary: the future is already written and can be clearly read in the examples offered us by industrially advanced capitalist nations (among which Italy endeavors to include itself).

Our research results show instead that in Italy control of business has not passed into the hands of managers. The growth in the number of managers, outstripping the increases in workers and production itself, reveals a separation between business *ownership* and business *management*. The entrepreneur or the owner-heir has delegated many of his functions and today firms' ownership and management lie in different groups. But in Italy we lack evidence of a divorce between business *ownership* and the real *control* of businesses. The reasons for the continued centralization of power are various in nature, some external, some internal to the organization. The very same factors on which the managerialists base their assertions lend themselves to a different interpretation.

a. Concentration of shareholding

In Italy concentration of shares still sustains control of the firm by the owners in many cases. The Italian economic landscape is dominated by individuals who represent, in the private sector, not only large enterprises but also themselves—as proprietors or heads of family "dynasties."

However, the Italian situation is not anomalous, but merely the most obvious case of a situation that is found in other capitalist countries. Even in the United States, stock is less dispersed than the managerialists would have us believe. Some discordant voices, isolated and without followers, have been raised to contest the well-known concept of managerial supremacy. Some of these studies are contemporary with Berle's.[50] More recently Berle and Means have been criticized for the inadequacy of their data sources, the use of scattered data, and their excessive reliance on estimates.[51] Followers of Berle and Means have been criticized for using their data without verifying them and for uncritically accepting the theory of managerial supremacy.[52] After reexamining the same firms analyzed by Berle and Means in light of more accurate information,[53] Philip Burch estimates that over 40 percent of them are controlled by a single individual or by one family (against the 6 percent claimed by Berle).[54]

Stockholders' control has weakened less than has been asserted. Concentration is less visible because of the tendency, for tax purposes, to divide shares among many members of the same family; further, many shares are tied up in trusts in the name of individuals who receive the profits without being the owners. The use of straw men allows important families to not appear in the Securities and Exchange Commission reports on stock ownership, which by law must list the owners of 10 percent or more of the shares of a corporation.[55] In fact, far from diminishing, stockholder concentration in the United States is said to be actually increasing.[56]

It is not unlikely that, despite tax erosion in those countries having an effective tax system, there still exists a stock concentration that nullifies the process begun by the creation of joint stock companies. Wealth generates wealth, and the nonconsumed surplus tends to be reinvested in the same areas that generated it. The financier does not have the same mistrust toward industrial stock as the casual investor does. The financier's knowledge of the market, his ability to influence it, and the opportunity to avail himself of expert advice assures him better results.

The huge number of stockholders and the existence of small investors who play the stock market give the impression that stock is heavily dispersed; but the passivity and lack of specialized knowledge characterizing the small investor are matched against the aggressiveness of financial groups with minority control, able to assume leadership positions: "... control of corporations by legal device, while excluding small stockholders from a voice in affairs, does not exclude the big interests."[57] What's more, diffusion has the effect of facilitating control, which is sometimes acquired with a very small block of shares.[58] Further, big stockholders tend to band together in coalitions which are difficult to oppose and which enjoy the support of large banks which they often own.[59]

b. The persistence of the power of the board of directors

A reexamination of a board of directors' role throws doubt on the proposition that it has been reduced to a legal fiction and that it has been deprived of authority by management. On the board are seated all representatives of propertied interests who often have together, if not individually, sufficient control of stock at least to interfere with decisions of top management if not to override them entirely.

An analysis of stock ownership made in 1960 on 232 of the largest enterprises listed by *Fortune* leads Villarejo to conclude that in about 60 percent of them, concentration of stock in the hands of board members was sufficient to assure them effective control.[60] For the remaining 40 percent the data were less certain, yet did not eliminate the possibility that control was exercised by a small financial group. Leonard Silk maintains that many board chairmen retain considerable power and that the technostructure, contrary to Galbraith's and Heilbroner's arguments, does not make the most important decisions nor does it in fact manage the firm.[61]

Even when it is not composed of stockholders, the board of directors can possibly resume an active role in long-term decisions by occasionally opposing management. Today in the United States we are witnessing a reversal of the passivity and dependence characterizing the board's past behavior. Theoretically the board fulfills two important functions: the first is to manage the firm, the second is to bear, even personally, the legal and financial responsibilities of bad management. The second function cannot be renounced and there are instances when directors, seeing themselves legally threatened by a misuse of the power they had delegated to managers, resumed partial control.

When, in an emergency situation or crisis (such as when the firm's operating procedure is publicly questioned), the board takes back the powers that it had delegated, conflict is unavoidable and management may get the worst end of it.[62]

While it may be true that the board often lacks adequate tools for carrying out effective action, it is also true that its function has not been superseded. Its tasks, which cannot be delegated, are to (1) determine the enterprise's goals; (2) set its growth rate (sometimes growth is anomalous or false); (3) evaluate the efficiency of top managers and if necessary replace them; (4) represent the firm's "conscience," that is, be the keeper of its ethical values, constitute its "window to the world," and be the channel of communication with the community and the public.[63]

To carry out these functions, the board must have adequate instruments: capable and full-time directors assisted by a staff of specialists; further, at least for some firms, respect for the demands of society at large may require that, in addition to representatives of capital and financial interests, some of the members be representatives of groups who are directly affected by the firm's operations.[64]

c. Transformation of industrial capitalism into finance capitalism

For other authors, the managerialists' limitations derive primarily from their exclusive focus on the industrial world, ignoring external connections and conditioning factors.

Large banks—which according to Bell were responsible for the weakening of the family enterprise—continue to exercise a predominant role in business. Modern business has not freed itself from bank control; in spite of its growing potential for self-financing, business is still heavily dependent on external capital. This dependence on the financial world, more evident in large corporations, is found in all types of firms and may be increasing.[65]

The influence of credit institutions is exercised not merely indirectly, through loans for new investments, but directly through stock ownership. Large banks and insurance companies are often the principal stockholders of many large manufacturing firms.[66] Evidence of this is the presence of representatives of financial interests on the board of directors in half of the very large industrial enterprises. There is, presumably, a strong concentration of economic power in a few very large financial institutions, whose indirect influential action is scarcely visible to the public and which, for this reason, have been labeled "silent partners."[67]

Just as in industry, it is difficult to identify the effective seat of control in banks. The "managerial revolution" could have also reached financial enterprises through a similar process of growth and stockholder dispersion. According to Allen, 75 percent of the large investment banks are controlled by management, since not a single stockholder possesses more than 10 percent of the shares in any of them. Besides banks there are new types of financial institutions, such as pension funds which, not having emerged from the entrepreneurial ventures of an individual or small group, seem to represent the purest case of an organization run by management for the benefit of multiple stockholders. Created to invest employees' pensions and sometimes controlled by labor unions, pension funds are in origin and in goal the opposite of the privately owned organization; the role of the stockholders is generally passive and their management seems to represent a clear-cut case of technocracy.[68]

The world of finance has been less studied than the industrial world, at least insofar as stockholders' control is concerned; also in this case, the diffusion of ownership does not automatically eliminate the prospect of control by minority stockholding groups.[69] According to some scholars, the withdrawal of the bourgeoisie from productive activities has not meant its disappearance from the economic scene, but rather its transition to the more modern, crucial and innovative activity of finance.[70]

Management is left the task of organizing the enterprise, a task that is primarily technical and organizational rather than financial.[71]

Not only does it seem that the heirs of the big entrepreneurs have shifted to finance, but also that a fusion of industrial capital with finance capital has occurred or that in any case a tight community of interests binds together the representatives of the various economic powers. Perhaps it is not exact to say that economic control has passed to the banks, but rather that "these families' interests transcend the banks and corporations in which they have principal or controlling interests; and the banks may merely be units in, and instrumentalities of, the whole system of propertied interests controlled by these major capitalist families."[72]

The habit of analyzing the individual entrepreneur and of considering the firm as an isolated entity has prevented many from perceiving the complex network of interdependence and alliances present in the modern economic world. Big capital, once concentrated in manufacturing and commerce, has spread to a number of economic activities. What appears to be a dispersion and thus a weakening is instead an integration of various economic activities, which has the effect of reinforcing a position of influence. A structure of ownership which includes many members of the same family permits them to keep control despite a differentiation in investments.

Furthermore, the great families' propertied interests are only one of the control centers of the modern economic world; the solidarity that ties industrial and financial circles together transcends kinship ties, and in any case integrates them within boundaries formed by common interests and goals. Again, the historically exact but now obsolete view of a group of capitalists competing among themselves must be replaced with that of organized capital, i.e., a structural integration of the large industrial enterprises and a close alliance between bankers and businessmen, described years ago by Schumpeter.[73]

Through this integration economic power is kept under the control of a small group. This is why the managerialists are wrong. They focused on the diffusion of ownership and the decrease in individual and family control of individual firms, but they ignored the existence of interlocking directorates and investments that were diversified but mutually reinforcing and they ignored the network of family relations creating a tacit system of alliance among economically differentiated enterprises.[74] Finally, the managerialists do not seem to perceive the existence of a "class solidarity" which maintains cohesion among members of the capitalist class on the basis of common financial interests and ideology.

Economic power has not in fact changed hands; it has only hidden itself from the eyes of the uninitiated.[75] This departure from the scene is calculated: the businessman "has a penchant for historical anonymity."[76]

d. The vitality of the family enterprise

No proof is needed of the vitality of the Italian family business.

While in small and medium-sized firms the figure of the entrepreneur still stands out, even in very large firms it is not difficult to identify the owner-stockholder. Even the ownership of Italian multinationals, whose stock is dispersed on the stock exchange, can generally be traced to a single family if not a single individual. The family name of the founder, which often gives the corporation its name, does not merely belong to the past. Many firms in our sample, taken from the Mediobanca list of the largest enterprises according to sales, have family names such as Pirelli, Buitoni, Marzotto, and Ferrero and are headed by one or more members of the founding family.

Patrimonial management of large companies, which in the United States constitutes an exception, is more common in Italy. It is difficult to establish whether this difference between the two countries is due to the less mature stage of development of the Italian economy or to the different structure of economic power in Italian society. In Italy, the large proprietor has not been seriously affected by taxation; there exists a strong tradition of inheritance of the entrepreneurial position and a strong emphasis on family which has been transferred to the business world.[77]

The efficient and vital family capitalism found in many developing countries (which would support the hypothesis of a connection between family enterprise and the first phase of industrialization) is also present in industrially advanced nations such as Sweden, France, Great Britain, and Australia.[78]

Patrimonial management does not necessarily prevent the emergence of professional management: the two can coexist in the same persons. The heir to a family business can afford the best professional training. Furthermore, it is unquestionable that functions that were once concentrated in the entrepreneur are now split (for the reasons of complexity and specialization cited by the managerialists). This delegation followed a logic: the head of the firm has delegated the less vital functions in order to concentrate on those crucial to corporate growth.

These vital functions can sometimes be better performed by remaining outside the firm. The management of great wealth may require its owners to hand over the management of a single line of business and to turn to external but supportive activities. The replacement of a father by his son at the head of a company, an event currently in decline in very large firms, is only one of the forms by which economic power can be transmitted.[79]

The great family "dynasties" described by Schumpeter, which the development of joint stock companies should have erased, are still found very much alive on the Italian scene. In Italy we witness literally the reverse of the tendency described by the managerialists. We see an increasingly active participation by owners in the management of firms, not so much with regard to daily operations and short-term planning as with the determination of long-term policies.

The representatives of the "great dynasties" have returned to the limelight by taking over the reins of power they had delegated for years, by establishing alliances and by operating through the industrialists associations over which they have resumed direct control.

e. Evolution of the entrepreneur?

The decline of the family enterprise is linked to the disappearance of its most conspicuous representative, the entrepreneur. There are those, however, who highlight his persistence, even if in forms that depart from Schumpeter's classical description. It is certain that the entrepreneur, in his role of financier, organizer, and manager of an enterprise created by him, is no longer, as he once was, a primary figure on the economic front. Interpretations waver from the extreme hypothesis of the entrepreneur's disappearance to a hypothesis concerning his transformation:

The entrepreneur as "dinosaur." One scenario leading to the disappearance of the entrepreneur starts with the observation of the continuous change that the firm undergoes or introduces. For example, technological innovation modifies size, structure, work relations and habits of a company. Similarly, mass production introduced by mechanization requires greater size and this in turn demands capital and specialized technical knowledge. In this changed environment, the dinosaur-entrepreneur disappears and the banker and the manager come into being.

The entrepreneur as "mutant." Another point of view instead emphasizes evolution, that is, the adaptive persistence of people, groups, and systems. Once established and entrenched, organizations consider change dangerous and erect barriers against it: change is considered not merely a challenge, but the seed of subversion against the established order. This attitude is shared by privileged individuals and groups: once they have reached an optimal position, they find any variation dangerous.

But opposition is not necessarily in the open. Active or passive resistance to the environment is only one of the ways to react to change. Another more intelligent way is to adjust flexibly to new requirements: mutations occur. Thus at first a firm may try to shelve a new technology, but when a competitor is ready to use it, the firm adopts it as well, because innovation ceases at that moment to be a disturbing factor and becomes a prerequisite to survival. A privileged social group has nothing against resting on its laurels, but when it is threatened by new emerging classes, its members adjust, changing their appearance and demeanor. The dinosaur disappeared not so much because it was confronted by a new hostile environment but because it was incapable of adapting to it; other species survived by adjusting to the new environment. Both the old captain of industry who used his intuition and the uncultured robber baron transformed themselves into the modern company presidents, highly trained and seemingly sensitive to social needs. This transformation does not necessarily occur in a brief period: it is a phenomenon involving more than the individual, and lasting generations.

The ebb and flow of history. A third way of interpreting the history of entrepreneurship is to view it as part of a cyclical process. Technological and market changes destroy certain roles and create new ones; they push certain social groups into the background and bring others to the fore. The entrepreneur and the enterprise operate in a world of change in which their positions are often determined by the struggles among bypassed groups, aspiring newcomers, and the entrenched leadership. Thus the tides may return some groups to the limelight, casting them afloat through the process of change itself; other groups may take a back seat. The entrepreneur disappears, the role of the banker grows and then shrinks when the enterprise is again able to rely on self-financing; the pure technician, needed to solve production problems, gives way to the organizer and ultimately to the "politician" (the one who handles relations between the firm and the external world, and who knows how to engage in long-term planning).

This role rotation represents the adaptive response of society and the enterprise to the different phases in the process of industrialization.

When relations with the external environment take place in an atmosphere devoid of tensions, when for example business relations with government are mutually supportive or indifferent, and when there is industrial peace, the capitalist-entrepreneur needs a less openly political role. When a firm's survival appears tied to its degree of market competitiveness, power is delegated to the "technician," and the role of managers takes a front seat.

The resurgence of owners in power roles (or in roles that allow them to connect directly with power groups) occurs when new social groups or forces threaten their existence: this occurs during serious economic crises, when government interference is considered to be excessive, or when union pressures threaten the survival of the enterprise. These elements are all present in the current Italian situation and help to explain the reappearance of the old, but domineering and alive, entrepreneurial class on the Italian economic (industrial and financial) and political landscape.

In this case the determining influence on the rotation of groups is no longer financial (need for new capital to expand) nor technological (professionalism of managerial tasks) but is political. It is not a coincidence that in the largest Italian firms the representatives of the propertied families have again taken over the reins of management, the leadership of industrialists associations (for decades delegated to people in backseat positions) and direct negotiations with labor unions, while at the same time effectively using the press and the mass media in general as a means of communication with the public and as an instrument of persuasion and pressure.

Among the industrialized countries, Italy offers the clearest example today of the return of capitalist-owners to a dominantly active role in the economy. (See Table 7.6)

7.3. Effects on society of the persistence of ownership control

Daniel Bell clearly describes the meaning of the division between property and control. When wealth and management of that wealth were concentrated in the same social class, family capitalism meant not only economic hegemony but also social and political hegemony.

Later, this class was divided into two groups: the owners (no

Table 7.6

Summary of the Two Theories

Hypothesis: managerial supremacy	Hypothesis: persistence of owner control
Control	*Control*
1. Diffussion of stockholdings—disappearance of the majority stockholder.	1. Financial concentration—large majority stockholders often allied with one another.
2. End of the entrepreneur and his replacement by the professional manager.	2. Transformation of the entrepreneur-owner into the financier-investor. Persistence of capital control over management.
3. Separation between ownership and *control*.	3. Separation between ownership and *management*.
Decision making	*Decision making*
4. The decision-making process takes place within the firm: it requires expertise (technical-organizational knowledge, developed through formal training and on-the-job experience) and information, both possessed by managers.	4. An important part of the decision-making process occurs outside management. Innovation decisions are not merely based on information stemming from within the firm. Knowledge concerning the external environment—economic and political knowledge—is as important as the technical and organizational knowledge possessed by managers.
The decisions are made by managers and not by owners.	The decisions are made by large stockholders.
5. The decision-making process is characterized by rationality.	5. Long-term decisions contain many elements of uncertainty and require ingenuity and intuition.
Power	*Power*
6. Given that it is impossible for a single person to possess all the necessary expertise, a complex decision will usually be a group process, and decision-making power therefore undergoes a process of decentralization: a. decision making is extended horizontally (collegiality). b. decision making is extended vertically towards the bottom of the hierarchy (decentralization).	6. The final decision-making power usually remains strongly centralized in an easily identifiable individual, often assisted by consultants who may be external to the firm and lacking formal hierarchical power. The delegation of power, which has occurred under the pressures of organizational and technological complexities, is limited. A restricted oligarchy has been created which shares power. Most managers are excluded from important decisions.

Table 7.6 (cont.)

Hypothesis: managerial supremacy	Hypothesis: persistence of owner control
Values	*Values*
7. Management is a professional and social group different from stockholders and has its own ideology (growth versus profits; social sensitivity versus specific interests), that is, a new "culture" with different guidelines for corporate behavior.	7. Management has not created a new ideology because it identifies culturally, socially, and economically with the ownership class; it reflects its values and tends to its goals.

longer entrepreneurs) and the managers; the first group kept the wealth, the other got the political and economic power. The consequence is "the break-up of the 'ruling class'. . . . Today, there is an 'upper class' and a 'ruling group.' Being a member of the 'upper class'. . . no longer means that one is a member of the ruling group, for rule is now based on other than the traditional criteria of property. . . ."[80] (A ruling class is "a power-holding group which has both an established *community* of interest and a *continuity* of interest."[81])

The end to family capitalism therefore generates a transfer of power. Detaching himself from the direct management of the economic medium, the industrial capitalist maintains his social prestige and his wealth, but loses political power. Ownership of the means of production no longer constitutes the basis for social domination. The decisive power in modern industrial society is exercised not by capital but by organization, not by the capitalist but by the industrial bureaucrat.[82]

The division between capital and control, and between the leisure class and the ruling class, is of great significance for its repercussions on social relations. A protagonist on the social scene disappears, and its rivals are in turn influenced by that event. The economic politics of capitalism and the class interests they served have been replaced with a kind of capitalism without capitalists.[83]

The manager is portrayed as being different from the capitalist in every aspect, both because he acquired a social position that the other inherited and because he is motivated by less egoistic goals. Thus, the reasons for conflict and class struggle should weaken[84]; further, the conflict between the firm and society should disappear, or at least should diminish in importance.

The discovery of a new managerial class, its coming to power and its different ideology—a discovery made by theorists and quickly harnessed and adopted by the interested parties and accepted by other social groups—had the effect of reassuring the rest of society about the phenomenon of the large corporation. Since the latter's range of influence is proportionate to its physical size, capital investment, and associated financial interests, it would be worrisome if this economic power were concentrated in the hands of an individual, a family, or a small interest group. Instead we are given the reassuring image of the giant led by an unselfish, aware, and knowledgeable elite that uses corporate resources for the benefit of the community.

The problem of industrial power in society is similar to the problem of neutrality in science: if people believe that the results of scientific discoveries benefit a small and uncontrolled group, they feel threatened and powerless; if instead, science appears neutral and independent, and the scientist at the service of the entire society, no danger is perceived to exist.

Capitalism is legitimated when the results it produces do not translate into profit for a particular group but seem to be distributed throughout a wider social group, thanks to the mediating role of the managerial group.

Managers as a dependent elite

The concept of managerial supremacy is based on the assumption that a power transfer has occurred and that the center of power has shifted. If this is not the case, then managers remain a subordinated category. In fact, writers opposing the concept of "managerial supremacy" are steadfast: "Under the owners of property a huge and complex bureaucracy of business and industry has come into existence. But the right of this chain of command, the legitimate access to the position of authority from which these bureaucracies are directed, is the right of property ownership."[85] Increasingly managers appear to be middle men, agents of stockholders, state bureaucracies, or in some cases, workers' councils.[86] Rather than an independent category, "they definitely form a segment of the small, much-propertied circle."[87]

Together with social origin and acquired status, ideological co-optation causes managers to avoid or reject new values and a new conception of corporate goals, and instead to restate and support the old capitalist ideology. Attitudes and behaviors once considered typical of owners have been transmitted to the new power representatives: "Although they have arrived at the top of the corporate hierarchy on the basis of only professional merit, managers are capitalist leaders as much as are heirs to large industrial wealth and it is not at all sure that they are less devoted to the capitalist order."[88] Indeed, they fulfill the functions they are delegated "with as much or more devotion as any owner could."[89]

It follows that the presence of managers does not constitute an element of innovation; by strengthening the institution of ownership and contributing to its legitimation, it helps keep the old power centers in place.[90] In this respect, managers are a conservative force.

Even if a new generation of managers were to wish to reverse the situation to its advantage, it would not be easy. The much proclaimed "power" of the managers is an illusory power; their influence in the firm is limited because their contribution, when not routine, remains purely sectoral. In society the situation is not any better, because of managers' limited prestige, their inability to play a political role, their weak integration as a professional group, and their lack of effective representation.[91]

We are reminded of Pareto's distinction between the "chosen" class, i.e., the elite, and the nonchosen class, which is governed by the elite.[92] Often mistaken for one of the ruling elites, managers really belong to the ruled class. They nonetheless enjoy advantages that distinguish them from other subordinated groups. According to Pareto, to keep itself in power the ruling class utilizes individuals from the ruled classes; these are divided into two groups according to the means they employ to help maintain power: one group uses force—they are the army, the police; the other uses skill.[93]

Managers look like the civil equivalent of the "centurions." They do not appear to be a ruling group but a subordinate one— a *dependent elite*.

7.4. Types of control and social relations

Determining which group effectively manages the firm interests us mainly for its implications for the relations between the firm and its employees, and between the firm and the environment. Identifying the locus of control—that is, of power—also permits us to locate those in the firm who are responsible toward society.

The seat of corporate control could vary with the dynamics of corporate development. If this is true, various questions arise: In which direction does the process of industrialization move, and how does control therefore change? If it is possible to reconstruct the past stages of its development, can one derive from them the future phases of its development? Do these stages represent a process common to all industrialized societies—which would thus be distinguished by their level of industrial maturity—or do they depend instead on the sociopolitical characteristics of individual countries? If the initial phase—constituted by the small private enterprise—necessarily leads to the large corporation and the multinational firm, what will be the next form of control of the enterprise? And what will be the characteristics of Italian industry?

We can summarize the various types of control in industry:

a. *Internal control: property ownership.* Power belongs to the firm's ownership. As a consequence, the firm pursues limited goals and is often insensitive to its relations with the environment. Its limits are the limitations of the market.

b. *Internal control: managerial.* Control rests with a group of professionals recruited not on the basis of social origin and economic status but on the basis of proven skills and experience. Power is independent of ownership. The firm's goals are broadened to include respect for all its members' and the surrounding community's needs. Its limits are moral limits, thanks to the new managers' ethical system.

c. *External control: financial.* Control is exercised by the big credit institutions—banks, insurance companies, investment funds, etc. In turn these institutions can respond to propertied owners (individuals or families who have shifted investments from industry to finance) or respond to a management that does not possess personal interests in them. The firm's goals and its relations with workers and society vary according to the situation and come under the two preceding descriptions.

These three types of industrial control have been illustrated in the preceding pages; they are often considered as different stages of maturity in the industrialization process, but they can be simultaneously present in the same historical period. For instance, entrepreneurial capitalism, characterized by the small firm, can long survive even though it is no longer the economy's dominant characteristic.

d. *Class hegemony*. As noted earlier, it may be simplistic to view control as occurring through stockholdings, technical-organizational ability, or financing.[94] To focus on a single individual (the erstwhile entrepreneur), family, or managerial group, or on the individual corporation or bank, yields but a limited perspective on how modern business operates. An important change has occurred: the reorganization of the propertied class into a privileged and powerful group of large economic entities.[95] The diversification of investments, far from meaning a loss of influence, allows investors to insert themselves into a complex network of economic activities and become part of a integrated group of owners. The high degree of "homophyly," due to common social class origin, education, life-style, standard of living, and ideology, ties the members of the hegemonic group closely to one another and predisposes them to support each other and adopt and defend a common front.[96]

Therefore this group controls not an isolated economic activity but the entire economy. A share of control is exercised by middle men, that is, by a group of professional managers who, in identifying with the hegemonic class, or at least in subordinating themselves to it, continue to guide firms in the pursuit of the same goals held by the old capitalist.

e. *State control*. State intervention represents a new opportunity for control of the corporation, replacing patrimonial capitalism or sometimes overlapping with it. Hypothetically, the substantive difference with private industry is not merely in the seat of control but in the corporation's goals, which should be more social than economic. It is in this type of enterprise that one might more readily expect to encounter a technocracy not contaminated by alliances with owners. But just as in large private firms, also in the state-owned firms there is a possibility that control, instead of being located in management, would be localized in external groups —in this case, in political parties or political factions. In Italy this is exactly what seems to occur. The economic and political might of the large state-owned corporations is such that no ruling group can escape the temptation to utilize it to its own ends.

In any case, important as it is, the state enterprise represents but a portion of the industrial panorama of capitalist countries.

f. *Public and social control.* The last alternative is not influenced by the ownership of the particular social group. It provides for the institution of a set of controls to be applied to any type of enterprise. Control is external to the firm and is exercised both by the public powers, through legislation, and by social groups, in particular those more affected by the firm's decisions. Such groups are labor unions, consumer advocate groups, environmental groups, and citizens of host communities.

The need for external control is born from the consideration that any organization, having been created to pursue limited goals, can enter into conflict with the remainder of society. Industry represents one of many influential groups in the modern world; it interacts with other groups, can challenge them, and can defy collective goals. Its size, enormous economic power, and fundamental function in modern society are all factors calling for more continuous control than other social groups. The corporation acquires, therefore, a public character.[97] The need to establish external control stems from the fact that even the existence of a technocracy does not ensure per se an enlightened and altruistic management, both because the selection criteria of managers take more account of technical and professional characteristics than they do awareness of responsibilities, and because managers are but an interest group and not the entire society.

The systems suggested for public and social control range from the development of more competitive markets to increased involvement of noneconomic groups in the economic and production decisions,[98] to divestiture (trust-busting),[99] and to state intervention through economic planning[100] or through appropriate legislation.[101] (See Table 7.7.)

The Italian situation: A summary

Perhaps because of the delay in its industrial development but also because of specific characteristics in Italian society, Italian industry has not in any major way come under the control of managers.

What appeared as a fundamental stage of development—the small enterprise and patrimonial capitalism—coexists with the more advanced phase of industrialization. The very large firm and the multinational corporation find themselves side by side with the small family business, which is alive and expanding, and some-

Table 7.7

Types of Industrialization, Ownership, and Control
in Capitalist Countries

Characteristics of industrialization	Characteristics of ownership	Locus of control
1. Small enterprise	Concentrated	Individual-Family
2. Joint stock company	Diffused	Professional management
3. Bank intervention (purchase of industrial stock by credit institutions)	Reconcentrated under financial groups	a. Management b. Families or large investors
4. Conglomerates Interlocking directorates	Diversified in multiple fields of economic endeavor	Class hegemony: Interconnected and organized interest groups
5. State-owned industry	Concentrated, but not in private hands	Two possibilities: a. management b. political parties
6. National economic planning	Possible stock concentration but subjected to limits and controls	Government and state planning agencies
7. Social control	Not decisive	Social environment—various groups: labor unions, consumers' associations, conservationists, public opinion

times they actually appear to be giving way to it. Even in very large firms, patrimonial and family control is often found.

Our research clearly shows that, partly due to the dual nature of the Italian industrial situation, the transfer of economic control from owners to managers has not occurred and that old (and new) entrepreneurs continue to prevail at the top echelons of firms.

The very large private firm remains under the domination of a few well-organized financial groups, which can usually be pinpointed to specific individuals, while the state enterprise is subject to the control of political groups. In both cases, just as in the family-run firm, managers are often excluded from making long-term decisions.

The concept of the corporation as a public institution is more advanced in Italy than in most industrially developed countries, and public and social control over corporate decisions is stronger. Political and social control over the firm in Italy does not appear to be so much the result of industrialization as of processes taking place in the entire society and within economic institutions.

Limitations on the firms' autonomy and power automatically reduce the likelihood that future managers will extend their sphere of influence. What for American managers was a long period of autonomy without controls (or few controls), and which in recent decades has been increasingly constrained by limitations imposed by the state or pressure groups, may not occur at all in the history of Italian managers. The evolution of Italian firms seems to consist of a transition from control by property owners to control by the public through state intervention and union demands, without intermediate phases: the stage of management control in the enterprise has been bypassed.

Appendix: RESEARCH METHODOLOGY

1. Research focus

Management can be considered as (a) an economic resource (a factor of production); (b) a system of authority; (c) a class or an elite.[1]

Our study treats management as an economic resource and attempts to measure the breadth of its decision-making power, that is, the characteristics and limitations of the authority system it represents.

For our study of management, we started with the individual manager's position in the enterprise, because the presence of authority permits us to identify an elite.[2] However, we did not assume that the hierarchical position is synonymous with decision-making power; it merely allows us to identify a putative elite—those who are able, in theory, to exert influence and control over people, resources, and the environment. Our study is an attempt to judge whether the managerial group genuinely constitutes an economic elite.[3]

From our point of view, the title of manager is indicative of a status and not necessarily of a role involving responsibility and command. Therefore, we found it necessary to penetrate the group and attempt to distinguish those who effectively exert power from those who are mere figureheads.

Identifying the group was facilitated by the fact that, unlike in other industrialized countries, in Italy the title of manager is recognized by the Civil Code[4]; the group is represented by a union and is covered by a special social security fund[5] in which all managers must enroll. Due to this list, we know how many people hold managerial positions.

2. Selection of the universe

The scope of the research was progressively narrowed through the application of a number of criteria:

a. Within the group of 100,000 managers, we concentrated on those in manufacturing; this is the most important area of the economy and the area in which we find the largest group (approximately half) of the managers.

b. Attention was focused on managers in large enterprises. We did this for two reasons: 1. by excluding the semi-artisan and small family-managed firms, we could focus the analysis on the executive function, separated from ownership. Our objective was to avoid the composite category of the entrepreneur-managers and concentrate exclusively on the professional managers.

2. One of the objects of study was to examine the managers' economic, social, and possibly political role and to learn whether the managers constitute a technocracy. Thus our universe had to be comprised of managers in large corporations, whose effect on the environment is most tangible, and whose economic power would seem to offer them the possibility of political power.

Therefore our universe was comprised of managers belonging to manufacturing industries with sales over ten billion lire in 1970.

The list of such enterprises is annually published by the Mediobanca, under the title *Principal Italian Corporations*. In 1970 there were 355 organizations listed, of which 149 were in the manufacturing sector; the others were credit (111), insurance (44), commercial (32), and transportation firms (9), etc.

From among the 149 manufacturing firms we proceeded to randomly select 50 firms for our research.[6]

This group of large firms is far from being homogeneous, since sales vary from a minimum of 10 billion lire to above 1,000 billion lire.[7] This fact not only made size one of the most important independent variables, but created a methodological problem in terms of selecting interviewees within each individual firm.

The selection of managers to be interviewed was based on the firm's organization chart. We selected at least one manager from each department or function and from each hierarchical level in each firm. The minimum number of managers selected from any firm was six and the maximum was seventy-five. The 663 individuals interviewed were therefore a reflection of the organizational terrain of our sample of firms.

In order to cover all departments and various hierarchical levels in a firm, we sometimes ended by interviewing more than half of all managers in smaller-sized firms. As a result, the smaller firms in the sample were overrepresented and the larger firms underrepresented in our interviews. To remedy this we applied a weighting system to all managers' responses, according to the percentage of interviewees in each firm on the total of managers. When the percentage shifted from the average, responses received a weight value smaller or greater than 1.[8] The "weights" were introduced into the computer, which made a series of trivariate analyses with and without "weights." A comparison of results obtained in this way showed no statistically significant differences. Therefore the weight system was dropped in subsequent data processing.

3. Research model

The first criterion for choosing the interviewees—namely, firm size—shifted the emphasis of the inquiry away from the manager to the firm. This procedure was also compatible with an initial hypothesis: that the independent variables—affecting not only decision-making power but other aspects of the managerial role as well—should be sought in factors outside the personal characteristics of the individual manager, and more precisely, in his work organization.

The causal relation among external factors and organizational characteristics on one side and attitudes and behavior on the other can be thus summarized:

Factors external to the organization	*Factors internal to the organization*
A. Technological and economic environment	a. Corporate characteristics
B. Individual's objective characteristics	b. Managerial role
C. Social and political environment	c. Managerial attitudes and behavior

Information concerning these factors was gathered in three questionnaires.

4. The questionnaires

We gathered data on the three main areas using three questionnaires:

a. a company questionnaire, the goal of which was to gather in each firm data on corporate characteristics through discussions with high officials, who were not included in the managers' interviews;

b. a questionnaire about objective data concerning the manager, using information existing in the personnel department files and completed during the direct interview;

c. finally, a questionnaire aimed at the manager and used in an interview lasting two hours on the average.

More specifically, we gathered the following information:

4.1. The company questionnaire

A. Technological and economic environment

1. Source of capital   Stockholders
   a. private individual or family
   b. private—large financial groups
   c. state
   d. foreign

2. Type of market	a. national
	b. international
3. Geographic location	a. North, Central-South
	b. industrial zone or depressed rural area

a. Corporate characteristics

1. Year the corporation was founded	
2. Manufacturing sector	a. traditional, with low capital investment
	b. traditional, with large capital investment
	c. modern, with high technoical content
3. Size	a. annual sales
	b. number of employees on the payroll
4. Growth	Sales increases over preceding year
	a. less than 15%
	b. more than 15%
5. Degree of modernization	a. new plants
	b. new products
	c. technological innovation (presence of a research department)
	d. long-term planning
	e. nonconventional use of computers
6. Degree of decentralization	a. type of organizational structure
	b. type of meetings
7. Labor-union policies	

4.2. Questionnaire about objective data

B. Objective characteristics of the individual manager

1. Birthplace	a. North, Central-South
	b. urban or rural area
2. Age	
3. Social class origin	a. father's profession
	b. economic sector of father's activity

4. Level and type of education
5. Seniority on the job
6. Age when nominated to the managerial position
7. Experience preceding joining firm   a. turnover
                                           b. mobility within departments

8. Breadth of experience   Index composed of:
a. education
b. knowledge of languages
c. time spent abroad
d. experience in other organizations
e. interdepartmental mobility

b. Corporate role

1. Hierarchical level
2. Corporate department
3. Type of function (line, staff)
4. Seniority in the firm
5. Seniority as manager
6. Speed of career advancement   time between hiring and promotion
7. Job mobility   average time spent at one job
8. Interdepartmental mobility   rotation in production, sales, administration departments, etc.
9. Role changes   changes in the content of executive duties
10. Number of direct subordinates   in percentage of total payroll
11. Peripheral or central location   manager's place of work with respect to the central headquarters

C. Social and political environment

1. Social environment   high intensity industrial area or low density industrial area

2. Labor union situation
2.1. degree of workers' unionization   % of workers enrolled in unions
2.2. degree and trend of labor conflict   hours lost in strikes in percentage of total payroll; changes in relation to preceding year

2.3. existence of a workers' committee	
2.4. labor union policies of the firm	open or closed attitude toward unions; judgments about the firm made by a panel of various union leaders
3. Electoral situation in the host community	prevalence of certain parties; shift toward the right or the left in the last elections

c. Managerial attitudes and behavior

4.3. Questionnaire for the interview with managers

1. Attitudes, perceptions, judgments

1.1. Description of corporate dynamics	type of structural and policy changes
1.2. Concept of authority and of changes that have occurred	authoritarian, charismatic, or functional concept of managerial authority. Changes following union pressures
1.3. Relationship between the corporate system and the social system	a. evaluation of the causes of and solutions to union conflict b. perception of the firm's social responsibilities
1.4. Managers' prestige in society	personal judgment and perception of public opinion
1.5. Participation of manager in political life	opinion on the opportunity for political participation and reasons for abstention
1.6. Unionization of managers	opinion on union representation for managers

2. Behavior

2.1. Decision making	a. scope of manager's professional decisions (decision maker versus routine manager) b. participation in the formation of new corporate policies (strategic versus tactical manager)

2.2. Professional and social associations   participation in technical, cultural, or political organizations

These three sets of data were analyzed jointly. To achieve this goal, the computer cards for each interviewee included, together with a manager's personal data and personal opinions, information on the firm to which he belonged and information on the sociopolitical environment. Chapter 4 illustrates at length the use of corporate data in relation to the management situation.

Considerable importance was attached to qualitative and interpretative data obtained in the interviews. Approximately half of the questions in the direct interview were of an open-ended type; although they were subsequently coded, they furnished interesting material, rich in clues which often facilitated the interpretation of the quantifiable data.[9]

The final draft of the questionnaires and the plans for their use were examined in a series of informal meetings and interviews with groups of corporate consultants, economists, sociologists, and corporate executives.

Given the rapid evolution of events in Italy, the results of the study were integrated with a set of conversations held in 1977-78 with managers at various levels and with leaders from workers' and managerial unions.

List of firms included in the study according to type of product

Textiles and garments	Bassetti	Rescaldina (Milano)
	Calzaturificio di Varese	Varese
	Gruppo Finanziario Tessile	Torino
	Lanerossi	Schio (Vicenza)
	Lebole	Arezzo
	Manifatt. Cotoniere Merid.	Napoli
	Marzotto	Valdagno (Vicenza)
	Snia Viscosa Tessile	Milano, Cesano Maderno (Milano), Napoli
Food	Chiari e Forti	Silea (Treviso)
	Ferrero	Pino Torinese (Torino)
	IBP - Ind. Buitoni - Perugina	Perugia
	Lavazza	Torino
	Talmone	Torino

Paper-making,	Cartiere Burgo	Torino, Romagnano Sesia (Novara)
publishing,	ILTE	Torino
printing	Ist. Geografico	Novara
	De Agostini	
	Mondadori	Milano
	UTET	Torino
Chemical	Ferrania-3 M	Milano, Ferrania (Savona), Savona
	Minnesota	
	Lepetit	Milano, Garessio (Cuneo)
	L'Oreal	Settimo Torinese (Torino)
	Mira Lanza	Genova, Mira (Venezia)
	Snia Viscosa Chimica	Milano, Pavia, Roma, Colleferro
		(Roma), Torviscosa (Udine)
	Anic	S. Donato Milanese
Oil	AGIP	Roma, Porto Marghera (Venezia)
	Esso Standard Italiana	Roma
	(Sarpom)	S. Martino Trecate (Novara)
	(Rasiom)	Augusta (Siracusa)
	Mobil Oil	Roma, Napoli, Milano
Electro-	Ducati Elettro	Bologna, Pontinia (Latina)
mechanical	Microfarad	
	IBM	Milano, Vimercate (Milano)
	Indesit	Orbassano (Torino)
	Magneti Marelli	Milano, Sesto S. Giovanni
		(Milano), Crescenzago (Milano)
	Microtecnica	Torino
	Olivetti	Ivrea, Milano, Torino
		Scarmagno (Torino), Pozzuoli
		(Napoli)
	Philips	Milano, Monza (Milano), Torino,
		Alpignano (Torino), Desio
		(Milano), Roma
	Selenia	Roma
	Zanussi	Pordenone
Rubber	Pirelli	Milano, Settimo Torinese, Arco
		Felice (Napoli)
	Boston	Bollate (Milano)
Machinery	Aeronautica Macchi	Varese

Machinery *(continued)*	Fiat	Torino, Grugliasco (Torino), Rivalta (Torino), Milano, Bologna, Firenze, Livorno, Perugia, Catania
	Galileo	Firenze
	Innocenti	Milano
	Nuovo Pignone	Firenze, Massa
	Riv-SKF	Torino, Airasca (Torino), Pinerolo (Torino), Villar Perosa (Torino), Milano, Firenze
Metallurgy *steel & iron*	Cogne	Aosta, Torino
	Italsider	Torino, Genova, Cornigliano (Genova), Servola (Trieste), Marghera-Venezia, Mestre, Bagnoli (Napoli), Taranto
	Mec Fond	Napoli
Construction	Cementir	Roma, Caserta, Spoleto, Perugia
	Ideal Standard	Milano, Brescia, Salerno
	Favvrica Pisana (Saint Gobain)	Torino, Savigliano (Torino), Milano, Pisa, Caserta
	Unicem	Torino, Milano, Guidonia (Roma), Catania

Notes

1. See Sylos Labini, *Saggio sulle Classi Sociali*, Bari, Laterza, 1975, pp. 168-74.

2. Official figures do not take into account the hidden economy and unreported labor. The Italian Institute of Statistics estimates that underground workers number between two and two and a half million.

3. See Charles P. Klindlberger, "Economia al Bivio," in Fabio L. Cavazza and Stephen R. Graubard, eds., *Il Caso Italiano*, Milan, Garzanti, 1974, p. 244.

4. Recent elections had these results (in %):

	1977	1980
Communist Party	35	30
Socialist parties	10	14
Parties to the left of the Communists	3	6
	48%	50%

5. The percentage of manpower occupied in firms below 10 workers is 19% in France, 13% in Germany, 7% in Belgium, and 3% in the United States. See Romano Prodi, *Sistema Industriale e Sviluppo Economico in Italia*, Bologna, Il Mulino, 1973, p. 37.

6. A high proportion of the small firms are service and maintenance companies, suppliers to the building industry, or producers of goods tailored to the tastes and habits of the Italian consumers. See Francesco Forte, "L'impresa —Pubblica—Privata; grande—piccola," in *Il Caso Italiano*, p. 347. On the other hand, they have recently begun to develop a remarkable export capacity.

7. Ibid., pp. 350-51.

8. When the Italian government and labor unions voiced concern about the sale of 11% of shares to the Libyan government in 1976, FIAT's president Giovanni Agnelli, as a reassurance, declared publicly that he and his family owned or controlled over 51% of the total shares.

9. Since 1957 state firms have been legally obligated to place at least 40%

of their new investment and 60% of their new plants in the South of the country.

10. Patrimonial management is "business management in which ownership, major policy making positions, and a significant proportion of other jobs in the hierarchy are held by members of an extended family." See Frederick Harbison and Charles A. Myers, *Management in the Industrial World: An International Analysis*, New York, McGraw-Hill, 1959, p. 69.

11. Article 2095 of the Italian Civil Code reads: ". . . The employees are divided into: administrative and technical managers, white-collars, and workers. The special laws and the corporative norms, on the basis of each product branch and the structure of the firm, will decide the requirements for membership in one of the above mentioned categories."

12. Although the functions and power of managers vary a great deal, their background tends to be similar. Apart from their common social origin, managers enjoy a high level of education (81% of our interviewees had a university degree, that is, 17 to 18 years of schooling). The great majority (71%) have urban backgrounds and most (66%) were born in the Northern industrial areas. They are well traveled and often speak more than one language. They show a very low job turnover (the average number of industrial organizations in which they worked is 1.82). An overwhelming majority (83%) have remained in the firm that granted them the title of *dirigente*. Even when dissatisfied with their current job and company, only 7% would consider looking outside for a better job.

CHAPTER 2

1. Most definitions of power go back to the definition provided by Max Weber: "Power (*Macht*) is the probability that one actor within a social relationship will be in a position to carry out his own will despite resistance, regardless of the basis on which this probability rests." See *The Theory of Social and Economic Organization*, trans. A. M. Henderson and Talcott Parsons, New York, The Free Press, 1964, p. 152.

2. "The corporation executive possesses power by virtue of his position of authority in a firm which is itself powerful." Power is exercised as "authority over subordinates, control of the disposal of resources, and great influence over persons and affairs *outside* the firm. The corporation is a vehicle through which power comes to be held and exercised. . . ." Robert A. Gordon, *Business Leadership in the Large Corporation*, Berkeley, Ca., University of California Press, 1966, pp. 305-6.

3. Carl Kaysen, "The Corporation: How Much Power? What Scope?" in Reinhard Bendix and Seymour M. Lipset, eds., *Class, Status and Power*, New York, The Free Press, 1966, 2nd ed., p. 238.

4. Ibid.

5. Perhaps the first sociologist to have described what he labeled the "seamy side of progress" was Elton Mayo in his well-known trilogy. See particularly *The Social Problems of an Industrial Civilization*, Cambridge, Mass., Harvard University Press, 1945.

6. Adolf A. Berle, *The Twentieth Century Capitalist Revolution*, New York, Harcourt, Brace, 1954, p. 183.

7. John K. Galbraith, *The New Industrial State*, Boston, Houghton Mifflin, rev. ed. 1968, pp. 173-74.

8. Robert A. Brady, *Business as a System of Power*, New York, Columbia University Press, 6th ed., 1951, p. x. In Ammassari's view, "Classical economics becomes philosophy, presenting the business enterprise as essential to society and indispensable to the productive process." See Paolo Ammassari, "Autoritá e potere nella societá industriale," *Quaderni di sociologia*, no. 37, 1960, p. 188.

9. Fritz Machlup, "Corporate Management, National Interest, and Behavioral Theory," *The Journal of Political Economy*, vol. 75, no. 5, October 1967.

10. The same democratic principles of which Western nations boast are sometimes sacrificed to business needs; the press and public opinion are indignant when a strike suspends a service, and they decry its cost to the community. See Ivar E. Berg, "The Impact of Business on America," in Ivar E. Berg, ed., *The Business of America*, New York, Holt Rinehart, 1968, p. 18.

11. Kaysen, "The Corporation," p. 234; see also Franco Momigliano, *Economia industriale e teoria dell'impresa*, Bologna, Il Mulino, 1975, pp. 260-61.

12. Henry Kariel, *The Decline of American Pluralism*, Stanford, Ca., Stanford University Press, 1961, p. 316.

13. Through national economic planning, the state in Italy plays a regulatory role over economic activities; by investing in state-owned firms, it takes on the role of a competitor. For some time the U.S. government has been an important purchaser of industrial goods; more than a third of the national product derives from government orders or government-related orders.

14. Galbraith, *New Industrial State*, chap. 27.

15. Brady concludes that "Business is in politics and the state is in business" (*Business as a System of Power*, p. x). Galbraith also notes that "The industrial system, in fact, is inextricably associated with the state. In notable respect the mature corporation is an arm of the state. And the state, in important matters, is an instrument of the industrial system" (*New Industrial State*, p. 298).

16. W. Thomas Easterbrook, "Some Comments of the Nature of Entrepreneurial Activity," in Richard Wohl, ed., *Change and the Entrepreneur*, Cambridge, Mass., Harvard University Press, 1949, p. 19.

17. In theory, by making itself an autonomous closed system an enterprise would obtain many advantages; autonomy would enable it to devote itself totally to those tasks it considers to be within the realm of its expertise: producing (without conflicts with employees), selling (without the constraints of competition or the unpredictable changes in consumer tastes), and expanding geographically (without submitting to government controls or delays). Since this degree of autonomy is not possible, the enterprise at least attempts to prevent political changes and tends therefore to behave fundamentally conservatively. In addition, because it can manipulate and ally itself with politi-

cal power, and because political power holders usually seek such a powerful ally, business can seldom behave in a socially and politically revolutionary
manner; it changes its attitude toward the state only if threatened by state
policies (interestingly, in such cases it tends to behave as a counter-revolu-
tionary force).

18. Berg, *Business of America*, p. 185.

19. Kaysen, "The Corporation," p. 238; Jean Meynaud, *La tecnocrazia.
Mito o realtà?* Bari, Laterza, 1966, p. 226.

20. *Power* (coercion) and *authority* (legitimation) are two extremes of a
continuum; they are different inasmuch as "institutionalized power" may be
"legalized," but "institutionalized authority" alone is "legitimized"; authority requires consensus, power demands compliance. See Walter Buckley,
Sociology and Modern Systems Theory, Englewood Cliffs, N.J., Prentice Hall,
1967, pp. 196 and 178.

McIver also distinguishes between "social power," which is the ability to
control another's behavior directly with force or indirectly through manipulation, and "authority," which means the preestablished right to determine
policies and to declare oneself the leader of other individuals. In this case the
emphasis shifts from *force* to *right*. See Robert McIver, *The Web of Government*, New York, Macmillan, 1947, p. 87. Michel Crozier distinguishes between "authority"—a form of power recognized as legitimate by law, by custom, or by the consensus of those who have submitted to it—and "power,"
realized in all forms of relation marked by phenomena of dependence, manipulation, or exploitation. See *La société bloquée*, Paris, Editions du Seuil,
1970, p. 27. For a distinction between "power" and "authority," see also
Robert Biersted, "An Analysis of Social Power," *American Sociological Review*, no. 15, 1950, pp. 730-38; Peter Blau and Marshall W. Meyer, *Bureaucracy in Modern Society*, New York, Random House, 1956, p. 71; and Peter
Blau, *Exchange and Power in Social Life*, New York, John Wiley, 1964, p.
117. Buckley asks whether the large enterprise should be considered a manifestation of institutionalized authority or institutionalized power, and concludes in favor of the latter definition (*Sociology and Modern System Theory*,
p. 200). Thus business power would be *control* without consensus, based on
sanctions.

21. Cf. Roy Lewis and Rosemary Steward, *The Managers*, New York, New
American Library, 1958, p. 194.

22. Already by the mid-fifties the literature on "social responsibilities"
was so abundant that Peter Drucker asked sarcastically (in "The Responsibility of Management," *Harper's*, 1954, pp. 57-72) how businessmen would still
find the time to handle their own affairs, when they were so busy with cultural and charitable activities, forest conservation, religious freedom, the intellectual refugees from China, etc.

23. Berg, *Business of America*, pp. 5-11.

24. Leonard S. Silk and David Vogel, *Ethics and Profits: The Crisis of
Confidence in American Business*, New York, Simon and Schuster, 1976,
p. 136.

25. K. Davis analyzes the fluctuations of American public opinion with re-

gard to business, linking them to periods of national emergency. Each time productive efficiency becomes a particularly important issue for the nation (as was the case during the nation's wars), the controls and restrictions to which business is subjected diminish ("Business and Government Relations," p. 434). A more recent case is the simultaneous reduction in severity of enforcement of antipollution laws and diminished public indignation concerning pollution—changes clearly related to the U.S. oil crisis and the growing national hostility toward the new policies of the Arab world. A similar decrease in concern about pollution has occurred in periods of unemployment; indeed, recent demonstrations organized by U.S. labor unions against ecologists who had blocked the construction of some nuclear centers, and the "Nuclear Power Is Safe" posters hoisted by workers, showed widespread acceptance of economic growth—and jobs—as a primary American value.

26. John Kenneth Galbraith, who developed the concept of "countervailing power," arguing that the power of the corporation was limited by labor unions, by internal competition, and by antitrust laws (*American Capitalism: The Concept of Countervailing Power*, White Plains, N.Y., M. E. Sharpe, Inc., 1980, reprint of 1956 ed.) later recognized the growing imbalance of power in favor of business resulting from consumer dependency and the declining strength of the U.S. labor movement. See *The Affluent Society*, Boston, Houghton Mifflin, 2nd revised edition, 1969.

27. In writing about managers, Berle stated: "As yet the community has not created any acknowledged referent of responsibility, no group from which they take their power mandate or get instructions in dealing with serious streams of events they can and do affect. There is no recognized body of doctrine by which [managers] themselves must test their choice as they act from day to day" (Berle, *Capitalist Revolution*, p. 181).

28. ". . . large owners and executives in their self-financing corporations hold the keys of economic power . . . no powers effectively and consistently countervail against them, nor have they as corporate-made men developed any effectively restraining conscience." C. Wright Mills, *The Power Elite*, New York, Oxford University Press, 1959, p. 125.

29. For a critical review of this theory of "managerial supremacy" see chapter 7 below, "The Powerless Elite."

30. Control refers to "the capacity to determine the broad policies of a corporation" (Maurice Zeitlin, "Corporate Ownership and Control: the Large Corporation and the Capitalist Class," *American Journal of Sociology*, vol. 79, no. 5, March 1974, p. 1090). Control can be exercised both through selection of directors and through orders transmitted to management. See Adolph A. Berle and Gardiner C. Means, *The Modern Corporation and Private Property*, New York, Macmillan, 1932, p. 66.

31. Giorgio Ruffolo, *La grande impresa nella società moderna*, Turin, Einaudi, 1971, p. 143. In *Capital* Marx also asserts that owners of capital are transformed progressively into the finance capitalist.

32. Arthur Cole, *Business Enterprise in Its Social Setting*, Cambridge, Mass., Harvard University Press, 1959, pp. 8-9.

33. Galbraith, *New Industrial State*, pp. 88-89.

34. Thorstein Veblen, *Absentee Ownership and Business Enterprise in Recent Times: The Case of America*, Boston, Beacon Press, 1967 (1st ed. 1923), p. 101.

35. See Daniel Bell, *The End of the Ideology*, New York, The Free Press, 1966, in particular chap. 2, "The Breakup of Family Capitalism."

36. Ibid.

37. Berle and Means, *Modern Corporation*, p. 93.

38. Gordon, *Business Leadership*, pp. 156 and 160.

39. Robert J. Larner, *Management Control and the Large Corporation*, Cambridge, Mass., Dunellen, 1970, p. 20. This process seems to be a function of firm size: the presence of family capital diminishes progressively from medium-large firms to large firms to very large firms. Minority control (at least 10% of the block of shares) found in 24% of the largest 300 firms, fell to 17% when the analysis was restricted to the 200 largest corporations, and fell to 11% when concentrating on the 100 corporations at the top of the list. See Robert Sheehan, "Proprietors in the World of Big Business," *Fortune*, June 1967, pp. 178-83.

40. Ruffolo, *La grande impresa*, p. 142.

41. Robin Marris, *The Economic Theory of Managerial Capitalism*, London, Macmillan, 1964, p. 18.

42. Confirms ibid. Irving Kristol also believes that "stockholder elections are almost invariably routine affirmations of management's will, because management will have previously secured the support of the largest stockholders; and for a long while stockholders have essentially regarded themselves, and are regarded by management, as little more than possessors of a variable-income security" (Irving Kristol, "On Corporate Capitalism in America," *The Public Interest*, no. 41, Fall 1975, p. 138).

43. Galbraith, *New Industrial State*, pp. 67 and 87.

44. Ruffolo, *La grande impresa*, p. 145. The stockholder's passivity, even as owner of a large block of shares, was pointed out by Burnham, who observed that a high percentage of stockholders are women who are limited to exercising second-party or third-party control. See James Burnham, *The Managerial Revolution*, New York, The John Day Company, 1941, p. 101.

Galbraith writes that among the 200 largest corporations, i.e., "those that form the heart of the industrial system," there are few in which owners exercise any important influence and that such influence as they do exercise is, moreover, diminishing. The exceptions (Du Pont, Firestone, and Ford) are due to the fact that in these cases the members of the owner family are part of management. Their importance derives therefore from the fact of belonging to the "technostructure." (*New Industrial State*, p. 83.)

45. Gordon, *Leadership*, p. 161.

46. Meynaud, *La tecnocrazia*, p. 238.

47. Cf. William R. Ripley, *Main Street and Wall Street*, Boston, Little Brown, 1927.

48. Peter Drucker, "The Bored Board," *The Wharton Magazine*, vol. 1, no. 1, Autumn 1976, pp. 19-25.

49. The Pujo Senate Committee already observed this phenomenon in

1913. It wrote that in large firms with diffused stockholders, "The management is virtually self-perpetuating and is able through the power of patronage, the indifference of the stockholders, and other influences to control a majority of the stock." See Robert A. Dahl, "Business and Politics," in Robert A. Dahl, Mason Haire, and Paul F. Lazarsfeld, eds., *Social Science Research on Business—Product and Potential*, New York, Columbia University Press, p. 7.

50. Concerning the limited relevance of the board of directors, and primarily of noncompany members, see Myles Mace, *Directors: Myth and Reality*, Boston, Harvard University, 1971. Similar conditions exist in British corporations. See R. E. Pahl and J. T. Winkler, "The Economic Elite: Theory and Practice," in Philips Stanworth and Anthony Giddens, eds., *Elites and Power in British Society*, Cambridge, Cambridge University Press, 1974. The study found (p. 106) that the majority of boards of directors examined were *pro forma* superfluous (because each was dominated by a single individual) or irrelevant (because composed of persons lacking in influence, e.g., retired executives, etc.). In case of serious conflict in the board it is not the norm for directors to voice opposition but rather to hand in their resignations. They conclude that "Capital is not synonymous with control" (p. 111).

51. Meynaud, *La tecnocrazia*, pp. 234-37. Technocracy is defined as "the government of technicians, that is to say, the predominance of experts and specialists in the social, political, and economic life of a nation . . ." (from *Dizionario Enciclopedico Italiano*, edited by the Institute of the Italian Encyclopedia).

52. Frederick H. Harbison and Charles A. Myers, *Management in the Industrial World*, New York, McGraw Hill, 1959, p. 69. For Robert Heilbroner, the transition is from "industrial dictators" to "corporate Caesars" and, finally, to a "faceless management." See *The Limits of American Capitalism*, New York, Harper and Row, 1966, pp. 24-25.

53. Frank Redlich, "Toward a Better Theory of Risk," *Explorations in Entrepreneurial History*, vol. 10, no. 1, October 1957, pp. 36-37.

54. *Power without Property: A New Development in American Political Economy*, New York, Harcourt, Brace, 1959, p. 19.

55. Galbraith, *New Industrial State*, pp. 55-58.

56. Burnham, *Managerial Revolution*, p. 102.

57. Ibid., p. 76.

58. Bell, *End of Ideology*, p. 43.

59. Burnham, *Managerial Revolution*, p. 150.

60. The impossibility of enjoying the high profits to which the entrepreneur was at one time accustomed, and the current more efficient system of taxation have induced the heads of firms to reinvest the majority of profits. Daniel Bell notes that while in 1929 only 30% of profits was reinvested, the percentage increased to 70% after 1945 (*The End of Ideology*, p. 44).

61. Managers' "rewards were not primarily money . . . but status achievements and, ultimately, some independent power of their own" (ibid., p. 43).

62. Ruffolo, *La grande impresa*, p. 152.
63. Galbraith, *New Industrial State*, pp. 174-75.
64. Meynaud, *La tecnocrazia*, p. 241.
65. Berle, *Power without Property*, pp. 91-101.
66. Burnham, *Managerial Revolution*, p. 213.
67. G. Paolo Pranstraller, in describing A. Frisch's position, *L'intellettuale tecnico e altri saggi*, Milan, Comunità, 1972, p. 130.
68. Meynaud, *La tecnocrazia*, p. 117.
69. Galbraith, *New Industrial State*, p. 71.
70. Meynaud, *La tecnocrazia*, p. 60.
71. ". . . I would limit the examples of technocratic phenomena to those cases in which the technician, whose real or supposed competence constitutes his right to intervene (his main weapon), has direct input into the centers where policy-formulation occurs . . ." (ibid., p. 117).

CHAPTER 3

1. See Mario Stoppino's definitions of power under the entry "Potere" in Norberto Bobbio and Nicola Matteucci, eds., *Dizionario di Politica*, Turin, UTET, 1976.
2. Meynaud also points out that the actual distribution of power does not necessarily correspond to the legal designation of authority; for example, in the technocratic system, the political man has the appearance of power, but in fact lacks it. See Jean Meynaud, *La tecnocrazia. Mito o realtà*, Bari, Laterza, 1966, p. 59. Hierarchical level and function are nonetheless two variables the research takes into consideration.
3. Frequently used in community studies such as Floyd Hunter's *Community Power Structure: a Study of Decision-Makers*, Chapel Hill, University of North Carolina Press, 1935.
4. Mary Parker Follet, "The Illusion of Final Authority," in Ernest Dale, ed., *Readings in Management: Landmarks and New Frontiers*, New York, McGraw-Hill, 1975, p. 394.
5. Leonard Sayles, *Managerial Behavior and Administration in Complex Organizations*, Englewood Cliffs, N.J., Prentice-Hall, 1966, p. 207.
6. Follett, "Illusion of Final Authority," p. 396.
7. Sayles, *Managerial Behavior*, pp. 218-19.
8. According to March, the decision-making process is more than a mere isolated event: it is analogous to a river that is constantly fed by streams and tributaries. See James G. March and Johan P. Olsen, *Ambiguity and Choice in Organizations*, Bergen, Universitetsforlaget, 1976.
9. March has often emphasized the nonrational aspect of organizational decisions. The frequently unclear objectives, the uncertain technology, and the turnover of chief actors over time all disorganize the decision-making process.

Because of uncertainty, many firms are in fact "organized anarchies" (see ibid.).

10. "It is often very difficult to say with much meaning who "makes" a decision in an organization or when it is made. Instead there seems to be a process of gradual commitment to a course of action." See James G. March, "Business Decision-Making," in Harold J. Leavitt, ed., *Readings in Managerial Psychology*, Chicago, University of Chicago Press, 1964, p. 454.

11. See the example in the following pages.

12. This is Franco Momigliano's definition, quoted by Giorgio Bocca in *Il Giorno*.

13. Herbert A. Simon, "The Executive as Decision-Maker," in *The New Science of Management Decision*, New York, Harper & Row, 1960, p. 1.

14. Ibid., p. 49.

15. Ibid., pp. 65-66. Others distinguish between critical decisions and routine decisions. See Philip Selznick, *Leadership in Administration*, New York, Harper & Row, 1957.

16. Simon, *New Science*, p. 6.

17. Some decisions considered innovative by managers we interviewed:

a. *Product Innovation*

"I heavily supported producing television sets. We had discussed them for years. When we finally began this line of production, it was because of me."

"I conceived, designed with the R&D office, and then put on the market a type of product that was adapted to the demands of the American customer for whom, in addition to a product's quality, the price is also important."

"When the opportunity to substitute natural gas for fuel oil heating systems emerged in Italy, the firm was undecided. To me it seemed a unique opportunity: I handled the problem by developing projections based on my analysis of consumer products. Initially a few billion lire were invested; as we were at that time competing with small wholesalers, initially we received lower net profits. However, currently these decisions are paying off. They are a product of my initiative and occurred without the support of the top men, or at least only with their skeptical consent. Eventually a new division devoted to the product was created."

b. *Methods and Organization*

"I supported changing the business account system, and the transition to standard costs." "I supported the introduction of the computer [there were many such answers]." "I 'invented' the product manager, who sets up a product's manufacture and follows it personally in all its phases. This is a technician who has to be very flexible and versatile in order to jump from one product to another."

18. For example, consider the financial risks that certain decisions cited by those interviewed carry:

a. *Research*

"I decided the firm should design some machine tools needed for a new product instead of buying them in the U.S. The order for the products amounted to 20 billion lire. Using our own patented design would save three-fourths of the cost; on the other hand we could have jeopardized or delayed production. The president asked me if I felt up to it. If I had not been, he would have bought the U.S. machine tools and we would have been completely safe. It was a decisive change of policy for the firm, an assertion of courage."

b. *Production*

"I decided it was necessary to install a new rolling mill process, and I argued that position. The cost was 10 billion. I also proposed and obtained the installation of a new electric steel plant (cost: 18 billion). I sign contracts for our foreign purchases necessary to complete production for a yearly sum of more than a billion lire."

c. *Market*

"I proposed to shift to a cash sales basis a firm that had made its success with credit sales. This improved our credit situation but risked alienating old clients."

"The no-discount price policy; allocation of extremely heavy investments in technical assistance; the creation of a spare parts inventory worth a billion. We continue producing spare parts even when a type of machine is no longer in production and this involves tying up machines and warehouses. Our spare parts yard is the second in quantity, and perhaps the first for quality in Europe."

19. Examples:

"I personally negotiated a 132 billion lire contract for supplies to the Ministry of Defense." "I insisted on doubling the amount allotted for the construction of the new plant, which generated changes in plans. I based my decision on my own market and growth forecasts."

"I am preparing the investment plan for the current year. The decisions and choice of priorities are mine. I am aware that in this way I determine a plant's size and thus its future."

Sometimes the importance of a decision manifests itself in terms not of growth but of a reduction within the firm. In such a case, following an immediate savings, there may be financial losses (connected to the loss of markets). An example is the manager who advised top management to cease producing an entire basic line of goods (large electronic calculators).

20. "I persuaded management to accept the Workers' Committee (*Consiglio di Fabbrica*), and to deal directly with the unions without going through the Industrialist Association."

21. "I urged management to decide to build a plant in the South. Many were against it and I had to fight to get my proposal accepted. Furthermore, I tried to bring about a policy of decentralization, which went against the firm's tradition and the habits of the 'old guard.' "

"I closed the unprofitable English branch without notifying the boss, who at first judged it an unwise decision."

"Contrary to the orders of the Management Committee, I assented to the union's request for new rules of compensation, in order to avoid open conflicts and endless strikes."

22. Examples of decisions considered routine:

"I make decisions that come under a department manager's jurisdiction, from selecting production equipment or taking disciplinary measures to proposing dismissals (which however must be approved by the personnel manager)."

"I make few decisions: office equipment purchases (tables, typewriters). I can change assistants. However, I am free to move about and make contacts. I can run to Naples or Venice, ask for meetings with the head of a large firm or with high-level politicians. Despite these undertakings, I am aware that all my decisions can be overturned by any strategic decision made by top officials. Strategic decisions are reserved for a few big-shots with whom I never communicate."

23. Herbert A. Simon, *The Shape of Automation for Men and Management*, New York, Harper & Row, 1965, p. 78.

24. We cite the following description of a sales manager's extensive (but neither innovative nor risky) decision-making activity:

"I give the firm my projections of sales of various products, based on estimates of market quotas achieved in the preceding year. The estimates are derived from an analysis of variations in increases in total consumption and export opportunities; I decide the prices minor clients must pay (the president intervenes in the case of major clients). I decide whether or not to continue production of a certain type of product, but only in the case of minor products. I evaluate the need to increase sales personnel, but I must obtain the personnel manager's approval for actual hirings."

25. Cf. Talcott Parsons, "Suggestions for a Sociological Approach to the Theory of Organization," in Amitai Etzioni, ed., *A Sociological Reader on Complex Organizations*, New York, Holt, Rinehart, 1961, p. 42.

26. See Daniel Katz and Robert L. Kahn, *The Social Psychology of Organizations*, New York, Wiley, 1966, p. 298.

27. Ibid., p. 298.

28. Alfred D. Chandler, *Strategy and Structure: Chapters in the History of the American Enterprise*, New York, Doubleday, 1966, p. 11.

29. Sayles, *Managerial Behavior*, p. 181.

30. Among the examples gathered, we mention the case of a manager who participated in defining the terms of his firm's merger with a foreign business, in a series of long and laborious meetings. He considers this operation to have been the most challenging and delicate in the firm's history. Another manager participates in planning financial policy by furnishing proposals and alternative courses of action. He further sets the terms of agreement for purchasing new firms and running their management, as well as the search for internal and external sources of financial support.

31. According to their managers, all fifty firms covered in the research had undergone substantial policy changes. The opportunity for consultation had thus been presented to most. Only 35 managers out of 633 (or 6%) were not able to cite examples of change. The tables below synthesize the various types of policy changes and their impact on managerial style and organizational structure, as described by the managers.

Types of Policy Changes
(in %, n = 543)

Technological: new productive methods	16
Financial: capital increases, stock changes, mergers, new investments	25
Market: market expansion or cut-back, new products	26
Personnel: new men at the top, new union and personnel policies	33
	100

Effects of Policy Changes
(in %, n = 633)

No transformation	6
Changes in managerial style:	
a) in one department	23
b) in the entire corporation	24
Changes in the organizational structure	10
Changes both in the organizational structure and in the managerial style in one department	14
Changes both in the organizational structure and in the overall managerial style	23
	100

32. Even a single agreement can have effects transcending the relationship between the firm and group representatives. For example, the determination of employment or salary levels, resulting from a union contract, also influences persons not belonging to the firm or unions.

33. In recent years many communities have become sensitive to problems involving pollution and environmental changes resulting from industrialization.

CHAPTER 4

1. The different definitions used for structure and types of technology are extensively examined below, in section 4.4.

2. See the arguments developed in section 4.4.2.

3. Firms are aware of this phenomenon, and job-specification manuals sug-

gest that periodic checks of the work content be made in order to verify whether it still corresponds to the existing job description.

4. Kurt Lewin applied the concept of "field" in psychology, borrowing it from physics. Behavior is conceived as the result of a system of forces operating within a space; hence, the importance of analyzing behavior by taking into account the individual's environment. While Lewin utilizes the concept of "field" to explain mental phenomena and psychological forces, our analysis considers the "field" to be the social space in which individuals operate. See Kurt Lewin, *Field Theory in Social Science*, New York, Harper & Row, 1951.

5. This statement is based on an individualistic and exclusively hierarchical view of power. A collegial decision-making system would have the effect of extending the individual's area of influence to others from which he had previously been excluded. This expansion could be achieved with a limited loss of individual autonomy (which is inevitable because of the reciprocal nature of the method). However, a participatory system is hampered by many technical aspects of the managerial function, by the time and cost that consultation entails, and last but not least, by personal motivations.

6. Anthony Jay, *Management and Machiavelli*, New York, Holt, Rinehart and Winston, 1967, p. 212.

7. Leonard Sayles, *Managerial Behavior and Administration in Complex Organizations*, Englewood Cliffs, N.J., Prentice-Hall, 1966, pp. 218-19.

8. In *The New Industrial State* (p. 74), Galbraith notes that large size allows the firm to control markets (both for supplies and sales) and to accept market uncertainty where it cannot be eliminated. This has the effect of increasing the firm's freedom to make decisions.

Another way of extending corporate power is to sharpen the firm's competitive edge by reorganizing resources and materials to increase efficiency. Yet another method is to establish new alliances or reinforce relations with other economically influential groups, resulting in a system of reciprocal supports. (One of many such methods is to trade seats on boards of directors and to develop interlocking directorates.)

9. These forces have been labeled veto groups (Sayles, *Managerial Behavior*, p. 219). Organizations have been defined as "decision making power systems interacting with their environment in conditions of uncertainty " (C. R. Hining et al., "Structural Conditions of Interorganizational Power," *Administrative Science Quarterly*, March 1974, p. 22). Thus their degree of autonomy, including their internal decisions, varies according to their relations with the environment.

10. We have labeled the *upper level* the stratum of managers who in the firm's organization chart depend directly on the chief executive officer (in Italy: the General Manager, Delegated Administrator, President) or on the Executive Committee. The latter echelon represents the supreme command, the focal point at which coordination of organizational activities occurs. The upper level is the point in the organization at which the division of the various organizational functions occurs. A subsequent articulation of tasks takes place at the second hierarchical level, and so forth, proceeding to even further specialized activities at the lower managerial levels.

11. Hierarchical distinctions are strongly felt by managers, to the point of constituting perhaps the greatest obstacle to their identification with the managerial group. Each rank is characterized not just by a specific function, but primarily a variation in status.

Though managers are homogeneous in terms of education, training, type of career, and role (involving supervision, coordination, and control) they are made different by the degree of power granted them, at least formally, by their hierarchical position.

12. Decentralization has been defined as the process of distributing decision making throughout the organizational structure. See Frederick H. Harbison and Charles A. Myers, *Management in the Industrial World*, New York, McGraw-Hill, 1959, p. 43.

13. The effect of type of organizational structure will be discussed in section 4.4.2.

14. In Figure 4.8, it is interesting to note the dominance of the R&D department at the upper level, and then its sharp drop below that level.

15. Personnel managers, however, are characterized by their approximately equal measures of decision-making and policy-making powers. This does not occur in other staff departments, and is probably explained by their extensive advisory activities with regard to organizational problems.

16. Out of a total of 663 managers interviewed, 373 belong to firms that have labeled themselves as production-oriented as compared to 290 belonging to firms defining themselves as market-oriented.

17. Other variables we analyzed, such as the year the corporation was founded, the firm's geographic location, its degree of hierarchical complexity, its production versus market orientation, and its trade-union policies, do not appear to have any effect on the distribution of power.

18. These categories were based on the criteria adopted by the Bank of Italy in its financial report. The *traditional sector*, with low capital investment, includes textile firms, clothing manufacturers, and the food industry (i.e., 17 firms in which 145 managers were interviewed). The *intermediate sector* (which the Bank of Italy calls "traditional with large capital investment") is the largest and more composite category. It includes the machinery, iron and steel, chemical (pharmaceuticals, plastics), and rubber industries (i.e., 24 firms with 382 managers interviewed). The *advanced sector*, which uses the most sophisticated technology, includes the electronics, optics, aviation, computers, and precision instruments industries (i.e., 10 firms with 136 managers interviewed).

19. Traditional firms: 37%; Intermediate firms: 38%; Advanced firms: 39%.

20. Organizational structure has been defined as a system of rules and goals that define the tasks, powers, and operational procedures of the organization's participants according to officially approved plans (Leonard Broom and Philip Selznick, *Sociology*, New York, Harper & Row, 1963, p. 222). Therefore, organizational structure defines the model of social interaction within the context of production. (See Charles Perrow, "A Framework for the Analysis of Organizations," *American Sociological Review*, vol. 32, no. 2, April 1967, p. 195.) Furthermore, the organizational structure codifies and

formalizes the power connected to the various positions, assuring each hierarchical level the degree of authority necessary in carrying out its functions.

21. See Alfred D. Chandler, *Strategy and Structure: Chapters in the History of American Enterprise*, New York, Doubleday, 1966, chapters 2 and 3. The multidivisional structure was developed in the United States between 1920 and 1940 by industries such as DuPont and General Motors. Outside the United States no examples were observable until 1960.

On the influence of technology on structure, see Joan Woodward, *Industrial Organization: Behaviour and Control*, London, Oxford University Press, 1970; Edward Harvey, "Technology and the Structure of Organizations," *American Sociological Review*, vol. 33, no. 2, April 1968; and Charles Perrow, *Organizational Analysis: a Sociological View*, London, Tavistock, 1970.

22. Peter M. Blau, "The Hierarchy of Authority in Organizations," *American Journal of Sociology*, vol. 73, no. 4, January 1968. It has been demonstrated that a participatory system is counterproductive in routine situations. See Charles Perrow, "The Short and Glorious History of Organizational Theory," *Organizational Dynamics*, Summer 1973, pp. 3-15.

23. This structural adaptation is so logical as to occur spontaneously. In a laboratory experiment, the groups who were charged with deductive tasks developed a centralized organization on their own, then switched to a decentralized organization when tasks were changed to inductive problems. See Victor H. Vroom, "Industrial Social Psychology," in Vroom, ed., *Handbook of Social Psychology*, London, Addison-Wesley, 1969, 2nd ed.

24. See W. J. M. Mackenzie, "Technology and Organization," in Amitai Etzioni, ed., *A Sociological Reader on Complex Organizations*, New York, Holt, Rinehart and Winston, 1969, 2nd ed. The firms that absorb innovation best are those that least respect the rules of the organizational chart. They create a system of relations among the various members but do not concern themselves with organizational "purity," with jobs overlapping, or with possible lapses in the continuity of policies.

25. See Tom Burns and G. M. Stalker, *The Management of Innovation*, London, Tavistock, 1961.

However the situation is not necessarily fixed, because during the development phase a firm can take advantage of a flexible structure, and, once it is established, shift to a rigid bureaucratic structure which can prove more efficient. (See C. Perrow, "The Short and Glorious History," cit., p. 14.)

26. See Theodore Caplow, "Organizational Size," *Administrative Science Quarterly*, vol. 1, no. 4, March 1957, pp. 484-505, and *Principles of Organization*, New York, Harcourt Brace, Jovanovich, 1965, pp. 25-28; Oscar Grusky, "Corporate Size, Bureaucratization and Managerial Succession," *American Journal of Sociology*, vol. 67, no. 3, November 1961.

27. See F. Stuart Chapin, "The Growth of Bureaucracy, an Hypothesis," *American Sociological Review*, vol. 16, no. 6, December 1951, pp. 835-56; Derek S. Pugh, D. J. Hickson, C. R. Hirving, C. Turner, "The Context of Organizational Structure," *Administrative Science Quarterly*, vol. 14, no. 1, March 1969.

28. See M. W. Meyer, "Two Authority Structures of Bureaucratic Organi-

zations," *Administrative Science Quarterly*, vol. 3, no. 2.

29. See Richard H. Hall, J. Eugene Hass, Norman J. Johnson, "Organizational Size, Complexity and Formalization," *American Sociological Review*, vol. 32, no. 6, December 1967.

30. See Richard H. Hall, *Organizations: Structure Processes*, Englewood Cliffs, N.J., Prentice-Hall, 1972, p. 229; Pugh et al., "The Context of Organizational Structure," p. 98; Harold Wilensky, "Hierarchical Control and Optimum Firm Size," *Journal of Political Economy*, 1967, no. 75, pp. 123-38.

31. See Richard B. Heflebower, "Observation in Decentralization in Large Enterprises," in Ernest Dale, ed., *Readings in Management: Landmarks and New Frontiers*, New York, McGraw-Hill, 1975, p. 206. The analysis of French bureaucracy by Michel Crozier effectively illustrates the disfunctions in an organization with many levels but which is centralized. In such an organization, those who have the authority to make decisions lack the necessary information, while those who possess information lack decision-making power. See Michel Crozier, *Le phénomène bureaucratique*, Paris, Editions du Seuil, 1963. In practice every increase in the number of organizational levels ("vertical differentiation") calls for decentralization. See Blau and Meyer, *Bureaucracy in Modern Society*, p. 93.

32. See Hall, *Organizations*, p. 133.

33. Technicians and professionals have internalized the rules and norms such that control is superfluous (see Pugh et al., "The Context of Organizational Structure").

34. In Europe this strategy apparently does not always affect the enterprise's structure (see Lawrence S. Franko, "The Move toward a Multidivisional Structure in European Organizations," *Administrative Science Quarterly*, vol. 19, no. 4, December 1974, p. 495).

35. We remind the reader that our research concentrated on large enterprises (with sales of over 10 billion lire annually). Firms with between 1,000 and 2,500 employees are the smallest in our sample.

36. We followed Chandler's criterion which defines the multidivisional structure as decentralized (see *Strategy and Structure*, in particular chapter 1). The definition is plausible in light of the fact that this type of structure creates units which are autonomous (differentiated by the activities and problems they handle) and self-sufficient (in that each contains all the services necessary to fulfill its function).

37. The change in FIAT's organizational structure toward a multidivisional system occurred in 1970 without substantial changes either in size or the number of products produced. However, such drastic change in the type of work relations and in the degree of autonomy has always been the result of the will of the power holders in the organization. It is obvious that such a decision, which implies considerable transition problems, is made only if it is believed that the firm requires such adjustments. Italian firms find themselves in a transition phase, and some firms have been more responsive to the need for change.

38. See Meyer, "The Two Authority Structures," p. 211, and Blau and Meyer, *Bureaucracy in Modern Society*.

39. In addition to the difference among hierarchical levels, the discrepancy already observed continues; the upper and middle levels are very similar with regard to degree of autonomy, but only those in the former group have a chance of being consulted on policy matters.

40. The analysis once again returns to the issue of the greater financial risk that technologically advanced industry runs and to the fact that the top tends to delegate the decisions on technical problems but not on large-scale innovations.

41. R. H. Hall points out (*Organization*, p. 133) that in large organizations, low-level managers and operational units are able to increase their power. Our comparison of size with decision-making power does not confirm this statement. Only when we add the variable of multidivisional structure does the impact of size become visible.

42. In practice, few people wish to participate in solving highly specialized problems. Instead, the nonspecialist, general character of policy decisions and their impact on all organizational members attracts the interest of many people; the results of widespread consultation may be disappointing. March points out that the higher the number of participants in a solution to a problem, the more the solution becomes impossible. See James G. March and Johan P. Olsen, *Ambiguity and Choice in Organizations*, Bergen, Universitets-forlaget, 1976.

43. This statement is serious because it seems to justify the exclusion from global decisions not only of managers but also of employees in general. It conflicts with the participatory systems currently in use in many European countries (such as co-determination and workers' councils in Germany, Holland, Yugoslavia, and the Scandinavian countries; workers' participation on boards of directors in Austria, Germany, and the Scandinavian countries; also, more recently, the development of factory councils (*Consigli di Fabbrica*) in Italy). The success of a participatory system requires training and information, two factors that the top echelons are often reluctant to grant in their effort to maintain a monopoly over decision making.

44. See Heflebower, "Observation in Decentralization," p. 207.

45. This situation should prevent an excess degree of decentralization, of the sort that could destroy the organization. See Harbison and Myers, *Management in the Industrial World*, p. 44.

46. According to Crozier, the power of an individual within the organization depends on the control that he is capable of exercising over a "source of uncertainty" that affects the attainment of an organizational goal. See Michel Crozier, *La société bloquée*, Paris, Editions du Seuil, 1970, chapter 1, "Du problème du pouvoir dans les sociétés avancées," pp. 27-46.

A strategy used to acquire power consists in what March and Simon describe as the absorption of uncertainty. This involves gathering a mass of information, drawing conclusions from it, and then passing on only the conclusions. The person receiving the conclusions therefore is unable to check their validity since he does not have the opportunity to examine the underlying data. See James G. March and Herbert A. Simon, *Organizations*, New York, John Wiley, 1967, pp. 165-66.

47. See Harold J. Leavitt, "Unhuman Organization," *Harvard Business Review*, vol. 40, 1962, pp. 90-98; see also G. Strauss, "Some Notes on Participation:Fact or Fancy, Power Equalization," in Harold J. Leavitt, ed., *The Social Science of Organization*, Englewood Cliffs, N.J., Prentice-Hall, 1963, pp. 41-84.

48. Another advantage of the meetings, mentioned by the managers interviewed, is that they are a way to keep up-to-date. Some low-level managers, complaining about their scanty knowledge of corporate programs and their own narrow perspective, limited to their specific field of operations, have suggested that "The best way for keeping up-to-date is an effective system of information to allow greater participation in corporate life." Also, "It is necessary to spread information and ideas." And, "By becoming acquainted at meetings with what is occurring in other departments, the manager develops a broad-scale view of organizational problems."

49. In fact "vertical relations" can become "diagonal" relative to the organizational chart. That is, the manager comes into contact with higher ranking managers to whom, however, he does not report. (See diagram in Figure 4.19c, where the relation between A and B is diagonal and ascendant, located outside the hierarchical channels of communication.)

50. This in spite of the fact that the fifty firms in our example are among the largest Italian firms, all of which are characterized by that degree of organizational complexity which should suggest the need for collegial decision making.

51.   Degree of Personal Influence at Meetings:
              Manager's Perception (in %)

Does not participate in meetings	4
Has little or no influence	6
Exercises some influence	27
Exercises considerable influence	63
	100

52.   Areas of Influence:
              Manager's Perception (in %)

Does not participate in meetings	4
No influence	2
Own department only	31
Other departments	56
Entire firm	7
	100

53.   Factors of Personal Influence:
              Manager's Perception (in %)

Experience and professional competence	84

Hierarchical position	12
Seniority in the company	4
	100

54.   Distribution of Managers according to
Focus of Meetings Attended (in %)

Departmental	31
Interdepartmental	26
Corporate-wide	43
	100

55. Figure 4.21 refers only to contacts made by middle- and lower-level managers. The upper-level managers are necessarily excluded from the analysis, because the only possible ascendant vertical relation—that with the CEO—is always hierarchical for them.

56. The same does not occur for participation in policy making. While participation in company-wide meetings considerably changes the power situation of the upper managerial level, it does not affect the other levels. Yet the difficulty is increased, mainly at the upper level, of distinguishing whether decision-making power or participation in meetings is the independent variable. One could suppose that the selection of those invited to the meetings is made on the basis of their actual decision-making power. Participation at meetings could therefore be seen as a consequence and not a determinant of their power situation. However, we believe such participation is decisive for the lower level because it permits them to exert an influence that would ordinarily be denied them.

57. As we shall see later, delegation of power varies also according to changes in corporate events. For example, it is influenced by market expansion (see Figure 4.28).

58. The Italian multinational's behavior is particularly interesting because unlike the foreign one, it is still often family owned and run. (The enterprises examined include such multinationals as FIAT, Pirelli, Buitoni, and Ferrero— all family businesses.) Hence, this type of firm is influenced by its dual nature. While objective factors such as size and geographical dispersion may force upon it the same approach as the non-Italian multinational's, its internal style makes its choices closer to those made by the patrimonial enterprise.

59. In a study of a country closer to Italy from the point of view of industrial development, we found that more mature private firms are now entirely led by professional management. However the owner continues to exercise control as chairman of the board or through the investment bank he owns. Thus the third- and fourth-generation entrepreneur continues to oversee corporate development although in a different way, but concerns himself primarily with financial activities and relations with industry, banks, and politicians. See Flavia Derossi, *The Mexican Entrepreneur*, Paris, OECD, 1970.

60. Concerning the impossibility of the exercise of control by those who

are outside the firm and do not possess the necessary technical knowledge, see chapter 2.

61. However, in his capacity as president of a firm he has not been considered in our study because he does not fall within the Italian legal and union definition of manager. Similarly, the other "technocrats" of private enterprise (the Agnellis, the Pirellis, the Marzottos, etc.) have not been included because of their substantial share of ownership.

62. Considered as such when sales have increased more than 15% over the preceding year.

63. C. Wright Mills, *The Power Elite*, New York, Oxford University Press, 1959, p. 135.

64. The differences are not statistically significant.

65. This category includes: the perception of the requirements of the managerial job; the most important incentives in one's work; the criteria on the basis of which the manager believes he is judged; the usefulness of unionized representation for the managers; professional risks; the opportunity for career advancement; and changes occurring in management relationships with employees.

66. We asked each manager to rank his profession on a scale of jobs that are similar in salary and university training (see chapter 6).

CHAPTER 5

1. Corporate authority is defined as the right and the power to act. It is conceived as directed toward the bottom of the organization. It flows from the very top of the corporation, reaching management through a process of delegation, and is exercised by managers toward the lower portion of the hierarchical ladder. As the term is generally used, authority is usually connected to a hierarchical system. See Joseph L. Massie, "Management Theory," in James G. March, *Handbook of Organizations*, Chicago, Rand McNally, 1965, p. 402. In the words of Robert K. Merton, "Authority, the power of control which derives from an acknowledged status, inheres in the office and not in the particular person who performs the official role" (*Social Theory and Social Structure*, Glencoe, Ill., The Free Press, 1957, p. 195). What we are examining in this chapter is therefore an authority derived from position, as distinct from other types of authority, such as charismatic authority and that conferred from legitimation (described by Weber) and authority deriving from competence.

2. See F. H. Harbison and C. A. Myers, in the chapter "The Executive as Rule Maker," in *Management in the Industrial World*, New York, McGraw-Hill, 1959, p. 47.

3. Ibid., p. 48.

4. Ibid., p. 47.

5. See James M. March and Herbert A. Simon, *Organizations*, New York, John Wiley, 1967, p. 90.

Weber states that factory discipline is based on submission to power; that one cannot overlook the concept of a power relation simply because it emerged from a formal contract which the worker freely signed. See Max Weber, "I Tipi del Potere," in Franco Ferrarotti, ed., *La Sociologia del Potere*, Bari, Laterza, 1972, p. 5.

6. See Sheldon S. Wolin's critique of the majority of organizational theorists, "A Critique of Organization Theories," in Amitai Etzioni, ed., *A Sociological Reader on Complex Organizations*, New York, Holt, Rinehart, 1961, p. 134. But perhaps these theorists limited themselves to describing the status quo, a situation that probably prompted the protest against authority that we will describe later.

7. Cf. Eugene E. Jennings, *The Executive in Crisis*, East Lansing, Mi., Michigan State University, 1965, p. 122.

8. Adapting to an organization is easier for the technostructure: "Here both the illusion and the fact of power are greatest. The individual will have increasing reason to feel that, by serving the organization, he can align it more closely with his own goals . . . And his higher position in the hierarchy will contribute to his impression of power" (John Kenneth Galbraith, *The New Industrial State*, Boston, Houghton Mifflin, 1968, p. 57). According to Etzioni, the *higher participants* (those occupying high positions in the organization) can be distinguished from *lower participants* from three points of view: a. the nature of the involvement; b. subordination; c. performance obligations.

	Nature of involvement (direction and intensity)	Subordination	Performance obligations
Employees (lower participants)	low, negative or positive	average	limited
Managers (higher participants)	high, positive	high	high

See Amitai Etzioni, "A Basis for Comparative Analysis of Complex Organizations," in Amitai Etzioni, ed., *A Sociological Reader on Complex Organizations*, New York, Holt, Rinehart, 1961, p. 75.

9. Identification is a process by which an individual's decisions are inspired more by the objectives of the organization or the group than by his personal goals. See Herbert A. Simon, *Administrative Behavior*, New York, Macmillan, 1957, p. 204-14.

10. Jennings points out the positive attitude toward authority and its representatives on the part of the middle class (*Executive in Crisis*, p. 123). Acceptance of rank-based authority varies according to culture: for example, the exceptional stability of management and the docility of workers in Germany are seen as the result of cultural models that value discipline and respect for authority. See Heinz Hartman, "Authority and Organization in German Management," in Stanley M. D. Davis, ed., *Organizational and Cultural Perspectives*, New York, Prentice-Hall, 1971, p. 408.

11. In the Fall of 1969, a full year after the French revolt of 1968, and

during a period of social unrest of international dimensions, Italian workers and students initiated a series of violent mass demonstrations against public and private authorities, demanding major changes in public policies and in the internal organization of firms.

This episode, referred to in Italy as the "Hot Autumn," produced a major shift in worker-management relations and indeed a different attitude on the part of employees toward authority, whatever its source.

An official document issued on February 1970 by the National Industrialist Association's special working committee acknowledged the shift of Italian society from a static hierarchical system to a flexible society having several power centers. It described the unrest and tensions as a search for a new power equilibrium; it recognized as a joint concern of business and labor unions the resolution of some social problems, such as the economic development of the Southern depressed areas, low-cost housing, and the improvement of transportation and educational and health services.

In May 1970 a law called "The New Employees' Bill of Rights" (better known in Italy as the "Statuto dei Lavoratori") dictated norms protecting "employees' freedom and dignity" and union activities within the plant. The law abolished company controls over workers' political, religious, and union affiliations, and sick absences (which were checked by the company physician). Article 18 forbids all nonmotivated dismissals of employees. While the first provision is seen by Italian industrialists as responsible for the extremely high absenteeism rate, the second had the effect of totally freezing employment.

12. For the two definitions, see Etzioni's classification in "A Basis for Comparative Analysis," p. 61.

Alvin Gouldner distinguished two types of organization: the representative organization and the organization centering on punishment. See *Patterns of Industrial Bureaucracy*, Glencoe, Ill., The Free Press, 1954.

Though one cannot define the Italian firm as solely *punitive*, neither is it *representative*.

13. Only in the first years of the postwar period do we find comparable situations. However, the majority of managers (who average 45 years of age) did not experience that period.

14. In firms in which union conflict levels (measured by the comparison between numbers of days lost due to strikes during the year of the interviews and the days lost in the preceding year) were decreasing, there was also a decrease in the percentage of managers who felt their authority had drastically diminished (nonetheless the figures remain very high):

Union conflict in firm	Managers declaring there has been a crisis of authority (%)
Decreasing	62
Stationary	69
Increasing	80

15. The simultaneous rebellion of the manager's children and his subordi-

nates had a shocking, but often beneficial, impact on the manager's revision of the concept of authority. The analogy between children and workers occurred frequently during the interviews, but not by chance, since in both cases we find a similar authority relationship and emotional involvement. "Today it is difficult to be understood even by one's own children," commented an interviewee in his fifties.

16. Perceived Changes in the Concept of Authority
(in %, *n* = 655)

Authority has not changed	10
Authority has partially changed (only for older or authoritarian managers or those in contact with blue-collar workers)	19
Changes have occurred at the individual level	9
The nature of authority has changed for everyone following:	
1. workers' reactions and union pressures	15
2. a crisis in traditional corporate values (the end of authoritarianism)	29
3. a crisis in the entire society which encompasses firms	18
	100

17. Location of Causes of and Solutions to Union Conflict — Managers' Perceptions (in %, *n* = 595)*

The firm	15
The workers and the unions	12
The firm and the unions	32
The lack of effective government action	22
The firm and the government	5
The unions and the government	6
The firm, the unions, and the government	8
	100

*There are 46 nonresponses, to which can be added 11 interviewees who do not believe that their firm experienced conflict.

18. During the survey, we asked several union leaders to evaluate the attitude that each of the 50 firms in the sample displayed toward unions. Four different groups were distinguished:

a. Firms that had always been "closed" to a dialogue with the unions;

b. Firms that were partially "open" to a dialogue;

c. Firms that have a long tradition of propensity for dialogue;

d. Firms that "opened up" only after 1969, under the pressure of the strikes.

The managers report that the greatest change in their relations with subordinates occurred in these last firms, which began by refusing to recognize the union or enter into dialogue with subordinates, but later modified their policies. This unexpected "opening up" was accompanied by the equally unpredictable decrease in discretionary power the managers enjoyed vis-à-vis their subordinates.

19.

| | | Firms' attitudes toward the unions | | |
	Closed	Partially open	Open before '68	Open after '68
Managers perceiving a crisis in corporate values (%)	27	27	30	41

20. "The underlying mistake was to have not understood that refusal to discuss issues with the unions not only weakened the unions but also deprived the firm of the opportunity for dialogue through a valid intermediary; that such a refusal was to unleash uncontrolled forces at the base, which would then end up subverting the system." (Comment by an interviewee.)

21. "It was like September the eighth [the day Italy withdrew from World War II and the army was left without clear orders]. Everyone had to make decisions by himself." "We all had the sensation of being trapped: on one side, there were the external pressures, and within the firm, a wall through which no directives passed." "We felt disoriented."

22. "What happened to the managers is what happens to the father who is stern with his children while the mother gives in on everything. The firm yelled that it was necessary to stick to one's principles, then it gave in precisely on those principles, overriding our authority and making us lose face."

23. It is interesting to note that these comments were made by managers who are relatively old, about 50 years of age. Not all managers deplore the loss of power: "One can no longer use the whip nor exercise favoritism, and this is good." "The Employees' Bill of Rights has made workers aware of the fact that they are human beings." ". . . Because of the Employees' Bill of Rights, the manager can no longer commit abuses. Now he must show the validity of his decisions. He is affected more by the bottom echelons. If he makes decisions unacceptable to workers, he risks a twenty-four hour strike. The atmosphere of rebellion has forced him to meditate on decisions and avoid excesses and arbitrary acts."

24. Jennings notes that a system based on authority is fundamental to the satisfaction of what is perhaps the strongest need of any manager—the protection and reinforcement of his image (*Executive in Crisis*, p. 123).

25. Probably our managers would see themselves in a description coined by *Le Monde* (May 21, 1970) for their French peers: "The nation's unbeloved" ("les mal- aimés de la nation").

26. We might have expected, for example, that those who do not attribute prestige to the managerial profession were at lower hierarchical levels.

27. That reasons for different perceptions of prestige are to be found outside personal characteristics is suggested by the fact that decision makers and strategists cannot be distinguished in this case from their colleagues handling routine and tactical decisions.

28. Level of conflict is measured in terms of the ratio of hours lost for strikes on the total manpower. On firms' labor union policies see section 5.2. Degree of unionization is measured by the percentage of workers enrolled in unions.

29. For an analysis of stress in normal managerial activity, see Robert L. Kahn et al., *Organizational Stress: Studies in Role Conflict and Ambiguity*, Wiley, New York, 1964.

30. Only a fourth of managers did not experience changes in the tasks they carry out.

30.   Changes in the Job (Cited by Managers)
                        (in %, *n* = 660)

No change	26
Recent transferral to the job	10
Job nonexistent earlier, recently created (independently of corporate changes)	1
Job recently created, following corporate changes	15
Job changed due to its own internal dynamics	4
Job changed following corporate changes	44
	100

31. Only in 4% of cases is the change perceived as negative, while 3% of managers report they experienced undesirable effects offset by positive ones.

                    Content of Job Changes
                        (in %, *n* = 659)

There have been no changes, or the manager was only recently transferred to the job.	52
Changes welcome to the manager:	
1. increased importance	24
2. greater professionalization and/or rationality of job	12
3. greater decision-making latitude and increased importance	5
Changes unwelcome to the manager:	
reduced latitude in making decisions and/or decreased importance	4
Changes producing mixed reactions:	
1. reduced latitude in making decisions but increased importance	1
2. reduced latitude in making decisions but greater professionalization and/or rationality of job	2
	100

32.   Forecast of Future Changes in the Job
                (in %, *n* = 635)

Does not foresee changes	35

Does not know or cannot predict content	16
Changes welcome to the manager:	
1. increased importance	27
2. greater professionalization and/or rationality of job	13
3. greater decision making latitude and increased importance	5
Changes unwelcome to the manager:	
reduced latitude in making decisions and/or decreased importance	2
Changes producing mixed reactions:	
1. reduced latitude in making decisions but increased importance	1
2. reduced latitude in making decisions but greater professionalization and/or rationality of job	1
	100

33. These and subsequent comments originate from managers belonging to different age and hierarchical levels.

34. It is interesting to note that these observations do not stem, as one might expect, from managers in technologically advanced firms, but mostly from firms using simple technology. They were made by managers from a variety of departments, from production to sales to personnel.

35. Differing attitudes seem to have translated into concrete changes in relationships with subordinates, at least according to reports given by interviewees. Only 6% of managers retained the old attitudes towards subordinates, and remained authoritarian; 16% believes that the change is limited to certain groups; the majority believes that they have established a "democratic" type of relationship with their subordinates.

Changes in Relationships with Workers:
Managers' Perceptions
(in %, n = 658)

No change	0
Persistence of authoritarianism	6
The firm has a long tradition of democratic relations	9
Changes imposed by the situation, more than by conviction	43
Movement towards relationships based on collaboration: delegation of power and greater responsibility	42
	100

CHAPTER 6

1. See Flavia Derossi, "A Profile of Italian Managers in Large Firms,"

in J. J. Boddewyn, ed., *European Industrial Managers West and East*, White Plains, M. E. Sharpe, 1976, p. 144-208.

2.

Incentives	Younger managers (25-40 years old)	Older managers (51-65 years old)
Recognition of ability	16	42
Self-determination	37	30
Participation in policy making	45	26
Increased salary	2	2
	100	100

3. One way to extend one's influence tangibly is to increase the number of one's subordinates; this indirectly increases the importance of the person in charge of the entire department.

4. From our question about participation in associations we ascertained that only 6 percent of the managers interviewed had ever played an active role in associations.

5. From 1967 on CIDA became part of CNEL (National Economic and Work Committee), the National Economic Council, CNR (National Research Committee), and participated on a consultant basis at ministerial meetings (in particular with the Ministry of Work). It deals also with international organizations, such as the ILO (International Labor Organization), the EEC (European Economic Community) etc.

6. Nevertheless, Talcott Parsons, while not equating the businessman with the independent professional, does not share the belief that the businessman has an "egoistic" attitude and the professional an "altruistic" one. He pinpoints some elements that are common to the two activities, e.g., "rationality, functional specificity, and universalism" ("Professions and Business Management," in Howard M. Vollmer and Donald L. Mills, eds., *Professionalization*, Englewood Cliffs, N.J., Prentice-Hall, 1966, pp. 56-58).

7. Cf. Morris L. Cogan, "Toward a Definition of Profession," *Harvard Educational Review*, vol. 23, Winter 1953, p. 49.

8. Cf. George Strauss, "Professionalism and Occupational Associations," *Industrial Relations*, vol. 2, no. 3, May 1963, p. 9.

9. Louis D. Brandeis, "Business: a Profession," in Ernest Dale, ed., *Readings in Management*, New York, McGraw-Hill, 1975, p. 371. While Brandeis recognizes that the free professional is in fact rewarded on the basis of his professional success, he notes that the professional does not consider financial rewards as a measure of success. Yet, he adds that the same attitude can be found in the businessman, for whom profit is a "side-effect" of success. For him, just as for the free professional, the true measure of success is given by the excellence of performance.

10. William J. Goode, "Community within a Community: the Professions," in *The Study of Society*, New York, Random House, 1967, p. 579.

11. Robert MacIver, "The Social Significance of Professional Ethics," in Vollmer and Mills, eds., *Professionalization*, p. 51.

12. Goode, "Community within a Community," pp. 580-81; see also Mac-

Iver, "Social Significance," p. 53. MacIver adds that, in order to provide an effective guideline, the professional ethic must take into account the specific ethical standards of the community in which the professional group operates (*ibid.*, p. 55).

13. Other societies more industrially advanced than Italy's have gone through these dilemmas but nonetheless have not experienced such open conflicts. In *The American Business Creed* it is stated that "The managerial definition of business responsibilities leaves the businessman at sea without a compass. The moral responsibilities towards others are numerous, conflicting, and incommensurable. By what standards shall he weigh competing moral obligations in making his decisions? It is not accidental that the codes of managerial behavior which appear in ideology are extremely vague." The authors add that the code of ethics is full of concepts lacking operational meaning, such as "fair salaries," or "prices as low as corporate needs will allow" and such others. See F. Sutton, S. E. Harris, C. Kaysen, and J. Tobin, *The American Business Creed*, Cambridge, Mass., Harvard University Press, 1956, p. 358.

14. Article 1 in the 1975 contract states: "Managers are employees for whom the conditions of subordination as laid down in Art. 2094 of the Civil Code are valid. The role they play in the firms is characterized by a high degree of professionalism, autonomy, and decision-making power; they perform their functions with the goal of promoting, coordinating, and managing the achievement of the firm's objectives."

15. See *Realta*, July 7-14, 1975.

16. *Realta*, January 6-13, 1975.

17. *Realta*, July 7-14, 1975.

18. *Realta*, August 4—September 1, 1975.

The definition given in the national contract signed in the same year for managers of commercial firms is less restrictive: "Managers are those people who report directly to the entrepreneur or to another executive delegated by him; they carry out corporate functions with broad autonomy, discretion and initiative; they are endowed with the power to convey orders to the entire firm or to an autonomous unit in it; they must be considered direct collaborators of the firm's general management."

19. The Arbitration Committee was already provided in the 1970 contract, but this time its functions are more clearly specified. Currently there exist 66 Arbiters' Boards, according to the number of regional unions that are members in FNDAI.

20. In the July 6, 1972 decree, the Constitutional Court judged in favor of the exclusion of managers from the "just cause" giving the reason that the relationship that binds the manager to the employer and the board of directors is based on trust.

21. The fact that the delegation of power is an ongoing process, bound to increase with time as new managers are recruited, is indicated by the fact that the number of decision makers is greater among younger managers (29-40 years old); the percentage of these is greater than the percentage of decision makers found among older managers (30% compared to 19%). Yet many

young managers have not yet had time to reach the higher levels of the hierarchy; as one might have expected, there are more older managers at the upper managerial level than young managers (32% compared to 19%). Despite their lower hierarchical rank, which puts them at a great disadvantage, the new generation of managers succeeds nonetheless in exercising greater decision-making power.

22. In the January 6-13, 1975 issue of *Realtà* (a date that precedes the contract), the FNDAI presented "a request for participation of managers in the formulation of corporate policy in cooperation with the RSA." However, Article 18 in the contract, although it introduces the issue of the institution of union representation for managers, reduces its function to the defense of corporative rights. Indeed, " . . . during the first hearing of a case, the managers' union representatives will be allowed to examine any questions concerning the application of contractual norms, therein included those relative to the qualifications of a manager as put forth by Article 1 of the present contract." As we see, we are a long way from discussing the manager's role in a firm's general policies! This phrasing remained unchanged in the 1979 contract.

23. Another possibility would be to let managers participate in a control body such as the Vigilance Council of the German co-management system as in the new law of July 1, 1978, for firms employing more than 2,000 people.

24. Article 7 of the RSA statute proposes to obtain the right to receive information systematically and be consulted on all aspects of an enterprise's activities, on work-related problems and corporate problems . . ." (point e); " . . . effective participation of managers in the formulation of strategies concerning growth, production, organizational plans, and corporate policies . . ." (point d).

25. Midy-Chimica's RSA in Melzo obtained approval of a different system to divide annual salary (13 monthly installments instead of 15). At the DeAngeli Institute in Milan, the RSA of managers obtained an increase in the managers' expense account based on the recognition that a portion of the expenses cannot be documented. The Montedison RSA won a corporation-backed social security fund (*Espansione*, July-August 1977, p. 38).

26. The RSA for the IRI Central Management disapproved of the creation of the 5th steel plant center in Gioia Tauro. The Alfa Sud RSA formulated proposals on corporate organization (ibid.).

27. An example of the first case can be found in the ANIC RSA's request that proposals for divestiture of some sectors be subjected to the approval of every employee, or that ANIC create a Strategy Committee for the examination of new corporate policy. But the IRI RSA's attempt to influence the appointment of their new CEO or the refusal of ENI managers to let politicians be appointed to high management positions could have a narrower scope.

28. The "Consiglio di Fabbrica," an offspring of the 1969 labor movement, consists of elected representatives of the employees and *must* be consulted by top management on every major company change.

29. At Alfa Romeo the Plant Committee accepted managers' presence

at production conferences only under the label "political representatives" (and not as representatives of their corporate function).

30. These and following comments are taken from the interviews and were made mostly by middle-level managers.

31. This attitude is not unique to the Italian manager. In fact, it can be found in many industrial countries in which the majority of interested parties would consider membership in a manager's union antithetical to the profession.

32. See chapter 5, Figure 5.1.

33. Thus, another image invoked by managers is that of "a monster with five heads."

34. Indeed, the industrial managers, who dominate with 59% of the membership (and make up 49% of the board), are looked upon with suspicion by the other, smaller groups.

35. Rather than the local federations, whose development is hindered by lack of finances from the center, one should note some voluntary, independent associations such as ALDAI (Lombard Association of Industrial Corporate Management) and its journal, *Dirigenti Industria* (Business Managers); or the UDDA (Democratic Union of Managers in Lombard firms) and its journal, *Dirigenti Impresa Politica* (Managers, Politics, Enterprise), which recently have shown considerable vigor.

36. This and following comments were made by managers in middle and low-level hierarchical positions.

37. FENDAC (the Confederation of Commercial Managers) accepted the concept of dialogues with cadres in its two last national assemblies (1976, 1977). The reasons for the different attitudes are many. The 9,000 commercial managers are closer in terms of insurance benefits to white-collar workers, with whom they share similar work. The typically small commercial firms are less stratified than industrial firms, and attribute less importance to hierarchy. The small group of commercial managers would gain an advantage if it were enlarged by admitting the cadres.

38. This appears to be the position of UDDA (the Democratic Union of Managers in Lombard firms), the most liberal of the independent associations.

39. In addition to the increase in minimum salary, the 1975 contract adds devices for automatic salary increases and increases based on seniority. The policy of increasing salaries according to seniority, typical of lower jobs, now appears to compensate the managers for their slower and less secure careers (one of the effects of the economic crisis). However, it contrasts with professional attitudes emphasizing merit over length of service.

40. Robin Marris, *The Economic Theory of Managerial Capitalism*, Glencoe, Ill., Free Press, 1964, p. 52-53.

41. For the moment it seems to be expressed primarily in UDDA. However, this front-rank group is small (note that the Milan UDDA has 400 members).

42. The stages in this evolution have been summarized by Lido Vanni in "Dirigenti e impresa: quale sistema?" *L'Impresa*, 2, 1977.

CHAPTER 7

1. Abraham Zaleznik, "Power and Politics in Organizational Life," *Harvard Business Review*, May-June 1970, p. 48.

2. In theory it is possible to conceive of an organization having a non-pyramidal structure, based little or not at all on hierarchy and authority, and in which the decision-making process is diffused. On a small scale, a successful experiment in purely functional organization is provided by the mixed work groups, whose participants come from various departments and are selected on the basis of their technical competence. Group members are not hierarchically connected—subordination is replaced by a horizontal relationship. Because of his temporary appointment, the program manager behaves more like a coordinator than like a superior.

3. Frank A. Heller, *Managerial Decision-Making: A Study of Leadership Styles and Power-Sharing among Senior Managers*, London, Tavistock, 1971, p. 38.

4. Participation of parties not having a direct stake in a decision is costly in terms of time and money (in that the consultants must temporarily be removed from their usual tasks).

5. Heller, *Managerial Decision-Making*, p. 38. One analyst of how workers' committees function in Yugoslavia and Holland stresses the role played by technical knowledge. When expertise is absent, participation paradoxically increases the distance between management (possessing the expertise) and workers' representatives (who lose power). See Mauk Mulder, "Reduction of Power Differences," in Geert Hofstede and M. Sami Lassen, eds., *European Contributions to Organization Theory*, Amsterdam, Van Gorcum. 1976, p. 85, and Mauk Mulder, *The Daily Power Game*, Leiden, Nijhoff, 1977.

6. It is nevertheless possible to conceive of an organization whose criteria for success are not productivity and market conquests, but instead the integration, satisfaction, development of skills, and active participation of its members. However, for this to come about, particular economic conditions are necessary, conditions which are seldom found in capitalist countries. In order to reduce the importance of market survival and thus production costs, there must be no competition for the internal market and little need to win foreign markets. The lack of national competition can usually occur only in a planned economy, in which every productive unit has its assigned task and thus is not interfered with by others. Production covers internal needs and is probably less diversified; prices are set by a central agency and do not compete with each other; there is no need for advertising because the consumer does not have a choice and because there is no surplus production; producers are protected by protectionist tariffs or by blocked imports. The productivity of an organization that does not give priority to rationality and costs, but rewards integration, individual satisfaction, and participation, is not necessarily low, especially over a long time. The starting time for a participatory system is lengthy, and such a system initially entails greater costs. In time, however, such an organization can prove itself more productive than the autocratic one, because of a number of factors which we will briefly mention:

a. the positive correlation between satisfaction and productivity;

b. the elimination of bottlenecks and difficulties where and when they occur, through the worker's or work group's initiative, without having to appeal to a bureaucratic decision-making apparatus. Thus a problem does not have to bounce along checkpoints in the hierarchical ladder with resultant delays in finding a solution.

c. the elimination or reduction of factors impinging on productivity, such as absenteeism, turnover, and, mainly, conflict.

d. the liberation of that part of human ability that concentrates on problems related to competition (market analyses, advertising, parapolitical relationships) and on appeasing tensions and conflicts. Usually a firm finds itself in a position of struggle, vis-à-vis the external world, trying to expand or maintain its existent share of national or international markets; within its walls, the firm suffers to the effects of labor unrest. The energy and skills absorbed in these activities, when released, can be dedicated to the solution of other problems.

7. See Harvey Leibenstein, "Entrepreneurship and Development," *American Economic Review*, vol. 58, no. 2, p. 72.

8. See James G. March and Herbert A. Simon, *Organizations*, New York, John Wiley, 1967, pp. 169-71.

9. Charles Perrow, *Complex Organizations: a Critical Essay*, Glenville, Ill. Scott, Foresman, 1972, p. 13.

10. Richard M. Cyert and James G. March, *A Behavioral Theory of the Firm*, Englewood Cliffs, N.J., Prentice Hall, 1963, pp. 27-29.

11. R. A. Gordon, *Business Leadership in the Large Corporation*, Berkeley, Ca., University of California Press, 1966, p. 95.

12. *Ibid.*, p. 95.

13. *Ibid.*, p. 98.

14. Several Italian newspapers are owned by large private and state-owned industrial corporations.

15. According to Mulder, there exists an increased tolerance for power, just as for drugs. Greater "consumption" has the effect of increasing the desire for it, while the person who does not experience it is less motivated to taste it. Two different mechanisms are created: influential individuals tend to increase or at least maintain distances between them and less powerful individuals (*downward power distance mechanism*); b. the amount of efforts applied by the subordinate to reduce such a distance diminishes with the growth of power inequality between the two groups (*upward power distance mechanism*). The effect is the polarization of any given social system into two groups having unequal shares of power and different attitudes toward it. (The less powerful tend to accept the leadership of the powerful, even when the latter have obtained authority through illegitimate means.) (See Mauk Mulder, "Reduction of Power Differences, p. 79.) Furthermore, the motivation to acquire power is one of the characteristics of a successful manager. However this is a case of an "altruistic" exercise of power applied to attain not personal goals, but those of the organization. (See David McClelland and David H. Burnham, "Power is the Great Motivator," *Harvard Business Review*, March-April 1976, pp. 100-10.)

16. Norman Martin and John H. Sims, "Power Tactics," *Harvard Business Review*, November-December 1956, p. 25.

17. "Coping with uncertainty is the variable most critical to power and the best single predictor of it." C. R. Hining et al., "Structural Conditions of Inter-organizational Power," *Administrative Science Quarterly*, March 1974.

18. Michel Crozier, *La société bloquée*, Paris, Editions du Seuil, 1970, p. 38.

19. The distortion that communication undergoes in climbing the hierarchical ladder is attributed both to excessive professional specialization and deliberate falsification of data. See James G. March, "Business Decision-Making," in H. Leavitt, ed., *Readings in Managerial Psychology*, Chicago, University of Chicago Press, 1964, p. 453.

20. C. Wright Mills, *White Collar: The American Middle Class*, London, Oxford University Press, 1951, p. 103; See also Jean Meynaud, *La tecnocrazia Mito o realtà*, Bari, Laterza, 1966, p. 261.

21. William Tousijn, "Il problema del potere dei tecnici. La conoscenza come fattore di produzione," *L'impresa*, July-August 1972, p. 286.

22. *Ibid.*

23. Business schools, which are often financed by firms, instead of teaching the values of the new technocracy, mainly transmit the attitudes of current management.

24. Michele Salvati, "Note sulla rivoluzione industriale," *Problemi del Socialismo*, November-December 1965, p. 915.

25. Cf. Brown, "The Controllers of British Industry."

26. "Large profits are required to achieve the position necessary to gain access to capital markets, and more generally, to easily obtain any form of financing . . . The other great bond of the capitalist market is to impose on firms the need for maximum development. In the fact of economic cycles, future profits and the solidity of the enterprise depend on development" (Salvati, "Note sulla rivoluzione industriale," p. 915).

"The conduct of the large corporation . . . whether under management control or ownership control, is largely determined by the market structure —the nature of competition, products produced and the constraints of the capital markets. Growth, sales, technical efficiency, a strong competitive position are at once inseparable managerial goals and the determinants of high corporate profits. . ." (Zeitlin, "Corporate Ownership," p. 1096).

27. Cheit, "New Place of Business," in Earl Cheit, ed., *The Business Establishment*, New York, Wiley, 1964, p. 179.

28. Robert J. Larner, *Management Control and the Large Corporation*, Cambridge, Mass., Dunellen, 1970. Michael Barrett Brown's research on English firms demonstrated that those controlled by management obtained higher profits than those managed by owners ("The Controllers of British Industry").

29. Professional managers are recruited with the goal of bringing corporate profits above the level achieved by owners. Everyone expects, therefore, that the manager would be more profit-oriented than the stockholder. It follows that, "The essence of the professional manager is his rigorous and exclusive

dedication to financial values." R. E. Pahl and J. T. Winkler, "The Economic Elite: Theory and Practice," in Philips Stanworth and Anthony Giddens, eds., *Elites and Power in British Society*, Cambridge, Cambridge University Press, 1974, p. 118.

30. Leonard Silk and David Vogel, *Profits and Ethics: The Crisis of Confidence in American Industry*, New York, Simon & Schuster, 1976, ,p. 202.

31. Villarejo, "Stock Ownership." In a study of the 200 largest firms, M. P. Allen found that, on the average, the chief executive officers owned stock worth over a million and a half dollars ("Management Control," p. 891). A recent study on the heads of the 500 largest enterprises found that 90% owned stock in the firm they were managing. In 30% of cases, the amount of shares owned was significant, as the stock value exceeded a million dollars (Burch, *Managerial Revolution Reassessed*, p. 176; also data in Nader, Green, and Seligman, *Taming the Giant Corporation*, p. 116).

32. Cheit, "New Place of Business," p. 178.

33. See also Flavia Derossi, "A Profile of Italian Managers in Large Firms," in J. J. Boddewyn, ed., *European Industrial Managers East and West*, White Plains, M. E. Sharpe, 1976, pp. 144-208.

34. Mills, *White Collar*, p. 102.

35. Theodore B. Bottomore, *Classes in Modern Society*, New York, Pantheon, 1966, p. 72.

36. An item in the questionnaire concerned differences between managers in private enterprises and state-owned firms.

37. C. Wright Mills, *The Power Elite*, New York, Oxford University Press, 1959, pp. 269, 297. Meynaud followed with, "The basic point in the notion of a managerial class is that it presupposes . . . an organization, or even a co-ordination of efforts" (*La tecnocrazia*, p. 263).

38. "One error which pervades this interpretation of the chances of power of managerial elements of the new middle class is the assumption that the technical indispensability of certain functions in a social structure are taken *ipso facto* as a prospective claim for political power." (Mills, *Power, Politics and People*. p. 57).

39. This characteristic is not found only in Italy. C. Wright Mills wrote about the social insulation of U.S. managers, who "are not organized in such a manner as to allow them to assume collective responsibility" (*White Collar*, p. 106).

40. In a study of entrepreneurs in Mexico, we found a significant tendency to join associations: only 10% of those interviewed did not belong to associations of any kind. Of the remaining entrepreneurs, 16% belonged only to business associations. But 70%, in addition to the latter associations, were inserted in a vast network of contacts. 63% sat on two or more boards of directors. Charity and cultural activities were very common, but political membership was non-existent. However, given the predominant role of the State in the politics of Mexican industrialization, (through protectionism, price-fixing, etc.), we were led to hypothesize a parapolitical function of membership in these groups. See Flavia Derossi, *The Mexican Entrepreneur*, Paris, OECD, 1970, pp. 187-89.

41. Mills, *Power Elite*, p. 281.

42. Nevertheless there seems to be a connection between political participation and participation in other types of association. Interest shown in political problems seems to be an indicator of greater openness toward social problems.

43. The businessman does not need to become a "politician" in order to influence political decisions. Indeed, shunning political roles is a strategy which keeps him out of the limelight; by entertaining informal relationships he gains greater flexibility and ability to exert pressure. Recourse to an open political role occurs as a last resort, when other types of relationships turn out to be ineffective.

44. The perception of the locus of power was derived from a question asking the managers to identify who had made the long-term policy decisions they had earlier described.

45. In Italy few if any managers have seats on the board. We remind the reader that the company president is not legally considered a *dirigente* (manager).

46. The rate of middle-management participation (5%) was so low that it was necessary to join together the two groups.

47. Percentage of managers who are unable to locate the seat of decision-making power, according to hierarchical level: upper level—8%; middle level —15%; lower level—15%.

48. Percentage of managers who are unable to locate the seat of decision-making power, according to corporate size (annual sales): 10-30 billion lire— 8%; 30-50 billion lire—14%; 50-100 billion lire—12%; >100 billion—19%.

49. For example, Robert A. Gordon, Daniel Bell, and E. J. Mason. Berle's theory is the basis of Galbraith's well-known work *The New Industrial State*. Berle returned later to the topic with publications such as *The Twentieth Century Capitalist Revolution* (1954), *Power without Property* (1959), and *The American Economic Republic* (1963). Even some Marxist economists subscribe to the theory of managerial supremacy. See P. A. Baran and P. M. Sweezy, *Monopoly Capital, An Essay on the American Economic and Social Order*, New York, The Monthly Review Press, 1966, pp. 15-17.

50. In analyzing the same enterprises that furnished data to Berle and Means, Anna Rochester and Ferdinand Lundberg concluded in 1936 and again in 1937 that a small group of families still controlled the industrial system through ownership of shares and control of the largest banks. See Ferdinand Lundberg, *America's Sixty Families*, New York, Citadel Press, 1938.

51. Lacking data for 73 of the 200 firms, Berle and Means proceeded by word of mouth. These blanks are due to the absence in the United States of an official list of the largest firms classified according to capital, sales and profits. *Fortune*'s list, on which the Berle and Means study was based, was believed for many years to be complete until it was discovered, with the publisher's own admission, that it omitted corporations that did not publish reports of their financial records.

We met with a similar problem in the course of our research in Italy, when we discovered that some firms with sales over 10 billion were not present on the Mediobanca list. They had not been included because they had chosen not to respond to the bank's annual questionnaire.

52. Philip H. Burch points out that Gordon reexamined only 65 of the 200 firms, interviewing managers in only half of them, and that Larner doggedly followed in Berle's tracks, limiting himself to up-dating corporate data using the same criteria. Burch also stresses that the dichotomy introduced by Larner—external versus internal stockholders, i.e., participants in management—should be replaced by the dichotomy managerial versus patrimonial control. The latter, in fact, can be exercised within the firm. See Philip H. Burch, *The Managerial Revolution Reassessed: Family Control in America's Large Corporation*, Lexington, Mass., Lexington Books, 1972, p. 3; and M. Zeitlin, "Corporate Ownership and Control: The Large Corporation and the Capitalistic Class," *American Journal of Sociology*, vol. 79, no. 5, March 1974, p. 1090.

53. The most important and reliable source is a report on the Investigation of the Concentration of Economic Power by the Temporary National Economic Committee: R. W. Goldsmith and R. C. Parmelee, *Distribution of Ownership in the Largest 200 Non-Financial Corporations*, monograph, no. 29, Washington, D.C., U.S. Government Printing Office, 1940.

54. Burch, *Managerial Revolution Reassessed*.

55. Zeitlin, "Corporate Ownership," p. 1086.

56. A University of Pennsylvania study showed that individuals reporting an annual income of over $100,000 owned approximately 20 percent of the stock in the entire country. The study—which inspired the *New York Times* to write an article entitled "Multimillionaire Stockholders Still Rule Big Business"—led Earl Cheit to remark that individuals owning such considerable stock are likely to exert a significant influence on the management of the firms in which they have invested. See "The New Place of Business," in Earl Cheit, ed., *The Business Establishment*, New York, John Wiley, 1964, p. 175.

57. Ferdinand Lundberg, *Who Controls Industry?* New York, Vanguard Press, 1938, p. 6.

58. The Patman Committee concluded that it is sufficient to own 5 percent of the holdings in the very largest firms to control them. There were cases of uncontested control with even smaller blocks of shares: Richard K. Mellon was still the largest investor in Alcoa with 2.98% of the stock, in Gulf Oil with 1.78%, and the second largest stockholder in General Motors with .84% of the stock.

59. The September 1, 1971 issue of *Forbes* described a case in which ownership of less than 2 percent of the stock allowed control of the Westmoreland Coal Co. by the Leisering family. The latter did not own any stock in Westmoreland, but through ownership of less than 2 percent of the mother firm—Penn Virginia Corporation—and through a complex network of family or friendship relations that according to *Forbes* tie it to other shareholders, the Leisering family was able to control up to 40 percent of the firm's voting shares.

60. Don Villarejo, "Stock Ownership and the Control of Corporations,"

New University Thought, Autumn 1961–Winter 1962, pp. 33-77, 47-65.

61. Silk and Vogel, *Profits and Ethics*, pp. 181-82.

62. Also because it may be useful to use it as a public scapegoat. The Board of Directors of Gulf Oil, the seventh largest American corporation, successfully opposed management after it was accused of illegal donations to American and foreign politicians. The Board appointed an investigation committee composed of two external members and chaired by a lawyer. On the basis of their report, the Board asked for and obtained the dismissal of the President, the Chief Executive, and two top-level managers. The decision was not unanimous and the length of the meeting (sixteen hours) indicates the existence of a conflict (one of the participants characterized the discussion as "brutal"). The issue was resolved with the defeat of management and a public disavowal of its policies. (*New York Times*, January 15, 1976, page one; and January 16, 1976.) Similar events occurred at RCA and Singer.

63. Peter Drucker, "The Bored Board," *The Wharton Magazine*, vol. 1, no. 1, autumn 1976, pp. 22-24.

64. Cf. Ralph Nader, Mark Green, and Joel Seligman, *Taming the Giant Corporation*, New York, Norton, 1976.

65. See the studies cited by M. Zeitlin (in "Corporate Ownership"), including the 1966 Patman Committee report concerning the growing power of banks.

66. Cf. M. P. Allen, "Management Control in the Large Corporation. Comment on Zeitlin," *American Journal of Sociology*, vol. 81, no. 4, 1976.

67. Daniel J. Baum and Ned B. Stiles, *Silent Partners: Institutional Investors and Corporate Control*, Syracuse, New York, Syracuse University Press, 1965.

68. Pension funds are not simply an organizational idiosyncracy, but are a considerable force in the financial world because they usually invest primarily in large firms, and often in such proportions as to assume some control. Through these institutions, employees in private and public corporations own a third of the shares existing on the stock market. According to Peter Drucker, we are witnessing a unique case of "socialism" if by socialism we mean ownership of the means of production by workers. See "Pension Fund 'Socialism,'" in *The Public Interest*, no. 42, winter 1976, pp. 3-4, and *The Unseen Revolution: How Pension Fund Socialism Came to America*, New York, Harper & Row, 1976.

In recent years in Italy the pension funds of the Bank of Italy played an important role at both FIAT and Montedison.

69. See Zeitlin, "Corporate Ownership," pp. 1104-06.

70. This change was perceived by Burnham, who, however, considered it a transitional phase: at first, owners did not lose contact with the means of production; rather they increased their control because ". . . through finance-capitalist methods a wider area than ever of the economy was brought, and was brought more stringently, under the control of the big capitalists." Only when control becomes more indirect (exercised at second, third, or fourth hand through various financial networks) do managers, who earlier were simple delegates of owners, succeed in annexing effective power and in depriving the owners of authority (*The Managerial Revolution*, p. 100).

Before Burnham, Veblen had described the transformation of the entrepreneur-capitalist—and not his disappearance—tying it to the separation of industry (conceived primarily as a productive unit) from business. The captain of industry, who begins as a technician responsible for production, becomes the businessman who dedicates himself to handling his considerable wealth. Through this process the entrepreneur loses his innovative qualities: awareness of financial risks makes him cautious, technological innovation is seen as causing plant obsolescence and thus decreased worth of capital invested. The monetary values that guide his decisions often make him ignore social goals. See Thorstein Veblen, *Absentee Ownership and Business Enterprise in Recent Times: The Case of America*, Boston, Beacon Press, 1967 (1st ed. 1923), p. 106 and pp. 108-9.

71. "It is on the supra-managerial level that members of controlling family dynasties are found. They may have hired executives to perform the *business* functions of their ownership; they have by no means turned over the larger economic and political interests of property to them." C. Wright Mills, *Power, Politics and People*, London, Oxford University Press, 1963, p. 75.

72. This is not a recent phenomenon. Zeitlin points out that a 1939 National Resources Committee study of the 200 largest businesses and 50 largest American banks brought to light the fact that almost half of the firms and a third of the banks examined belonged to eight "interest groups" which, though different, were united by the common control of one family and/or investment bank (Zeitlin, "Corporate Ownership," p. 1102).

73. Joseph Schumpeter, "The Sociology of Imperialism," *Imperialism and Social Classes*, New York, Meridian, 1955 (1st German edition, 1919).

74. Analyses of kinship ties among owners and managers, and, above all, studies concerning relationships within the ruling class are sorely lacking.

75. The "corporate Caesars" have been replaced by a usually faceless group labeled "management," whose individual names are unknown to the public. (See Robert Heilbroner, *The Limits of American Capitalism*, New York, Harper & Row, 1966, pp. 24-25.) While those dominating American industry at the turn of the century had famous names, today the heads of large enterprises are practically unknown. In fact, they prefer to remain anonymous. (See Silk and Vogel, *Profits and Ethics*, p. 108.)

76. See Ivar E. Berg, "The Impact of Business on America," in Berg, ed., *The Business of America*, New York, Holt Rinehart, 1968, p. 150. The fact that several years ago 200 of the largest American firms refused to divulge the names of their thirty largest stockholders to the Committee on Government Operations chaired by Senator Lee Metcalf (*New York Times*, August 22, 1975) leads one to suspect that the fear expressed by President Roosevelt in his time—that in practice industry was controlled by a hundred men, that is, by an "economic oligarchy"—may still be warranted.

77. Yet, even in the United States, at least in medium-large firms (to which the majority of our principal firms can be compared), we are witnessing increased hereditary transfers of positions of corporate leadership. In half of those companies the owner-president still passes on the reins to his son or to a member of the family at his retirement. A 1964 analysis conducted by the

Young Presidents Organization (which grouped firms according to ones with sales over a million dollars, and with presidents appointed before they were 40) found that 44% of those presidents headed a patrimonial firm; 28% of them were the founders; 25% had attained control through purchase; and finally, 3% had married the owner's daughter. Therefore, "family dynasties are still playing a role in American corporations. . . ." See David Finn, *The Corporate Oligarchy*, New York, Simon and Schuster, 1969, pp. 104, 115, 119.

78. An analysis in *Fortune* (September 15, 1968, p. 202) showed that in Sweden 15 families—some of them related to one another—control a third of the national production. A 1966 study estimated that more than a third of the 120 largest English firms were controlled by an individual or family. See Michael Barrat Brown, "The Controllers of British Industry," in Ken Coates, ed., *Can the Workers Run Industry?* London, Sphere Books, 1968.

79. An interesting example is the third generation of Rockefellers, of whom none out of the five male heirs remained in Standard Oil, the origin of the family fortune. They all hold strategic positions in financial, cultural and political areas. The five brothers devoted themselves to different but equally important areas in the life of the country. John focused on the foundations and financing of scientific (such as the Population Council) or cultural activities. Laurence was an entrepreneur in the aeronautic industry. David managed one of the largest banks in the United States (Chase Manhattan Bank). Winthrop was involved in regional politics and Nelson, former Vice-President of the United States, was a major figure in national politics. See Edward Jay Epstein, "The Great Rockefeller Power Machine," *The New Yorker*, November 24, 1975, pp. 42-73; and Peter Collier and David Horowitz, *The Rockefellers: An American Dynasty*, New York, Holt, Rinehart & Winston, 1976.

80. Daniel Bell, *The End of Ideology*, New York, Free Press, p. 45.

81. *Ibid.*

82. See John Kenneth Galbraith's introduction to the 1971 edition of *The New Industrial State*, p. xix.

83. This is the central idea in Adolf A. Berle's book *Power without Property* (1959).

84. Ralf Dahrendorf, *Class and Class Conflict in Industrial Society*, Stanford, Stanford University Press, 1959, pp. 275-76.

85. Mills, *White Collar*, p. 101.

"In Italy there are no managers because there is no real delegation of power on the part of the top. Before appointing managers, one must be convinced that they should exist and be willing to share power. Instead the Italian manager never had authority, a fact underlined by recent events. There still prevails a centralized conception of power in the Italian socio-political structure, and the political will to delegate power has always been absent." (From an interview with a manager belonging to a state-owned firm.)

86. Clark Kerr, Frederick Harbison, John Dunlop, and Charles Myers, "Industrialism and Industrial Man," *International Labour Review*, September 1960, p. 10.

87. Mills, *White Collar*, p. 104.

Meynaud, too, doubts that it is possible to consider managers as an autonomous group. He refuses the definition of a "managerial class" because the characteristic that makes managers similar to one another—the possession of technical-scientific knowledge—is not sufficient (*La tecnocrazia*, p. 259).

88. Jean Meynaud, *Rapport sur la classe dirigeante italienne*, Lausanne, Ed. de Science Politique, 1964.

89. Mills, *White Collar*, p. 103.

90. On the contrary, says Mills, the lesser the visibility behind the screen provided by management, the greater the freedom of action of the owner class has to act. Mills asserts that "The powers of property ownership are depersonalized, intermediate, and concealed. But they have not been minimized nor have they declined" (*White Collar*, p. 101).

In an interview granted to H. G. Wells in 1934, and published in the *Express*, Stalin asserted that "Capitalism will not be destroyed by 'organizers of production' or the technical intelligentsia. . . ." To do so, he said, the intelligentsia would have to sever its ties to the capitalist world and this is utopian. (Reprinted in *The New York Times*, December 6, 1976.)

91. After having questioned whether the technical intelligentsia would detach itself from capitalism to modify society, Stalin added that in any case, ". . . in order to transform the world, one must have the power to do so. It seems to me, Mr. Wells, that you seriously underestimated the question of power. . . What can the best-intentioned persons do if they cannot pose the problem of taking power and do not have power in their hands?" *Ibid.*

92. Wilfredo Pareto, "Elite, forza e immagini del potere," in C. Wright Mills, ed., *Immagini dell'uomo*, Milan, Comunità, 1969, p. 239.

93. *Ibid.*, p. 324.

94. See Charles Perrow, ed., *The Radical Attack on Business*, New York, Harcourt, Brace, Jovanovich, 1972 (a collection of papers by New Left representatives) and the writings of some U.S. Marxist economists, including Paul Sweezy and Paul Baran. The vision of a class hegemony is shared by many of the non-Marxist writers cited in this chapter.

95. Mills, *Power Elite*, p. 147.

96. Frank Parkin observes that, with respect to their counterparts in socialist countries, elites in modern capitalist societies present greater uniformity from both the social and functional standpoints, due to their being recruited from much smaller circles. As a result, they tend to share the same goals and political convictions. The uniform nature of elites in capitalist countries grants them a greater stability, enabling them to respond more effectively and usually without internal conflict to the crises in the system (because there is no polarization of interests). See Frank Parkin, "System Contradictions and Political Transformation" in Tom R. Burns and Walter Buckley, eds., *Power and Control: Social Structures and Their Transformation*, Beverly Hills, Ca., Sage, 1977, pp. 139-41.

97. Cf. Giorgio Ruffolo, *La grande impresa nella società moderna*, Turin, Einaudi, 1971, pp. 235-40; David Vogel, "The Corporation as Government: Challenges and Dilemmas," *Polity*, autumn 1975, pp. 5-37; Robert Dahl, *After the Revolution*, New Haven, Yale University Press, 1970.

98. Carl Kaysen, "The Corporation: How Much Power? What Scope?" in

Reinhard Bendix and Seymour M. Lipset, eds., *Class, Status, and Power*, New York, Free Press, 1966 (2nd ed.), p. 239.

99. Cf. Irving Kristol, "On Corporate Capitalism in America," *The Public Interest*, no. 41, autumn 1975, p. 219.

100. Ruffolo, *La grande impresa*, chapter 11.

101. Such as antimonopoly and antitrust legislation in the United States. The most recent proposal for the control of the large enterprise in the United States suggests to change its legal status and consider it as a public institution. Corporations would have to be subjected to a series of economic, legal and political controls administered by government agencies. Control would be enforced by placing public officials and representatives of interest groups on the boards of directors; by obliging corporations to furnish financial information which is currently off limits; by establishing the personal responsibility of the directors in cases of illegal conduct; and by the right of employees to divulge corporate information without being penalized. See Nader, Green, and Seligman, *Taming the Giant Corporation*.

APPENDIX

1. Cf. Frederick H. Harbison and Charles A. Myers, *Management in the Industrial World*, New York, McGraw-Hill, 1959, p. 69.

2. By "elite" we denote individuals who occupy formal authority roles in various social institutions, such as finance, industry, university, and church. See Philip Stanworth and Anthony Giddens, *Elites and Power in British Industry*, Cambridge, Cambridge University Press, 1974. C. Wright Mills also asserts that elites are groups "in command of the major hierarchies and organizations of modern society." (*The Power Elite*, New York, Oxford University Press, 1956, p. 4.)

3. According to Pahl and Winkler, before classifying the category of manager as an economic elite, it is necessary to demonstrate that they control the allocation of capital: "In a capitalist society, effective economic power lies with those who have the ability to conceive and carry through schemes for the profitable allocation of capital" (R. E. Pahl and J. T. Winkler, "The Economic Elite: Theory and Practice," in Philip Stanworth and Anthony Giddens, eds., *Elites and Power in British Society*, Cambridge, Cambridge University Press, 1974, p. 115). This definition is in the spirit of Marx and Weber who consider elites as groups controlling the distribution of resources.

4. Article 2095 of the Italian Civil Code distinguishes the category of managers from that of white-collar employees and blue-collar workers: "Subordinates are divided into administrative or technical managers, white-collar workers, and blue-collar workers. The special corporative laws and norms, relative to each sector of production and the particular structure of the enterprise, determine the prerequisites for belonging to one of the above-mentioned categories."

5. INPDAI was created in 1929 by the National Association of Managers and was recognized as a public body by Law No. 967, in December 1953.

6. See below the list of corporations which participated in the study. They are divided according to type of product manufactured.

7. The smallest of the firms examined, the Officine Meccaniche Galileo, had annual sales of 11 billion lire in 1970. FIAT, the largest, announced sales of 1,700 billion in the same year.

8. This method was suggested by Herbert H. Hyman and was programmed for the computer by Jorge Garcia Bouza.

9. Note, for example, the "open-ended" responses cited in chapter 5.

About the Author

Flavia Derossi was the founder and until 1974 the director of the Center for Industrial and Social Research in Turin. Educated at the University of Turin, she has taught courses in industrial sociology and management at a number of business schools in Italy and has extensive international experience as a researcher and consultant. Among her many publications are *The Mexican Entrepreneur* (1971), *Old Age in Industrial Society* (1967), and (with Magda Talamo) *Report on Carbonia: The Social Consequences of an Economic Crisis* (1965). Dr. Derossi is currently a management consultant headquartered in New York City.